Who's Hiring Who

MORE THAN 600,000 JOB
OPENINGS THIS MONTH!
HOW AND WHERE
TO GET THEM

Library of Congress Cataloging in Publication Data

Lathrop, Richard
    Who's hiring who.

    Includes bibliographical references.
    1. Applications for positions. 2. Employment
interviewing. I. Title.
HF5383.L34   650'.14   75-44412
ISBN 0-913668-55-9

Who's Hiring Who

Richard Lathrop

TEN SPEED PRESS 1🔟

Contents

Foreword:
What this book
will do for you

The simple aim of this book is to double your prospects for finding the job you want. And to cut the time it otherwise would take in half.

Impossible?

Not at all.

In fact, government research shows that when those applicants who need it are given strong guidance, their rate of placement does just that: it *doubles*. And it doubles even though such guidance is limited to the single question of career choice.[1]

But the question of career choice is only one of the areas in which job seekers need help. Far more serious, far more pervasive are the thorny questions of how to cope with the job market itself when trying to find work—questions for which almost all applicants are totally unprepared simply because they have had neither the experience nor training that would help them to cope with such problems.

So it is the aim of this book to provide sound guidance in *both* areas—choosing your career field (if you need to make that choice) and dealing successfully with job-finding problems that throw most applicants for a heavy loss.

The importance of such help becomes clear when two highly disturbing facts are considered:

1. During the ten years prior to this writing approximately 20 million Americans annually suffered extended unemployment averaging 70 days. And they were desperate days, indeed, for many. Worse, in recession years like

---

1. See Appendix A: Footnotes, page 256.

1974, the average duration of unemployment tops 100 days and nearly 30 million Americans suffer the agonies of such extended unemployment.[2]

2. *Despite such horrifying statistics, only a tiny fraction of the tens of millions who seek employment each year receive the expert help they MUST have if they are to find the best possible job in the shortest possible time.*

Does Fact Two have anything to do with Fact One?

Of course it does. If Fact Two were not true—that is, if job seekers all received the help they critically need—the time taken to find work would be shorter and literally millions would be subtracted from this country's yearly ccunt of the unemployed.

For example:

If practical ways are found to provide expert help to all job seekers (and they can be), if that is done and the average time taken to find employment during "normal" years is reduced just *four* days—from 70 to 66—the annual count of people without jobs will drop one million. If it is reduced to 63 days—nine weeks instead of ten—*two million* will not be around to be counted when the government makes its unemployment surveys. They will be on the job instead. *And total unemployment will drop 10 percent!*[3]

Does the potential for such telling reductions in average job-finding time really exist? According to job-market analysts, it does. They observe that most job seekers make one critical mistake after another when looking for work—mistakes that inevitably delay their employment for days, weeks, even months.[4] Guidance that will help prevent such mistakes, they say, will inevitably shorten the time to find employment—probably by greater margins than those indicated above—in both good times and bad.

So what does that have to do with the way things are and the way they should be?

As suggested by the government research mentioned at the outset, instituting practical ways to provide all applicants with

---

2. See Appendix A: Footnotes, page 256.
3. See Appendix A: Footnotes, page 256.
4. See Appendix A: Footnotes, page 257.

the expert job-finding help they need would cut national unemployment rates significantly, permanently, and at relatively little cost. In fact, such studies indicate that a really comprehensive program of help to job seekers beginning with an introduction to the job market and how to cope with it at the high-school and college levels would reduce such rates 50 percent during "normal" times. *Fifty percent!* Or even more.

On that score, considerable evidence shows that a short job supply is only *half* the nation's unemployment problem during those years when joblessness is below 6 percent.[5] Incredible as this may seem, no national program exists to minimize the effect of the other half—simple failure to help applicants find and land suitable jobs—jobs that are open and waiting to be filled.

Instead, our national approach to applicants seems to assume that they are born with a job-market gene—a gene that tells them by instinct how to cope with the searing problems almost all job seekers face. It would be as logical to assume that everyone has the inherent ability to take over the presidency of Continental Can. Right now. Today. With great success.

On the contrary, the best the job market offers—in the absence of the kind of guidance this book provides—is a castabout system of job hunting. That system leaves you to figure out by a tortuous, hit-or-miss, trial-and-error approach which measures are most likely to turn up the job you are looking for. It leaves you to wrestle from an extremely weak stance with some of the most muscular problems encountered in a lifetime and exposes you to numerous traps and hazards that can bring you to the brink of despair and blight your life for years to come.

But that is not the only cost.

With your career—your life ahead—at stake, grappling alone with grotesquely unfamiliar job-finding problems can be a shattering experience. Perhaps you have already learned just how soul-destroying it can be. So much so, in fact, that when all the costs imposed by lack of adequate support for job seekers are weighed out, they add up to the nation's number one public health problem. In fact, mountainous evidence indicates that employment problems are, by far, the greatest single cause of heart disease—

---

5. See Appendix A: Footnotes, page 257.

the nation's primary killer. Not to mention other studies showing a strong correlation between the dismally poor results produced by a malfunctioning job market and increased mental hospitalization and suicide.[6]

Considering such costs, one wonders why study of the job market and how to cope with it is not a standard course in every high school and college in the country, preferably required. And why the government isn't funding massive research into the job market's gross failings as an operating system to determine why it is producing such disastrous results so programs can be developed to reduce such failings.

Fortunately, such costs are not ones *you* have to pay. By picking up this book you have already set yourself apart from millions of applicants at your level who fail to put the importance of their job hunt in proper perspective and, instead, leave the outcome to the mercies of ill-conceived applicant-support systems and highly erratic fate.

And you've done more than that.

You've put yourself in a position to convert your job hunt from a frustrating, if not agonizing, problem to a challenging opportunity—the opportunity to move *now* into work close to the peak of your abilities and interests, work that is perhaps more exciting and rewarding than you ever thought it could be.

That should be your goal. The guides in the following pages will help you achieve it.

But don't just read this book. *Study* it. Absorb every word of it. Doing this will give you an entirely new insight into your opportunities and how to make the most of them. *Who's Hiring Who* should be a dynamic factor in your success—not only now but for years to come—as it has already been for thousands upon thousands of others.

RICHARD LATHROP, DIRECTOR
National Center for Job-Market Studies

6. See Appendix A: Footnotes, page 257.

*I was totally unprepared
for what I was about to face.
When I stepped out of that office
I didn't know what I was stepping into.
There were opportunities
and I missed them,
there was money
and I wasted it,
there was time
and I fumbled the days away.
I should have grasped what was happening to me,
but I didn't;
a man falling down a flight of stairs
doesn't count the steps.
I had very little job-hunting experience
and I didn't know that job-hunting is a fine art.*

Allen R. Dodd
The Job Hunter—Diary of a "Lost" Year
McGraw-Hill

*Because your next job will probably determine
the quality of your life for years to come,
finding and landing it
is one of the most important moves
you will ever make.
With stakes like that in the balance,
you will want to avoid the haphazard approach
most applicants take.
Here's how to proceed.*

1
This is what
WHW is all about

Applicants sometimes victimize employers—not very often, but still frequently enough to make a point about it. Such victimization occurs when an applicant faces an employer knowing *more* about the key factors controlling hiring decisions than the employer does. And it can occur at *any* job level, from the production line to the executive suite.

Gaining such knowledge is not hard to do. In fact, by the time you have finished your study of this book, you will be way ahead of most employers you talk with in terms of insight into the dynamics of the hiring process. You are likely to find them terribly impressed—impressed to the point where they may be tempted to hire you on the spot.

Let's take an example.

Some time back, a reader of a previous edition of *Who's Hiring Who* (we'll call him Joe Jones) stopped by our office to discuss progress in his job hunt. Jones had worked for only one employer (his father), had general administrative experience—certainly nothing spectacular about it—and had never looked for a job before. He had many nice things to say about WHW and how much it had helped him. This pleases us, of course, and disposed us to encourage him to say more while paying close attention.

Working wonders

Jones told us that he was getting an unexpectedly strong response to his bid for a job as assistant to a marketing manager for one organization or another—although he had no direct marketing experience. Application of WHW techniques, he said, worked wonders in opening employers' doors. Once through the door, he added, interviews frequently closed with an invitation to lunch. Sometimes with top officials in tow. Jones was delighted that he was getting far more attention than he had expected and wondered whether he should be aiming higher.

When we asked Jones to describe his approach, all seemed in order. For example, his qualifications brief (résumé) was a good, accurate—even if enthusiastic—account of his abilities and experience supporting his marketing objective. We suggested a few minor changes and asked him about interviews.

Discussion indicated that Jones always came into interviews with strong advance information about the employer's operations and problems. He took deliberate pains to identify with the basic interests of the employer in everything he said, and, in the main, spent more time talking about those interests than in talking about his own qualifications. Probably equally important, he worked to make a friend of everyone he talked with— even the receptionists (or, perhaps, *particularly* the receptionists). Now he wanted to know whether to accept one of the offers he had already received.

We suggested that he try a few more employers—larger organizations than he had contacted before—and that he bid for somewhat higher pay to see what happened. As the door closed behind him, a member of our staff remarked that Jones appeared to be a fast learner, to say the least.

Voice from a cavern

Nothing more was heard from Jones for about two weeks. Then came his follow-up call. His voice reverberated on the phone, creating the impression that he might be calling from a vaulted cavern of some kind.

"I have just been appointed as special assistant to the Assistant Secretary of Commerce," he said, a shade breathlessly. "Heard a couple of weeks ago at a friend's housewarming that the Department is setting up new programs to expand foreign tourism in the U.S. Shot right over here. The pay is $6,000 higher than I hoped to get. I'm calling from my new office now. It's big enough for two simultaneous ping pong tournaments with spectators." Then a pause. "Did I do wrong?"

Did he? The fact that he raised the question indicates that maybe he had.

The important point here is this: It is possible to learn the lessons in WHW too well. It is easy enough to victimize employers by playing on their own unfamiliarity with the dynamics of the hiring process (and *most* employers do not fully know what they are doing when they try to fill a job) but if you victimize an employer, you may also victimize yourself. A job over your head can be a good deal worse than one that fails to use all of your talents.

In any event, to learn the lessons in WHW, you'll need a wide-open mind. If you are typical of most applicants—and it's best to assume you are, at this point—you are about to learn in the following pages that the job market is vastly different from your current concept of it. More than that, you are likely to discover that you probably put too low a value on your abilities and experience and that *most* of your ideas on the best ways to find the job you want are seriously wide of the mark.

Here's a brief example.

Suppose, right now, you were asked, "What pay do you want?" —one of the most routine questions asked of job seekers. How would you answer it?

Immediately, you're faced with a dilemma. If you put the figure too high, you've priced yourself out of the job you want. Put it too low and the employer may pick you up for substantially less than planned, at great cost to you. Or your low figure may inspire the thought that you must not be the hot candidate you originally appeared to be.

The truth is, most job seekers come through with a self-defeating answer to that question. Yet a correct response in a few words can literally add thousands of dollars to your earnings and greatly enhance your future prospects.

But that isn't the only question of its kind for which you are, at this moment, probably terribly ill prepared. Contact with thousands of applicants has shown us that there are hundreds of such questions—all of great importance to your success— for which you are now likely to have wrong answers and must find better ones.

You will find those answers in the following chapters.

So, right now, decide to discard—at least for the time being— every last idea you have regarding the best steps to take to find the job you want. Decide that you are going to take a fresh look, free of all preconceptions, at the way the job market operates and what you must do to deal successfully with the prickly problems it poses. Do that and you will be open to an entirely new view, a new approach that will greatly enhance your prospects for finding that ideal job.

Importance of your job search

So that you can decide just how critical your job hunt is in your total life scheme, let's put a kind of frame around the importance of the effort ahead.

Reflect on it.

A job is not just a job. Half of your waking hours are devoted to it. Its quality ramifies through all other aspects of your life. It determines your productivity and how far you will go in achieving full self-realization. It governs your happiness, the happiness of your family, where you live, and how well. The quality of the job you land now will inevitably affect the quality of your next one. It will even determine the kind of education and opportunities your children will have and, consequently, *their* future prospects. Not to mention whether your retirement years will be beautiful or bleak.

With all that and so much more hanging on the outcome, good sense says you should proceed with your job-finding campaign as though your life depends on it. In fact, most of it does.

When you get right down to it, aiming for a really good job doesn't require more effort than setting your sights on a poor one. And aiming high leaves you in far better control of the outcome. Consequently, it is plainly your duty—your duty to yourself, your family, your new employer, even to society— to proceed with your job search in ways that will produce work as close as possible to the peak of your abilities and at the highest possible pay.

Yet, few job seekers—even though their careers, their lives, are on the line—sense that such urgent considerations require a carefully planned approach. (Most people spend more time learning to play *Monopoly* than they ever spend learning to play the job market.) And, unhappily, it is generally not in the interest of people who know better—the employment agencies and other applicant services—to show them a better way.

The castabout alternative

So that you will know what to avoid and the strong advantage you will have if you plan your approach, it is important to understand this: Most people—and that includes others who want the job you want—do a very poor job of job finding. In the absence of adequate guidance, their only alternative is to cast about in the job market while painfully learning lessons by trial and error that have already been painfully learned, at least in some small part, by tens of millions of applicants before them—at a great cost in time, money, morale, and employment. Virtually all make critical—and entirely avoidable—mistakes, mistakes that delay the day when they are hired.

Their first impulse is to check the help-wanted ads—an exercise that produces the first inklings of impending despair. And then the employment agencies. After all, they're in business to find people jobs. (It doesn't matter that this is an inaccurate assumption.) But, barring great good luck, the contacts with agencies also prove both frustrating and fruitless.

Direct visits to employment offices of various companies here and there usually come next—often producing canned brush-offs from clerks with canned smiles who cannot possibly appreciate either the height of the job-seeker's abilities or the growing depth of the dark despair inside. Or, instead of the visits, unguided job seekers often elect a busywork direct-mail approach —letters and résumés to hundreds of employers. Unfortunately, the quality of such mailings in the great majority of cases is so low as to kill all interest at the employer's first glance. And from that moment on, the application, prepared with so much pain and hope, is on the skids to the burn basket.

Along the way, most applicants deal with many employers and counselors who are in a position to make critical decisions on their employment (and lives) but who simply do not seem to know what they are doing. And the job seekers concerned know of no way to defend themselves against such ineptitude. After all, how could they? They, too, are taking an inept approach to a critical problem.

Then the outcome. After an extended period of intense confusion, discouragement, and deep frustration, most applicants accept a job—more or less by chance—that is significantly below the peak of their abilities. They do it so often, in fact, that

11

employment that uses substantially less than all of one's talents is considered a normal thing.

To avoid such an outcome, plan now to *plan* your job search. Providing that plan and showing you how to carry it out are the primary aims of this book. By the time you are finished studying WHW, you will know how to aim for a job at the peak of your abilities and how to land it. You will be able to conserve your time and energy in the process while proceeding with the confidence that comes from *knowing* you are on the right track. And once you've landed the job you want, you will be able to move ahead in your career as fast as your personal development allows.

In short, with WHW's help, you should find that you begin to take a new approach to your career—one that puts your progress in your personal control, not in the hands of fate (and highly erratic hiring systems) where most people leave important career questions.

How to use this book

The guidance in the following pages applies to every career-minded applicant who wants to find challenging and well-paid work that leads to future advancement—that is, the best possible job in the shortest possible time. *Everyone.* Graduates, housewives, executives, production workers, dropouts, junior and senior managers. Regardless of field of work. And WHW points to other courses of action where long-term planning and action can achieve a dramatically successful transition from one career field to another.

You will find that this book is written first to cover the basics —the things everyone must know and do to cope successfully with job-search problems. Then it goes into other things that should be done *if suitable to your ability level, age, education, and experience.*

Determining those steps that are suitable for *you* to take is not hard. Here's how to go about it:

First, read all of this book so you will understand its scope. Then apply this rule of thumb: Take action on every recommendation in WHW that makes sense to you. Do it even though it involves more work (or

courage) than you anticipated. When you have a
question about any particular course of action, talk
it over with an employment counselor at your school
or local public employment office so you will have
the benefit of another point of view. But push yourself to do everything that seems sensible, even though
you'd rather not. On the other hand, *don't* do those
things recommended in WHW that simply do not
make sense to you.

Applying this rule to the planning of your job search will assure
that your approach to your next job is a great deal more effective than that of countless other applicants at your ability level.

And keep this in mind: The campaign ahead will yield results
in direct proportion to the effort you put into it—and the care
with which you follow WHW's guides.

For most people, the job market offers
traps, blinds, false leads, and even mirages
which block the way to their goals.
Yet, it offers countless rewarding opportunities
for those who know their way around in it.
This chapter will orient you
to its most unfamiliar aspects
so you will know what to expect and how to cope.

"As a marine in Viet Nam, I went through a lot of hairy fire flights. Believe me, they were damn scary. But, in all that time, nothing frightened me as much as this _____ problem of finding a decent job."

"I've never had to look for a job in my life. Now I *must* find another one immediately, but how to do it has me completely baffled."

"This employment business has me more than a little chilled. I had the notion that at age 42 I was in my prime. Some of these employment officers look at me as if I had one foot in the grave."

"Man, those cats make you feel like ____ when you ask them for a job. Don't they know I'm human, too?"

Such is the refrain that anyone who helps job seekers hears every day. To us, the underlying message comes through loud and clear. These people are asking, "Why isn't anyone around to give me the help I *really* need to find the work I want?"

You may be in the wrong job now. Or just graduated. Or released from military service. Or mergered out. Or laid off. Or afflicted with little Hitler for a boss. Maybe you simply came to work one day and found your desk gone and nowhere to be found—as sometimes happens.

Whatever the reason that caused you to pick up this book, take heart. If you find that you pull a blank when it comes to planning your next step, you have a lot of company. Most people of ability don't get much well-rounded experience in the job of finding a job. Yet your job-finding job is certainly as demanding as any other you will ever have in terms of the know-how and effort required for success. To say nothing of raw courage.

People faced with the need to find a good job frequently are overwhelmed with the apparent complexity of the task. Matters are not helped at all by the fact that the job market is a terribly lonely, discouraging, and sometimes savage place to be— especially for those who are unfamiliar with it.

Mindless monster

Bluntly stated, the national job market—if it can be said to exist at all—is a chaotic mess. It is highly disorganized and riddled with conflict. It is almost entirely unregulated, has no central communications system, and no coordinating or moderating influence to guide its operations. It presents a bewildering front and few guideposts to people seeking employment. If offers excellent, inept, and abusive applicant services in such an appalling mix that job seekers frequently can't tell the bad from the good—until too late. It exploits applicants far more than it assists them and offers the most help to those who least need it. Its operations and services usually cost too much—for both applicants and employers. Its ways of matching people with jobs resemble sorcery more than science. It is woefully short of information on its basic stock in trade—job openings. And it has no goals of its own looking toward more efficient operations and lower unemployment rates.

As if all that isn't bad enough, the so-called job market is constructed along feudal lines. It contains few buyer-seller relationships as in most markets. Instead, it operates on a benefactor-supplicant basis and *you* are cast in the role of supplicant. (Small wonder people find it demoralizing.)

In short, the job market currently sits in our midst like a mindless monster with its finger on everybody's fate but under nobody's control.

Can it be brought under control?

You will begin to bring it under your personal control when you decide that employers are no more your benefactors than you are theirs. You will bring it under control when you decide, in line with the guides in this book, to take yourself out of the hat-in-hand supplicant business and when you understand that you are offering employers value *at least* equal to any pay they may offer you. With those as your attitudes, you will look on the whole employment process as one in which people get together to explore the possibility of a *mutually* beneficial relationship.

And the job-market monster will begin to come under *full* control when educators and national planners start to act on the understanding that applicants—in the national interest and as a matter of right—are entitled to far more information, guidance, and help than they now get when they go out to find a job.

Until such control measures begin to take hold, people by the millions will continue to be utterly dismayed as they meet soaring obstacles in their search for work. Under such conditions, applicants quickly begin to assume that something must be wrong with *them*. They can't bring themselves to believe that the job market itself contains elements that seem deliberately calculated to bring them down with despair. But it does—despite the fact that employment operations are the largest and most important single sector of economic activity in the nation and countless people have been wondering for decades why they work so poorly.

As bad as all that is, it still is not the worst of it. You may sense that people whom you thought were fast friends are also acting like there's something wrong with you. They may even begin to shun you altogether. Moreover, if you are male you may even feel somewhat unsexed, less a man, disinclined to seek female attention.

It can make you feel unclean—if you let it. And it won't matter at all that your unemployment may be due to a change in U.S. foreign-trade policy or a hare-brained management decision four echelons above yours, or some other factor over which you had absolutely no control. They'll still wonder. In truth, they *have* to. Otherwise, their own sense of security would erode.

But the most devastating blow to your ego and feelings of self-worth can come when your spouse finally wonders out loud whether, maybe, the whole family is going down the tubes simply because you haven't the strength, ability, adaptability (or whatever) to pull your share of the load.

Steel yourself, my friend, against such developments. Recognize that they stem from the barbarically inhumane and counterproductive system we have in this country for dealing with the problems of job seekers.

Understanding all this is critically important for you. With such understanding you will know when to blame that system and not yourself if things get out of hand in your job search. You will use the available applicant services with your eyes open to their major limitations. You will even be able to turn many weaknesses in the system to your own great advantage. And you will understand that attempting to negotiate the treacherous hazards of the job market without a strong plan of approach is *not* likely to produce a good job—much less the one you really should have if all your talents are put to full use.

Aim for that ideal job

On the other hand, many people seem to believe that they are entitled to have that ideal job delivered to them wrapped in red velvet as a matter of right without effort on their part—like citizenship or air to breathe. It doesn't seem to occur to them that a career change is terribly important business that warrants hard planning and hard work. While they recognize that getting from one grade to the next in school requires long months of heavy effort and expense, they seem to feel that getting from one job to the next—a far more critical undertaking in one's life scheme—should require no effort at all.

Simple good sense says that you should pour all of the energy and ability you can muster into the task of landing the best possible new position. Look on your search as a full-time job with overtime until your goal is achieved. After all, you will be living with the results of your effort for a long, long time to come.

The truth is, almost anybody can find a job. The basic question is whether just a job is what you want. Or is it better to move in the direction of a career—that is, employment that uses all of your abilities, experience, and potential for growth and that will produce the best long-term results for you?

The question answers itself, but it's easy to be distracted by other considerations. Let's take an example.

We know of openings involving a high prestige product in which any applicant who is qualified can start earning $12,000 a year within a month. What will make you qualified? You must be mature in your outlook, able to speak well, think on your feet, follow simple instructions, and be a hard worker. That's all. No degrees, no technical knowledge, no special training are required. What's more, these openings are generally available wherever you want to live and work, virtually for the asking.

Sound like great jobs, don't they?

For some applicants, these jobs offer a fine career, one that represents everything they could ask for—much time outdoors meeting and dealing with people of all types in beneficial ways plus an exceptionally strong prospect for advancement to the $20,000–$30,000 level in a relatively short time if they apply themselves.

For others, these jobs—involving door-to-door sales—are nothing less than plain, unmitigated drudgery. Or worse. Regardless of the fine pay and strong prospects for the future that they offer.

The point is this: Your next job should closely fit your entire personality if it is to be an exciting part of your life rather than just a day-in, day-out, onerous chore. It should take advantage of your best training and experience; it should tie in closely with your strongest interests; it should challenge all of your abilities; it should give you room to grow in directions that provide spiritual satisfaction as well as adequate compensation, and it should be located in a place where you would like to live.

But does such employment exist?

You can bank on it. It does.

Two million job openings

Barring a depression, this month—now, as you are reading this —there will be at least one million *new* job openings in the U.S. *At least!* In "normal" times when unemployment is ranging between 4 and 6 percent, there are about two million new openings per month in the nation. In boom times, three million. *Per month!*[7] This does not count the sales openings like those described above, for which employers have almost unlimited applicant needs. And it doesn't count the latent jobs—that is, openings that don't exist until the day an applicant walks in and convinces an employer that he/she needs help and the help

---

7. See Appendix A: Footnotes, page 257.

needed is standing right here on the other side of the desk. These latent jobs are also uncountable and are filled every day in just that way.

Nor do those figures count the openings left over from the prior month that are still unfilled. We have no way of knowing but it appears that there may be just as many old openings begging to be filled as there are new openings per month. For example, even in the depths of the 1974-75 recession, the available job supply—according to the best government guess —never dropped below two million. During most of that recession—the heaviest and deepest since the Great Depression— the estimated number of acceptable openings available *each day* ran closer to three million.

Yet—and this point needs heavy stress—*only 1 in 5 jobs in the basic two million available each day are likely to be advertised with employment agencies.*[8]

The reason is simple enough.

Employers most often go "outside" to find personnel only when they have jobs that are hard to fill. They do it when the jobs are undesirable because of low pay or bad working conditions. And they do it when the jobs have exceptionally heavy education and experience requirements or qualified people are hard to find for other reasons. Of course there are exceptions but, in the main, those openings that are widely publicized are likely to be those that you will find *least* interesting. Or if you do find an interesting opening that has been highly publicized, you are least likely to land it simply because of the flood of applicants competing for it.

All of which helps to explain why so few people find employment through help-wanted ads and employment agencies.

So how do employers traditionally fill the four out of five jobs that are *not* publicized?

- They fill them with their friends or people recommended by their friends.
- They fill them with friends of their employees.
- And they fill them with people who have applied directly to them without knowing that any opening existed.[9]

8. See Appendix A: Footnotes, page 258.
9. See Appendix A: Footnotes, page 258.

If you were an employer, it's highly likely that you would do it that way, too. From an employer's point of view, the "insider" system outlined above makes a great deal of sense.

So the message is clear. If you are going to find one of the better jobs among the millions upon millions each year that go unpublicized, you will have to use your own resources to do it—not those of such "job-delivery" systems as agencies, computerized placement services, help-wanted ads, job banks, etc. They never hear of such openings.

Providing you with those resources is what this book is all about.

Who gets the best jobs?

Regardless of the kind of work you are looking for, here is another critically important point for you to understand: The best jobs do not necessarily—or even usually—go to the best qualified people available. Instead, they go to the best qualified APPLICANTS—*that is, people with the basic qualifications for the jobs who <u>know</u> how to get hired.* Consequently, you should aim to become an extremely capable *applicant*— one who knows how to cope with job-market problems that throw other applicants seeking the job you want for a total loss, one who does a much better job of presenting his/her qualifications to employers. The guides you need to do this are in the following pages.

Directly related to the uninformed approach most applicants take to finding jobs is the equally uninformed way in which most employers fill them. It's a factor that confounds countless applicants every day. The inability of employers to get at your basic qualifications can be extremely unsettling unless you are prepared for it and know how to deal with it.

The simple truth is that most employers are specialists in fields other than employment. Usually, they are rank amateurs when it comes to the highly demanding task of successfully matching experience, personality, and abilities to the detailed requirements of the openings they need to fill. As a result, their notions about the best ways to discover how your abilities relate to their need for competent help are usually foggy at best. If you depend on employers to lead the way in making a sound determination of your qualifications, chances are they will botch the job—and horribly. This means that it will often be up to you to help employers with this unfamiliar problem. *You* will have to be prepared to control the situation so that you can be sure employers gain a good appreciation of the abilities you are offering them. This, also, is covered in detail later on.

How to focus your efforts

Now, let's get the major "job-help" services in perspective so you will know right here at the start how much—or how little —reliance to put on them.

A report from the Department of Labor covers a study in which thousands of job holders were asked how they found their employment—certainly one of the most comprehensive surveys of its kind ever made.[10] Here is what the job holders said:

- One percent found their employment through private employment agencies.
- Three percent successfully used public employment agencies.
- Five percent succeeded through help-wanted ads.
- Six percent got their jobs through school placement services.

So much for the job-help systems that dominate the national job market. Obviously, they are not very effective. According to the study, only 15 percent of the job holders surveyed directly attributed their employment to such systems. So how did the other 85 percent land their jobs? Here's how:

- Twenty-four percent found their jobs through direct contacts with employers—going to them and asking for a job.
- Forty-eight percent found their jobs through friends or relatives.
- About 13 percent reported that they used a combination of the above techniques or other means to find employment.

Several important points need to be made about these findings:

1. *Most job seekers, by far, (at least 72 percent) found work through their own efforts.* Undoubtedly, most of these used the costly, time-consuming, and unrewarding "castabout" system of job hunting described earlier. If they succeeded, however inadequately, with that system, your prospects

---

10. See Appendix A: Footnotes, page 258.

with an organized and informed approach will be substantially better.

2. Only 4 percent said they found work through employment agencies. There's little question that this dismal record stems, in part, from the fact that few applicants know how to use such agencies for best results. Since you will know how, your prospects with agencies should also be substantially better than those indicated by the study.

3. Five percent said they found their jobs through help-wanted ads. While that's not very many, it still is 20 percent more than succeeded through employment agencies. That indicates that you should keep the help-wanted ads in perspective, too. Don't rely on them too heavily but still give them the attention they're due. There are enough nuggets among the dross of underpaid openings and non-jobs listed to warrant a quick review every morning over coffee and heavy digging on Sunday.

The key point here is this: The odds are at least three in four that you will find your next job through your own efforts— *not* those of organized applicant services—especially if you rely heavily on friends and acquaintances to help you (while making many more along the way).

Get help

So, in the main, you're on your own during your job hunt. And that's one of the cruelest aspects of the job market— its loneliness. Few people appreciate the genuine agonies of unemployed job seekers. Keeping your balance as you walk the high wire between difficult decisions and repeated discouragement can be tough going indeed unless you have a knowledgeable expert to back you up whenever you wonder about your next step.

Professional career counselors are available to provide such support. Their fees normally range between $25.00 and $40.00 an hour and their counsel can be worth every cent of such fees. If you can afford it, find one. (However, be *very* careful in your selection. Many near-racketeers operate in this field. More on that later.) Otherwise, your best bet is to make friends with a good counselor at your local public employment office. The quality of support you receive will probably not be nearly as high as with a true professional, but it is likely to be far, far better than none.

The way to establish a good relationship with a public employment counselor is this: Ask the telephone information operator —dial 411—for the number of the local state employment office. Call to find the office that serves people in your category and then visit it. Tell the receptionist you would like to get the advice of the wisest and most experienced counselor on the staff who helps applicants in your category. Do what you are asked to do to register for the office's services but do not, in any way, let that slow down your own job-finding efforts.

Then, thereafter, call on your counselor at least once a week —in person or by telephone. Call whenever you have a problem with the best approach to take or need an informed judgement on your next step. Seek your counselor's advice on your qualifications brief (résumé) and how it can be improved, on the latest openings listed with the office that may be suitable for you, on how you should improve your interviewing techniques, and additional employers you should contact. In fact, seek support whenever you simply want to talk over your situation or when you encounter *any* job-hunting problem on which your counselor should have helpful ideas. Deliberately weigh, if you will, on your counselor's conscience and never let him/ her forget you as long as you need a job.

If you first connect with a counselor who is not very helpful, see the manager of the office and request that another be chosen to help you. It's your right. Moreover, there are no fees for such help. Your taxes have already paid for it.

Leave no stone unturned

So there it is. Because of the way the job market is currently structured, confusion, frustration, discouragement—even despair —are endemic among job seekers. The best way to prevent such demoralization is to enter the job market knowing its hazards and how to avoid or minimize them while making the most of every step you take.

Concentrating most of your effort—at least 80 percent of it— on the "hidden" job market (that vast number of openings that employers never release to agencies or help-wanted columns) is essential to your success. On the other hand, you should pay due attention (but not more than 20 percent of your effort) to the services of organized job delivery systems. And, if at all possible, get the continuing help of a sympathetic and concerned counselor. It can be critically important to the maintenance of your morale and the success of your search. Whatever you do, keep in mind that no stone should be left unturned in your job hunt. Look on it as a full-time project until success is achieved.

Don't you believe it.
If you really want to work
and let employers know you will work <u>hard</u> for them,
many will want to hire you for that alone.
Then you can get the experience you need to move ahead.
And, even if you have a great deal of experience,
this chapter will give you broad insights
into job-market dynamics.

3
Suppose you have "nothing to offer"?

Maybe you've never worked for pay a day in your life. Or you may feel that school didn't give you much that's of use in getting a job. Or it could be that you've just come out of the Army and feel pretty sure nobody's hiring combat infantrymen these days. (Except, maybe, the Godfather.)

Whatever the story's been up to now, you can still make a great case with employers—one that will make them *want* to hire you —if you know how to do it.

Let's suppose the Army has just given you a passport to civilian life, and you're out in the real world again. It's probably good to know that you can reenlist if you want. Even so, you may feel that nothing happened on the military scene that will help you find a civilian job.

Well, let's look at it. You could be wrong.

In the Army, you probably did at least some of these things:

- You may have operated a vehicle—perhaps a very heavy one. (That's a leg up on a good paying job as a truck or delivery driver, as a cabbie, or as a heavy-equipment operator.)
- You may have maintained or repaired those vehicles. (Auto or heavy equipment mechanic or maintenance worker.)
- You maintained, assembled, and disassembled weapons. (Tool maintenance or repair or production assembly worker.)
- You may have helped put up structures of one kind or another. (Construction worker or helper.)
- Undoubtedly, you helped police the post. (Building and grounds maintenance worker.)
- You probably filled out forms till you were blue in the face. (Clerk.)
- You may have checked in or maintained supplies. (Supply clerk, warehouse worker.)

- You might have read maps. (Driver, surveying crew member.)
- You may be a sharpshooter or have stood guard duty. (Security guard, border patroller, police work.)
- Maybe you dug bunkers. (Nursery or landscaping assistant.)

Whatever you did, most of your military experience has some application to civilian work and gives you something to offer employers. On top of all that, you also learned how to work closely with others and how to carry out orders. *Every* employer wants both of those abilities.

A great talking point

Okay. So you have proved you can do things employers pay for—not necessarily that you are a top expert in any of them or that you want to make any of them your life's work. But, unless you are unusual, these things are not all you have to offer employers. The basic fact that you want to do a good job for any employer you choose to work for is a heavy asset and a great talking point if you present it right.

Whether you are just out of military service, just out of school, or in a reentry phase after having dropped out for a while, there are two important things to do some thinking about right now:

1. What you do best.
2. What you most *like* to do when being constructive.

For example, maybe you like cooking, repairing things around the house, making plants grow, sewing, caring for kids or pets, repairing bikes, or tinkering with cars. It's possible you enjoyed arranging furniture for special meetings at school, or running a slide projector, or acting as a monitor on the bus. It could be that you are an especially good car or bike driver, or that you were top honcho in calling the shots with the kids you hung out with in your neighborhood. Maybe just talking with others to get them to think the way you do turns you on.

The things you have enjoyed doing and doing well could be much different from any of those just listed but, whatever they are, think about them. Recall as many as you can, even if you don't see how they relate to any job you might take. Getting these things in mind is important in deciding just what kind of employer to aim for and what kind of work you will do best and most enjoy.

As you think about these things, you may also want to give some thought to this: The odds are at least even that you tend to underrate yourself when you think about your abilities and the value they will have for you and your employers in the future. Chances are also high that you probably underrate the satisfaction and pleasure you will get from a job that gives you a chance to put your abilities to good use.

Step one — think about what you do best

Give it hard thought. Ask people who know you what *they* think you do best. After they stop kidding around and get serious, they'll probably come up with things you didn't think about. Then, start lining them up, either in your head or on paper, so you can complete the following *Abilities Checklist* —the first important step in your job hunt. This will help you put your finger on your best experience and strongest abilities so you can begin to decide just what kind of job is best for you—the one you will be happiest with and will find easiest to land.

ABILITIES CHECKLIST

Completing this list is the first step to take in your job search. Before doing it, read the qualifications brief for Jordan Pruitt on pages 42 and 43 to get an idea of the kinds of information you should include below. Be sure to include everything you can think of that fits the topics below, no matter how unimportant it may seem.

1. List the courses in school or military training that you liked most (or disliked least) including those in which you received the best grades.

   a. _____

   b. _____

   c. _____

   d. _____

   e. _____

2. List any school activities not involving studies that you particularly enjoyed and any accomplishments in school that made you feel proud.

   a. _____

   b. _____

   c. _____

   d. _____

   e. _____

3. List any kinds of tasks you have done well or really enjoyed in the past—at home, school, in military service, or elsewhere—whether or not you were paid for them.

   a. _____

   b. _____

   c. _____

   d. _____

   e. _____

4. Write down, as nearly as you can recall, good things people have said about you or work you have done for them.

a. _____

b. _____

c. _____

d. _____

e. _____

5. Now, read all of the statements below. Think about each one. Which will most truthfully fit the attitudes you will bring to your job when you get it? When you have decided, go back and check off those that fit you the best.

a. I would most like a job requiring:
☐ handwork
☐ brainwork
☐ both

b. I would like to work:
☐ indoors
☐ outdoors
☐ both

c. I like to:
☐ work where I can think my own thoughts
☐ work with details
☐ work with ideas
☐ work with people
☐ work with tools, equipment, and other things I can touch
☐ work alone
☐ work as part of a team
☐ express my ideas
☐ see the results of my work
☐ help others
☐ work hard
☐ keep very busy
☐ keep things in good order
☐ take on new tasks
☐ look for other things that need doing when my own work is done
☐ do a better job than others performing the same work
☐ learn new things
☐ fill requests fast and accurately
☐ stick to a job until it is well done

☐ maintain a good appearance

☐ _____
    (add any other things like those above you can think of)

☐ _____

d. I have:
   ☐ the ability to make friends easily
   ☐ a good sense of humor
   ☐ a strong sense of responsibility
   ☐ a cheerful outlook

   ☐ _____

   ☐ _____

e. I am:
   ☐ energetic
   ☐ a fast learner
   ☐ good with words
   ☐ good with my hands
   ☐ accurate with details
   ☐ easy to get along with
   ☐ careful to follow directions
   ☐ dependable and always on time
   ☐ neat in work habits
   ☐ cooperative with others
   ☐ not a clockwatcher
   ☐ willing to do extra work
   ☐ self-disciplined
   ☐ imaginative

   ☐ _____

   ☐ _____

f. I want to:
   ☐ obtain more training after work hours
   ☐ move ahead on the job
   ☐ make my own opportunities
   ☐ do an outstanding job for my employer
   ☐ contribute to the support of other family members

   ☐ _____

   ☐ _____

When you have completed this form, take *Step Two*.

Step two — get advice

It could be that your completed *Abilities Checklist* will be all
you need to develop your own qualifications brief like the one
shown for Jordan Pruitt at the end of this chapter. If so, good.
However, more than likely it would be a good idea to check it
out first with somebody who knows about the job market.
To do that, arrange to see an employment counselor either at
your school, military separation center, or the local public
employment office. (Read *Get help* on page 23, first.) Then
ask these questions and take notes on your counselor's answers
if you can.

- Can the counselor give you more help in checking out your
  strongest abilities?
- Are there any tests you can take that will help pinpoint
  your interests and aptitudes?
- What kinds of jobs are most likely to use your abilities?
- Does your counselor know of any openings now that might
  use your abilities?
- What kinds of employers are most likely to offer work in
  line with your abilities and interests as shown in your
  Abilities Checklist?
- Can your counselor tell you where to find such employers
  and give you a list of their addresses, telephone numbers,
  and the people to contact?
- Can your counselor show you how to use the *Yellow Pages*
  to track down more?
- How should you dress when you contact employers?
  What is the best way to handle interviews?
- In view of your abilities, what is the pay range you should
  aim for?
- Can your counselor help you develop a qualifications brief
  that shows your best abilities and experience?
- Does your counselor have more ideas on how you can find
  the work you want?
- Where can you get typing help with your qualifications
  brief? Where can you get it reproduced?

When you go to see the counselor, take your checklist and the
above questions with you so you will be sure to cover them all.
Don't be nervous about putting such questions to your coun-

selor. It's his/her job to give you all the advice and help possible. And your talk with the counselor will give you beginning practice for the time when you begin to tell employers just how good you are.

Step three — develop your qualifications brief

Let's face it. Few job seekers at your level come in to employers with a qualifications brief (or résumé). So why should you have one? Well, for several reasons. The first and biggest reason is that you are likely to find a better job faster with a qualifications brief than without one. Two, it will save a lot of talk when you try to explain to employers what you have to offer. Without a piece of paper to guide them, employers often fail to ask questions that bring out your strongest qualifications. Third, your brief will save you much work in filling in details on company applications. All you have to do is fill in information on the applications that is not covered by your brief and then write, "Please see attached qualifications brief" for the rest. Finally, most employers just naturally assume that an applicant who comes in so well organized has a lot more on top than one who doesn't.

In short, your qualifications brief will make your job hunting easier, shorter, and more likely to produce a job you will enjoy.

Before starting to put your qualifications brief together, read the one for Jordan Pruitt again. As you do, you will see how he has lifted statements directly from the *Abilities Checklist* that fit him and put them into his brief. You should do the same thing and try, with the rest of it, to make your presentation just as readable and interesting as his is. When you tackle the job of writing your brief, you may run into problems finding the right words. If so, get the help of your counselor or a friend who is good with language. (A friend may also be willing to type it for you, if that's not one of your strong points.) However it's done, try to have it look and sound as much like Pruitt's as possible—just as neat and easy to understand.

When writing your qualifications brief, show your name, address, and a telephone number where you can be reached at the top. After that, state the kind of job you are looking for PLUS a phrase like the one in Pruitt's brief that indicates that you can be relied on to do a good job. Here are some more examples:

- Sales clerk *where friendly, efficient treatment of customers is important.*
- Stock clerk *where there is a need for an employee who is good with detail, learns fast, and likes to work.*
- Construction worker—*especially with a company looking for reliable, energetic, and hard-working help.*

If you and your counselor are unable to decide on the specific kind of job you want (after giving it a strong try), simply lead off by asking for an "entry-level job" followed by a phrase like one of those shown in italics above.

After showing the general kind of job you want, show where you went to high school or college and, if you were graduated, when. State which subjects produced the best grades for you at school and include a word on any special success or activities in school that show that you go out of your way to do well.

Next, describe your work experience in school, at home, or elsewhere. Include any statements you can that show *how well* you did. Another look at Pruitt's brief will show you how to do this by describing the reaction of other people to things you have done.

Now—and this is important—cover "other qualifications." As in Pruitt's case, this can be a straight pick-up of some of the items you checked off on your *Abilities Checklist* plus others you think of.

Finally, show your birthdate. You can also include your height and weight if you want—particularly if size is important in the kind of work you want to do. If you're married, that should be indicated along with number of children. In addition, you can add anything else here that shows that you are responsible and a good citizen, just as Pruitt does when he mentions support for his sisters.

Step four — now run with it

All right. So you've developed your qualifications brief, asked your counselor to suggest improvements, and had 25 or more copies reproduced. (Good, clean Xeroxing is okay.) Now what do you do?

First of all, it's important to understand two things. One is this: As a normal thing, no one else can land a job for you—not your parents, relatives, or friends, not even employment agency or school job counselors. All they can do, usually, is help point you in the right direction. After that, it's up to you. *You* are the one who has to go after any leads they may give you. *You* are the one who has to uncover additional possibilities and track them down. And *you* are the one who has to convince an employer that hiring you is worth the substantial amount of money he/she will pay for your work. (The amount of money involved over a single year is usually more than most of us ever see in one lump sum.)

Then, there is another basic point to think about: Finding good people is one of the most important things employers ever do. When you contact employers, you are helping them with that job. You are *not* asking for a favor. Instead, you are offering them strong value—the value of your abilities, energy, and loyalty. You are giving them the opportunity to take advantage of that value. You are *not* imposing on them. Consequently, if anyone seems to turn you off or put you down as you seek employment—and it *does* happen—chalk it up to the fact that you have run into someone who apparently doesn't know his/her job, one you probably shouldn't be working for anyway.

Once you have those two basic ideas firmly in your head, the general idea is to work as hard as you can to get out of your current job (the job of finding a job) and into one you will enjoy. You are looking for a far better job that puts pay in your pocket every week or so.

Here's how to do it:

First, rely on your friends. Tell *all* of them what kind of work you're looking for. Include relatives and acquaintances, especially those who have jobs themselves or who are in contact with many other people. Tell everybody—even the postal carrier, the corner grocer, the dude (or chick) who gasses your wheels, your parents' friends. *Everybody.* Ask for their ideas and suggestions. Ask them to give you a quick call if they hear of a job you might want. Go immediately to see employers they name. (Maybe they'll arrange it for you.) Doing that will put you on the path down which you are *most* likely to find the job you want.

Second, go see employers—at least two or three a day—who employ people in the kind of work you want to do. *Don't worry about whether they have any openings right now. Don't even ask whether they do.* Employers never know whether somebody will resign the day you see them or the next. So, instead of asking whether they have any openings, tell them you want to show them why *you* should be the next one to hire as soon as a job opens up. Contacting employers in that way pays off in job offers at a faster rate than any other system except contacts through friends.

The last two points above are so important, they bear repeating:

1. Go see employers who you know have people on their payrolls doing the kind of work you want to do.
2. *Don't* ask if they have any openings. Instead, go with the idea that you will convince them that YOU should be the next person to hire when a job opens up.

In addition, here are some other key tips that will speed up the day you are hired as you contact employers:

- **See your future supervisor.** With each organization, try to see the supervisor you would be working for if you get the job you want. If it's construction work, see the foreman on the job. If you want a job as a supply clerk, see the head of the supply department. In small organizations (less than 25 employees) ask to see the manager. In larger ones, call first and ask the switchboard operator for the name and location of the head of the department or section you would like to work in—motor pool, shipping, maintenance, warehousing, production, sales, typist pool, personnel, accounting, whatever.

- **Come on strong.** When you know which people you want to see, go to see them directly or call to arrange a time. If you call, come on strong at the beginning after introducing yourself with something like this: "Mrs. Fellini, I'm sure I can do a great job in your department when one opens up. May I come to see you?"

But be prepared for resistance.

For example, Mrs. Fellini may come back saying, "We don't have any openings."

Still, hang in there. You could say, "What I'd like to do is show you that I'm the best applicant to hire the next time you do. May I come see you?"

When Mrs. F. tries another turn-off by asking, "What's your stock-handling (or whatever) experience?" don't cave in simply because you don't have any. Instead, stress *related* strengths and say something like this: "In school I showed that I work hard, fast, and carefully. People have always liked the jobs I've done for them."

By this time, Mrs. Fellini is probably beginning to realize that you are no run-of-the-mill applicant, but still, she might say, "We need better experience than that."

Even with that, you could still keep it going by saying, "I learn fast and you can count on the fact that I'll work hard for you. I'd like to prove it to you. Can I come see you?"

With a never-say-die approach like that, Mrs. Fellini may well say, "Okay, kid (she calls everybody "kid"), you've earned yourself a hearing. Come on in."

Or she may still say no.

Don't let that discourage you. Instead, ask her if she could suggest someone else who could use your abilities. Then thank her.

If you haven't found a job within a week or two, call her again. One thing is sure, she'll remember you. This time, she may be *very* glad to hear from you because a member of her crew has just told her he/she has accepted another job.

Either way, whether calling or talking in person (the better way to go since you can present your qualifications brief), try to take an approach like the one described above. Do everything you can to get across the idea that you very much want to work for the person you are talking with and that, if you do, you can be counted on to do a great job.

- **Contact company employment offices.** In every sizeable company you visit, go by the employment office. Give them a copy of your qualifications brief. Let them know if you have already made other contacts in the organization. Ask them if there are other departments in which your qualifications fit. If they have nothing to offer now, ask them to recommend other employers you should see, and also to name any employment agency counselor in town they depend on. Then go see the counselor as well. (Be sure to read all about employment agencies in Chapter 12 first.) And keep in touch with the agency counselor at least once every week until you've found the job you want.

- **Check the help-wanted ads.** Each day and especially on Sunday, check out the help-wanted ads in your newspaper. When you see a job listed that looks interesting and the address is provided, try to be there with your qualifications brief in hand *before* they open on Monday. If only a telephone number is given, call, using a strong approach like the one with Mrs. Fellini described above.

- **Report to your employment counselor.** Call or see your employment counselor at school or the public employment office *once a week.* Tell your counselor what you have been doing. Ask for advice on any job-hunt problems troubling you. Ask whether the office has any new openings in line with your needs. Ask to be notified immediately if a suitable opening comes to his/her attention. Continue to do this until you've found the job you want.

Repeat contacts like those we've been talking about above pay off in a big way. But be ready for it. Unless you're lucky, you're going to hear a lot of negatives. Some may sound rude. Don't let them slow you down.

Calling employers back every week or so literally *doubles* your chances of finding the job you want. The reason is that employers pay less and less attention to applications in their files as time passes by. They begin to assume after a couple of weeks that you are no longer available, or that you're not all that interested. After a month, they're pretty sure of it and are unlikely to check with you when a good job opens up. Because of that, keep this in mind: It's a lot easier and cheaper for you to keep an application alive than to start up another one with another organization. It's only when you are told that the organization has recently laid off people in your category who are up for rehire before they take on anyone else that you should cool your repeat contacts.

But it could be that there's *no* way that you're going out to see employers with a qualifications brief. It's not that you're trying to avoid a little extra effort. It's just not your style. You're not out for anything fancy in the way of work. All you want is a job in one of the small businesses close to home.

All right. At least do this: Go see the employers you want to work for. Three, four, or five a day. Look your best—clean, neat, smiling, friendly, up. Every time ask to see the manager. (Write down their names if you can.) When you see them, tell them that the next time they're looking for a really *good* employee to please call you. Be confident but respectful. Try to get them to believe that you can run rings around the crew working for them now but don't jive. Be prepared to tell them what kind(s) of work you could do for them. Then give them a 3 x 5 card on which you have written something like this: "The next time you need a really great employee, please call me," along with your name and phone number or a number where you can be reached. If they're too busy to talk with you when you come by, just hand them the card and split. Or ask someone there to do it.

But don't let it hang there. Go back to see them every week or so. Using their names (Mr. Smith, Mrs. Smith, or whoever), tell them that you still want very much to work for them. Always ask whether they might have an opening for you soon. Give them another card with your name and number in case they've mislaid the other one. Make it clear as you leave that you can be counted on to learn fast and do a great job.

Do that and you'll have a job in half the time (or less) than if you go around asking people if they have any jobs open today. And you'll enjoy it more.

What employers want

Employers admire applicants who put out a lot of well-directed effort to find the job they want. They want people working for them who are energetic, friendly, cheerful, and interested in their jobs. They want them to pay attention, ask questions, and learn fast. They want them to be there on time every day, to care how well the job goes, and to get the work done quickly, neatly, accurately, and with little waste. They like them to be willing to do extra work and to look for other work to do when their own work is done. They want people who will do everything they can to increase production while cutting costs and problems. In short, they want people working for them whom they like and who will do everything possible to make their jobs easier and get *them* promoted.

When you go out to see employers, be prepared to show that you meet those needs. Be attentive, respectful, alert, quick to smile, and ready to state your case after the employer has taken the lead. Normally, the best way to start off is to say, "I have a qualifications brief. Would you like to see it?" while offering it. But, whether or not you use a brief, be sure one message comes through so employers can't possibly miss it: "You can count on me, Ms. Smith, to do an outstanding job for you."

Doing that inspires employers to offer you a job at their first opportunity, maybe then and there, even though you may not have the experience they normally look for. It's the surest way to get the job you want.

One more thing.

Some people don't go along with the typical employer values outlined above. They're not ready to adjust to employers' likes and dislikes. That, certainly, is their right. But they're in for a heavy time when they go out to find a job.

When you get right down to it, there are two kinds of jobs out there—good and bad. The kind we hope you're aiming for offers pleasant working conditions, fair pay, the chance to get ahead, reasonable security, and consideration for you as a person. The bad kind offers none of these things. People who have no concern for the needs of their employers are most likely to end up in such poor and unrewarding jobs—if they succeed at all.

Don't be one of them.

QUALIFICATIONS BRIEF
FOR JORDAN PRUITT

Following is Jordan Pruitt's qualifications brief. Read it carefully. When you do, look for ways in which he:

- Has indicated the kind of job he is looking for *and* what he offers employers right at the beginning under his name and address.
- Has shown how he succeeded at jobs he has tackled in the past.
- Has used the comments of others to show how well he did those jobs.
- Has picked up statements from the *Abilities Checklist* that show that he is an applicant with strong abilities.

When you write your qualifications brief, try to make it as much like Pruitt's as you can. Use the same kind of language. Include the same kinds of information. Show what you've done and, where possible, how *well* you've done it. Stress strong abilities and personal characteristics near the end.

JORDAN PRUITT

1146 Sixth Street, South, Milwaukee, Wisconsin 61733
Telephone: 588-5323 (Please leave message with Joe Witzky.)

Applying for:

Printshop or carpenter's helper with an organization looking for a
dependable, hard-working employee.

Education:

Schulmeister High School, Milwaukee. Had to stop in junior year
to earn own support. Best subjects: Arithmetic, geometry,
printing, and wood-working shop. (Three A's, two B's.)

Work experience:

In school, type-set and printed programs, handbills, schedules,
and school forms. Many compliments on them. Maintained presses.
Sometimes repaired them. Also did about a third of the set construction for school plays. Liked doing it. After the first year, the stage
director put me in charge.

Part-time and summers did handiwork for people in neighborhood--
fixed plumbing, repaired porches, gutters, electrical fixtures.
Got many repeat calls from customers. Also made bike deliveries
for neighborhood snack shop. People joked about how I delivered the
order before they put it in. Mr. Corby, the shop owner, asked me
to stay on.

At home, helped paint the house. Got my part done faster and better
than my older brother. Often did major house-cleaning chores and
minor repairs around the place. Learned how to work fast to get
these jobs done. Took care of my little sisters when my mother had
to be away at work.

Other qualifications:

Make friends easily . . . energetic . . . like hard work . . . not a
clockwatcher . . . always on time . . . enjoy helping others . . .
neat work habits . . . learn fast . . . have a work permit . . . own
a car . . . good in basketball.

Personal:

Born June 17, 1964. Single. 5' 8", 140 pounds. Strong--not afraid
of heavy work. Part of all my earnings help support my sisters.

The ideal job for you will make the most
of your best experience and personal assets.
Finding your strongest qualifications
is likely to take hard thought and study
but, once you fully know them,
you will know where and how to aim your efforts.
Here's more on how
to take a good look at your abilities.

4
Explore yourself
for the right job

A startling thing usually happens to people who find themselves under the guidance of a good professional career analyst and counselor. As a *normal* result, they discover (usually to their ecstatic delight) that their abilities and potential for enriching employment are considerably greater than they thought. The results are sometimes so profound that we have heard more than one clergyman describe the revelation involved as akin to a deeply moving religious experience.

"Know thyself" is an ancient admonition that most of us have heard but, unfortunately, few of us heed. As a result, most of us are strangers to ourselves. Yet, only by understanding yourself can you know what you are capable of becoming. But be prepared. Gaining such understanding is likely to furrow your brow.

There's an old tale told about Michelangelo that bears on this point. Asked how he visualized his magnificent monuments to man in rough-hewn stone, he replied, "My friend, the figure is already there. I simply carve away the stone that covers it." The procedure for determining your best abilities is like that. The work is just as hard, and the figure of yourself revealed in the process can be just as inspiring.

So, before anything else, explore yourself. Get to know the product (yourself) that you are about to put on the job market. Doing this permits you to aim for employment at the *peak* of your abilities—the kind of employment you will land most easily and quickly. It can produce a massive payoff in terms of immediate and future rewards.

Employers don't bother

Most people neglect to define their greatest strengths before entering the job market. Many seriously handicap themselves by leaving it up to employers to figure out the jobs that best fit them. Employers, of course, can't be bothered. They offer employment and pay on the basis of abilities that *you* communicate to them. If your assessment of yourself is vague, your communications regarding yourself will be vague. And employers, if they respond at all, play it safe. Because of the cloudy picture they get from most applicants, they tend to offer employment at the *base* of the abilities the applicants communicate to them—not at the hazy peak which they are unlikely to perceive when you yourself see it only in dim outline, if at all.

But that's not the worst of it. Many applicants aim themselves in the wrong direction entirely simply because they don't know what their abilities are or where they can be put to best use. Take, for example, the man who shot off a letter to us, apparently without much thought, saying, "Get me one of them executive jobs." Somehow, that letter created the impression that this man had not analyzed his goal in terms of his abilities. His qualifications brief confirmed the thought.

But that's not unusual.

Our mail indicates that *most* applicants who have not had adequate guidance steer themselves toward the wrong job goals as a result of failure to analyze their own abilities first. Some of these will be seeking the job *you* want. If you avoid their error, obviously your prospects for landing it will be better than theirs.

The unhappiest aspect of all this is that great numbers of people get started in the wrong direction with their first job and then compound the error by building their careers on the initial mistake. They get in deeper and deeper with each promotion. In effect, terribly inexperienced young people are determining—without planning or guidance—the futures of the adults they will later become. All too often, those futures are dim indeed.

Life-long entrapment of this kind comes from the habit of basing career decisions on work experience rather than personal ability. It's a habit that introduces the heavy hand of fate into your life's work in a way that can corrode the whole course and character of your future. Avoid it.

Stress ability, not experience

Ability, basically, is what counts in determining your best job field and the specific type of job you should aim for—not experience or past duties performed. Fortunately, ability is a built-in factor. It's there for you to discover and bring out and hold up to employers so they can see it and put it to work, even if you have never worked a day in your life. But, again, discovering your own best abilities is not always—or even usually—easy.

Let's take an example to show what we mean, one that shows how your job experience and even your education can directly handicap you in your job search when emphasis on ability would lead to highly rewarding employment. We'll call our man Kirby (not his name) and take up his story in high school.

Chronicle of a failure

When he was a sophomore, somebody told Kirby that there was a big need for engineers and that they made a lot of money. This clicked because Kirby's father was already an engineer and Kirby liked his father. More than that, he liked his father's standard of living. So Kirby took courses heavy in mechanical drawing and physical science. However, he enjoyed the school's athletic program a great deal more, and his grades in the technical courses were low.

In the summer before graduation, Kirby found a job as an engineering aide. Unfortunately, he goofed off for lack of interest and his father had to enter the picture to buck him up and keep the employer from firing him.

After graduating in the lower half of his class, Kirby took a summer job as a lifeguard with a community swimming pool. He was reprimanded twice for excessive attention to (and from) the female customers and was also responsible for an expensive foul-up when he punched the wrong button in the pump room. This almost got him fired again.

When the summer ended, Kirby entered a pre-engineering course at a state polytechnic institute but quit after the first year because of lack of interest and low grades.

He enlisted in the Army. Nothing distinguished him during basic training except that his superiors leaned heavily on him for being overleave after graduation. (He was taking in the

World Series and it ran to seven games.) Based on the technical emphasis of his education and employment to that point, he was assigned as a stock clerk responsible for a sizeable spare-parts inventory for a small missile base. Some time later, he was a central figure in an official investigation because he had issued an obviously defective part that resulted in a serious accident. He came close to being courtmartialed. The general conclusion of most of his Army associates was that he was highly likeable but a damn poor soldier.

When he was released from military service, Kirby aimed himself in the direction of his past experience and goal—engineering employment. Then he fell into the hands of a competent counselor who soon spotted the fact that Kirby was persistently aiming for work for which he had no talent and didn't like. He was letting fate decide his career.

Probe the past for accomplishment

The counselor probed Kirby's background. What about the record when he was doing what he wanted to do? That's where ability is usually revealed. Since most people are good at something, the counselor assumed that even Kirby probably had some strong points despite a heavily fortified personal conviction of worthlessness.

As a result of her probing, this is what the counselor found:

In high school, Kirby consistently got high grades in English and social studies. He was the school's star athlete and persuaded the athletic director to establish crew as a regular part of the school's sports program by lining up strong student interest and some second-hand racing shells that could be purchased from available PTA funds. During the summer as a lifeguard, he organized a swimming team that swept all of the meets in its league.

While at the missile base, he talked the executive officer into undertaking a survival hike in the Santiago Mountains during which he displayed unusual ability to make the best of almost intolerable conditions and to bolster the morale of the other men. During off-duty hours, he wrote a grimly humorous story of the hike that aroused strong interest in the editorial office of one of the nation's leading sports magazines, although it was not finally accepted. Another article on bush league baseball in West Texas also received favorable editorial attention.

In the absence of key officer personnel, Kirby had also volunteered to conduct a tour of the base for a group that included the mayor of the nearest town. His excellent appearance, affable manner, and concentration on the human and humorous side of the operation made friends for the Army of everyone in the tour and produced a laudatory letter from the mayor.

So Kirby failed at almost everything he was supposed to do. It was only when he was enjoying himself that he did well.

Most of us are like that.

Boiled down, the things that Kirby enjoyed most made him an expert in athletics and outdoor activities. They showed that he had strong leadership qualities, drive, high persuasive ability, an unusual understanding of what makes people tick, and a talent for writing. This, then, was the outline of the requirements of the ideal job for him. Kirby's qualifications brief on the next page shows how he made the most of it despite a strong and consistent record of failure on previous jobs. Read it now to see what we mean.

JAMES CREED KIRBY

Area code 412, 362-4751

3434 Hanover Avenue, NE   Hyattsville, Md. 20034

JOB OBJECTIVE

Public relations assistant - especially where the aim
is to motivate large groups to positive action in the
field of athletics, physical development, and outdoor
activities.

PUBLIC RELATIONS - U.S. ARMY, 1975-1980

While assigned to stockkeeping and supply duties at a West Texas missile
base, was asked to conduct tours of the base for interested civilian groups
of visitors although this function is usually handled by officers. Enjoyed
this duty tremendously. Press and public comment regarding our base took on a
warmth previously unknown in that unit. The Mayor of the nearest city addressed a letter commending the base for ". . . the impressive caliber and
high level of performance of its personnel . . ." and adding that ". . . PFC
Kirby opened our eyes to the importance of this base and the dedication of
the men who man it." Also during this tour of duty, persuaded the Executive
Officer to organize a 7-day survival hike in the Santiago Mountains. It was
more rugged than I had anticipated. At its close the Exec took note of my
performance as ". . . unusually resourceful and undoubtedly an important
factor in the success of the mission. Noteworthy aspects of leadership were
displayed in your ability to organize effective action and bolster the morale
of others under conditions of extreme stress." Authored a grimly humorous
account of this hike - now under consideration for publication. Another story
on bush league baseball in West Texas is also under editorial review.

OTHER EXPERIENCE

During summer vacations, served as an engineering aide one year and lifeguard the next. Organized a swimming team among youngsters of the pool
(17 and under) which swept all of the meets in its league in its first year.

PERSONAL DATA

Born June 7, 1947. 5'11". 170 pounds. Marriage imminent. Presentable.

EDUCATION

Pre-engineering studies for one year at Maryland Polytechnic Institute prior to
military service. Strongest subjects: English, History, Social Studies. Varsity letters in high school for swimming, football, and crew. (Persuaded head
of physical education department to organize this team.) Captain of football
team and crew (both winners). Plan to obtain degree in Marketing and Public
Relations with Psychology minor through evening studies.

QUALIFICATIONS BRIEF FOR A CHRONIC FAILURE *(See text)*

This shows what happens when you emphasize your abilities instead of your
experience. Comparison of this brief with the text account of Kirby's dismal
work experience will show you how to give proper weight to those things you
have done which reflect your strongest abilities while minimizing the rest.

Finding your best job field

How can you discover the outline of the ideal job for you? Doing it involves uncovering your abilities, desires, sources of satisfaction, even your dreams of what you would like to do. Fortunately, because everything you are is, after all, within your head, such self-knowledge is really within close reach. Time, thought, and a self-discovery plan of action are all that are required to get at the core of your personality and make-up.

The *Career Analysis Guidelines* at the end of this chapter provide the plan. You can provide the time and thought. It won't be easy but it should be interesting, if not exciting. With the insight gained, you will be much better equipped to aim your abilities and energies in the direction of a richly rewarding life in the years ahead. This applies whether you are in high school and wondering where to go from here or in mid-career and unhappy with the way it has gone up to now.

As you reflect on the things the *Career Analysis Guidelines* suggest that you do, keep this in mind: A professional career analyst, if you retained one, would lead you through essentially the same process. The requirements in terms of your time and effort would be just as demanding as those imposed by the ten steps covered in the *Guidelines.* But there would be one major difference. With a career analyst guiding you, you would be spurred to complete the task rather than see the substantial fee paid for such guidance wasted. So, as you proceed, keep in mind that completing this self-analysis successfully is worth a great deal to you in terms of saving the high costs you would otherwise incur to achieve the same benefits. More important, it promises to provide you with a strong new sense of direction and confidence in your career development.

To get it done, set a schedule for yourself. Allot time—several days, at least—to complete the ten steps covered by the *Guidelines.* Take each step thoroughly, carefully, and conscientiously. *But see that it gets done.*

When you are finished, you should have a firm idea of where your strongest abilities lie. You will have identified those kinds of work in which you can make your greatest contribution during the years immediately ahead. You should know the types of duties you want to avoid. You should also know a number of areas in which you can improve your performance if you apply yourself. With such knowledge, you will have pinned down the type of job you will find easiest to land and from which you can expect the greatest long-term rewards and satisfaction. And you will be thoroughly prepared to develop a high impact qualifications brief to aim at those employers most likely to offer such work as shown by the final step of your analysis.

As indicated before, completing this analysis will give you self-knowledge and a sense of career direction matched by few others you will ever encounter. We hope you make the most of it.

CAREER ANALYSIS GUIDELINES

Preparation

Find a quiet place to work. Clear your workspace of everything except a scratch pad and a large sheet of paper 24 inches wide and 18 inches long. (That's newspaper size. Shelf or wrapping paper will do.) Have two pens or pencils on hand—one black and one red.

Now, with the long side of the paper horizontal, divide it into six columns as follows: Allow six inches for column 1, four inches each for columns 2 and 3, three inches each for columns 4 and 5; and four inches for column 6. Head the columns as follows: 1. General Abilities; 2. Dislikes; 3. Persisting Correctable Limitations; 4. Specific Abilities; 5. Specific Functions; and 6. Ideal Job Content. (See illustration at right.) If you are well into your career, you may find that you need two such pages, but it's best to wait and see. When this is done, proceed with Step One.

Step One
Defining Your General Abilities

First, start thinking about your high-school experience—ALL of it. Reflect especially on those aspects of your experience (other than purely social) that you most enjoyed and those things that you did best. Forget about the things you were *supposed* to be doing best at the time; instead, concentrate on those things that turned out best. Try to stand outside yourself and take a detached view. Consider your performance in comparison with others. In particular, recall every aspect of your performance in which you excelled or for which others expressed admiration. Also, consider those things you did that had an effect and influence on others. Pay no attention to the relative importance of any of these things in your career to date.

CAREER ANALYSIS WORKSHEET

1 General Abilities	2 Dislikes	3 Persisting Correctable Limitations	4 Specific Abilities	5 Specific Functions	6 Ideal Job Content

> **CAREER ANALYSIS WORKSHEET**. Your career analysis worksheet should look this after you have followed the instructions for drawing it (on page at left). Or, if you wish, two 24″ x 18″ copies including guides for completing each column (printed at each column head) may be ordered from the National Center for Job-Market Studies. To order, send $2 with your name and address to NCJMS—CAW, POB 3651, Washington, D.C. 20007. Multiple copies for group or class are available at lower cost.

Now, start writing. In columns 1, 2, and 3 of your large worksheet, insert the subhead "A. High School." Briefly identify, item by item, every study or school activity in which you did well or from which you gained special pleasure. Be sure to consider the *elements* of various studies. For example, you may have done very well at English composition, may have found it exciting, but may have been sufficiently poor in the rest of your English courses to get mediocre grades. Perhaps you also got a special charge out of calling the student dress code into question, mobilizing student opinion, and persuading the school administrators to change it. This, plus other things, might result in a list something like this in column 1: Creative writing, history, public speaking, acting, typing skill, newspaper reporting, debate club, swim team record, student leadership, persuading officials to change policy (policy formulation).

Next, reflect on those aspects of your high school experience that you found especially unappealing—anything that stands out in your memory as more than routinely bad. This can include subjects (or elements of them), activities, or simply reactions to situations. For example, you may have blown your top over what you considered to be bad teaching and unreasonable discipline. If so, your list under DISLIKES in column 2 might be something like this: All math courses, physics, contact sports, mediocrity of some teachers, authoritarianism.

Third, column 3, CORRECTABLE LIMITATIONS, should show a list of those personal limitations that also were evident in high school and *that you know are still part of your make-up*—that is, limitations that you know have kept you from doing your best. Be honest about them. For example, you might recall that you failed to seize opportunities for interesting studies and activities, devoted too little time to studies to get the most from them, and usually tended to let others provide leadership when you felt you could do a better job. In that case, you might describe these in column 4 like this: Lost opportunities, lazy about studies, non-leadership.

Now, write "B. College" in columns 1, 2, and 3, if that is part of your experience. Take the same approach as that indicated above in describing abilities, dislikes, and limitations. Write in all *new* courses of study (or elements of them) that provided bonuses in pleasure or that feeling of sound accomplishment. Where you find that your college experience repeats your high school experience, don't write it down again. Instead, put a red asterisk by the related high school item. For example, you may have excelled in debate at both levels. The red asterisk technique will reflect this reinforced interest and ability.

As your next subcategory in columns 1, 2, and 3, consider your "Summer or after-school employment." Take the same approach. Use the asterisk technique to indicate repeated items. Give due consideration to your relationships with coworkers, your boss, and others contacted on the job. For example, you may have been a playground director during the summer and after school. You may have chalked up positive enjoyment or accomplishment in developing unusual special events, increasing attendance by organizing a system of rewards to kids who brought friends, gaining city-wide publicity for your playground, and developing increased parent participation. You may have most disliked disciplining the kids, record keeping, dealing with irate parents. In terms of limitations, you may have lacked tact in dealing with your superiors, associates, and subordinates.

Then proceed in the same way with your "First fulltime job," "Second job," etc., taking each up in sequence. Hang on to the asterisk technique. *Go into more detail as you get closer to the present.* Consider new elements as they occur, new kinds of problems met and handled. Identify each briefly. Identify dislikes and limitations.

After covering your whole employment experience job by job, show "Other activities" in columns 1, 2, and 3. Identify the elements of your hobbies, outside activities (other than strictly social), associations, and unpaid work (including personal property maintenance as well as volunteer work) that you did best or enjoyed most. Cover it in the same way as your school and unemployment experience. For example, suppose sailing is a consuming outside interest. Have you become involved in maintenance, boat or sail design, navigation? Have you taken part in races or organizing them? If so, did you help with the planning, publicity, financing, staff recruitment, officiating, social affairs, etc.? List all of these elements that you handled well or from which you gained special pleasure in column 1. Take care of the other aspects in columns 2 and 3.

That concludes Step One. If you haven't already, maybe you should take a break.

Step Two
Identifying Your Strongest Abilities

Go back over everything in column 1. Ask yourself which of these items *really* stand out as sources of pleasure for you—even delight. Underline all you find of *different* types in red.

Next, review the column 1 list again with this question in mind: Which items in this list loom over the others in terms of providing satisfaction for a job well done? Underline them in black—again choosing items of different types.

When you are finished, five to ten items should be underlined—some once, some twice. A number of them are likely to have one or more asterisks beside them.

To this point, you have been thinking in detail about what you have been doing until now. You should have a more precise idea than before of those areas in which you perform well and enjoy yourself. You have defined some active aversions and have pulled out a number of characteristics that hold you down and that you probably can change if you work at it. With the next step, you will begin to determine the content of that ideal job.

Step Three
Identifying Specific Functional Abilities

Concentrate now on the items underlined in column 1. Examine each of them for the major *specific abilities* (personal characteristics that you applied to the situation) and *specific functions* (types of activities or duties required by the situation) each contains. Write the abilities in column 4. List the functions you are capable of performing in column 5.

Suppose, for example, that you obtained special satisfaction from organizing a mountaineering club in school. Major *abilities* that you applied to this task probably included the following: Verbal ability (oral and written) to persuade others to join and obtain the consent and cooperation of school officials and adult supervisors, leadership, creative imagination (on publicity to get others to join up), technical knowledge, mountaineering skills (probably requiring a combination of additional abilities including physical strength, endurance, coordination, balance, courage, judgement, determination, etc.). These would go into column 4.

Functions you had to perform in organizing the club may have included organizational and program planning, coordination of effort, supply and logistics (to get members, supplies, and equipment to climbing sites), communications (correspondence, reports to members), records, training (including first aid), advertising and publicity, financing, budgeting, procurement, and/or supervision of some or all of these. It doesn't matter that many of these may have been performed in simple style if, in fact, you performed them. That you did indicates ability in those areas. List them in column 5.

Proceed in this way to analyze *each* of the underlined items in column 1, to determine all of the innate and functional abilities demonstrated in your experience to date. Include them in columns 4 and 5. To avoid repetition, use the red asterisk technique to identify those that crop up repeatedly. As you do, ignore any that you feel are of no real significance, but if you must err, err on the side of too much detail rather than too little.

Step Four
Getting Advice

You may not get too far into the Step Three procedure before discovering that analytical ability is *not* one of your stronger characteristics. As a double check on your efforts, take a list of your underlined items from column 1 to your school counselor or to a public or private employment agency. Tell the receptionist you need advice regarding your career goals. Ask him/her to let you see the wisest, most experienced, most helpful counselor on the staff. Give the counselor your list and this report. Show the counselor the *Step Three* text above and ask whether he/she can help you define your strongest abilities and functional strengths. This advice won't cost anything, and your counselor should enjoy providing the help you need. Employment or recruiting officials of any sizeable organization are likely to be helpful in much the same way.

After developing your lists on best abilities and strongest functions in columns 4 and 5, use a red pen to underline those abilities you *most enjoy* exercising, those functions you most enjoy performing. Use the black pen to underline those you know represent your greatest strengths in terms of accomplishment. Limit your underlines to five or ten of the most significant items of *different* types. More than likely, some—perhaps all—will be underlined twice and have asterisks after them.

Step Five
Determining Content of the Ideal Job

Now move to column 6. As the first subhead, write in "A. Specific job content." Under it, list the abilities and functions you have just underlined in columns 4 and 5. First list all with two underlines. Then rank the rest according to your interest in them—with the highest first. *With this list, you have a specific idea of the content of the ideal occupation for you—one that will give you the greatest satisfaction and lead to the strongest possible opportunity for maximum personal development in the foreseeable future.* With it, you have the facts you need to develop a strong objective on your qualifications brief—one that shows the type and level of the job you want, your strongest abilities, and what you can do for your employer. You have the information you need to develop the rest of your brief in a way that concentrates on your best qualifications and backs up your objective with explicit proof of your ability to perform effectively in the type of job described. But you are not finished yet. Some refinement is necessary to be certain that you have not overlooked important aspects of your make-up—refinements in terms of your innate interests and requirements that will determine *where* you should look for that ideal job.

Step Six
Assessing Your Personal Relationships

Now take a close look at your personal relationships to determine whether you will be happiest in a job that requires strong contact with others or one that leaves you pretty much on your own. Or something in between. How do you stack up with others you know in terms of the effectiveness of your dealings with people? Is your persuasive ability high or low? Do people naturally warm up to you or do you tend to keep them at arm's length? Ask others how they feel about these questions to arrive at a fair and factual answer concerning whether you are most, moderately, or least effective in cooperative personal relationships. Write your conclusion in column 6 under "B. Personal relationships." Give it due consideration in terms of your objective since the degree of your effectiveness in dealing with others is an important factor to consider in choosing your job.

Step Seven
Determining Your Flexibility

Reflect on your freedom to take the kind of work you want without too much regard for immediate or future consequences. Do you need a strong element of security in your job to be happy with it? Is it essential that your income be steady, that your job provide medical, insurance, and retirement benefits? Can you afford to gamble a little—or a lot—

with the future in order to take advantage of possible prospects for exciting work that may offer a strong pay gamble? Turn these questions over in your mind and determine how you feel about them. Equally important, reflect on the effect on your family if you accept a job that contains a large element of adventure. Give as much weight to their feelings as your own. After weighing these questions, decide whether your job security requirements are high, moderate, or low. Write your conclusion in column 6 under "C. Security requirements."

Step Eight
Determining Your Best Working Environment

Consider the surroundings that will make you happiest, considering everything else you know about your abilities and aspirations. Consider the kinds of people you want as associates, the physical surroundings, climate, location, and conveniences that are essential to your happiness and that of your family. Consider the need for good educational facilities, recreation, cultural facilities, and housing. Note all of the environmental requirements that *must* be met by your next job in column 6 under "D. Environment." Then add others that would be desirable. Keep both in mind as you plan your job search, but remember that flexibility on this score will greatly broaden your opportunities.

Step Nine
Establishing Pay Goals

Formulate ideas on your immediate and long-range pay goals. Are you willing to start low in exchange for the prospect of a high return later? Do you want a job that offers the probability of steady progression at moderate levels along with high fringe benefits? Are your immediate pay requirements high relative to your experience so that you will trade other advantages in order to earn at a high rate to meet some long-range goal? (For example, working on Alaska's North Slope offers many discomforts and disadvantages but exceptionally high pay.) In any event, if you are in a quandary regarding the pay you should be aiming for, discuss your specific abilities list (item A in column 6) with a competent employment counselor to get a feel for the *range* of pay you should be aiming for in light of your other requirements. Write this range, the minimum you will accept under normal circumstances vs. the maximum you can reasonably hope to get, in column 6 under "E. Pay requirements."

Step Ten
Designating Best Fields of Work

Now, give consideration to the broad fields of work that will interest you. Keeping everything else you have learned about yourself in the back of your mind, would you be happiest in business, industry, services, education, or government? Write in those general areas that are appealing under "F. Fields of work." Now, try to be more specific. Recall any fields of activity you previously thought you could become very excited about—airlines, resorts, marine biology, professional athletics, etc. The range, of course, is extremely wide. So that you will get a better idea of these areas, spend some time thumbing through the index to the *Yellow Pages* of any large metropolitan area. Write down on a separate sheet of paper those product or service areas that look most interesting to you.

As a further guide, reflect on your "intake activities"—reading, listening, and viewing habits. Think about the kinds of articles, books, or programs that most frequently seize your concentrated attention (except those that serve purely as distractions). Do they concern politics, business, new trends in science or mechanics, ecology, agriculture, space, population, etc. Do you tend to zero in on everything you come across on certain subjects such as weather, children, gardening, do-it-yourself projects, cooking, through the whole gamut of human and natural phenomena? Try to pin these interests down as specifically as possible. For example, suppose detective stories are one of the sources of your greatest pleasure. Does this mean that you would enjoy being directly or indirectly involved in police, investigative, security, intelligence, penal, border patrol, or customs activities? Reflect on it. Define as precisely as possible all of the activities engaged in by employers that interest you. Get the help of an employment counselor in designating the types of employers engaged in the kinds of activities that most interest you. List all that look most interesting and promising in column 6. Use this list as a source of strong clues to the types of organizations you should contact in your job search.

Failing to give it proper attention
can be costly in many ways
—frustrating disappointments,
time and money wasted,
a job at lower pay than you are qualified for,
and plain, long-term unhappiness.
Because of this, your qualifications brief
is likely to be the most important thing
you will ever write.
Here's how to do it.

Probably you've noticed that we don't say much about
résumés in this book. For two reasons:

1. The word *résumé* is a pretty fancy piece of language—
   almost elitist in its connotations. The term implies, and
   perpetuates the notion, that résumés are only for high
   level white-collar types. Too bad, too, because *all* applicants who want to get ahead in their careers—from high-
   school dropouts on up—critically need a piece of paper
   showing their strongest abilities and experience if they
   are going to make the most of their current opportunities.
   Yet, even among those who recognize this need, many
   feel uncomfortable with the word "résumé." It just doesn't
   go down very well, for example, with some heavy-duty
   truck drivers, or, often, with the people who might hire
   them. Moreover, its frequently mispronounced—like
   "ree-zoom" instead of "rez'-oo-mā'." Countless people have
   been made to feel unnecessarily idiotic when they discovered they had been making that mistake.

2. Far more important, by dictionary definition, a résumé is
   "a summary of experience submitted with a job application." And that's just about all most résumés do; they
   summarize experience—experience that, typically, is good,
   bad, and indifferent. Unhappily, they say almost nothing
   about *abilities.* Yet, your abilities—obviously—are far more
   important to your success (and to your employer) than
   your experience. Because of this failing, our analysis of
   thousands of résumés shows that fully 78 percent fail to
   do justice to the people they describe. And the bulk of
   the remaining 22 percent only barely do an adequate job.

All of this helps to explain how highly competent people can
mail out as many as 500 résumés without obtaining a single
interview. Because of their major shortcomings, résumés

simply don't work very well as a means of getting jobs. No wonder they are so heavily discredited these days by men and women who have been doing basic research into the job market's operations!

Don't use a résumé

All right, if you are not going to have a résumé summarizing your experience, what should you have? Clearly you need something that adequately reflects your *qualifications* for the job you want—not just your experience.

Qualifications? What are they?

A quick trip to the dictionary provides the answer. Qualifications, it says, are "any qualities, accomplishments, or abilities that suit a person to a specific position or task."

There's a clap of thunder in that definition. (A true genius must have written it.) Once its implications are read and absorbed, then its importance becomes abundantly clear.

Of course! Obviously you are more than a sum of your experience. You are a living human being with a set of personal *qualities* and interests that suit you to a particular kind of work. Your past *accomplishments*—more than any other single factor—indicate what kind of work that should be. And your *abilities* (which, more than likely, have not been fully used in your experience to date) are critically important in determining how well you will do at such work.

When you look at it that way, the need becomes evident. You critically need a brief statement that stresses the qualities, accomplishments, and abilities that qualify you for the job you want—not a résumé that summarizes only your experience. And your *qualifications brief*, like a lawyer's brief, should make a highly persuasive case for you—a case for hiring you above all other applicants.

Not only do *you* need such a brief. Employers do, too, if they are going to improve their performance in hiring people. The résumé tradition over the past 30 years has trapped them into unduly emphasizing experience in the selection process when stress on *qualifications* (as defined above) would undoubtedly produce much better results. (This factor alone may well explain why personnel turnover is so high. For example, it runs as high as *46 percent*—nearly half—in manufacturing industry during some years.)

All right. Accepting all that, in what specific ways will your qualifications brief be sharply different from the résumés likely to be compared with it? Here are some of the most important ones:

- Your brief will focus on the needs of *employers* where résumés almost always focus on the needs of the applicants they describe.

- Unlike résumés, your brief will define your *abilities* more than the duties you have performed in the past.

- It will clearly indicate *how well* you perform when operating at or near the peak of your abilities where résumés typically leave this vital question unanswered.

- It will stress your accomplishments (an important part of your qualifications) where résumés, in a much less meaningful way, describe responsibilities (not part of your qualifications) and often obscurely, at that.

- It will reflect your character and personality as a live human being—critically important elements of your qualifications— where résumés tend to ignore these factors and, instead, describe their authors in excessively dry terms like the specifications for piston rings in some wholesale auto parts catalog.

- Most important, because of all these major differences from résumés, your qualifications brief will aim you in the direction you should go for easiest success in your job search and greatest self-fulfillment—not necessarily in the direction you have traveled to date.

So, from here on out, we'll refer to this key document in your life as your "qualifications brief" or simply as your "brief." If you want to cut that back to "qualbrief" or "QB," feel free.

An important key to success in your search

Let's assume that (as outlined in Chapter 4) you've counted up all of your personal assets and interests plus the kinds of tasks you have always done best and have come up with an outline of the duties of the job you would be best fitted to hold. Then you went to your counselor at the local State unemployment office for advice on the job fields that could most readily use someone with the talents shown in your list of personal assets, interests, and best past performance. Now what do you do?

Keep this in mind: *No matter how you approach the problem, you will enter a kind of sales campaign when you offer your services in the job market. The services you are selling are likely to cost employers at least $100,000.00 over a period of years. In many instances, the cost will range well over half a million.* No small item in anyone's budget.

You may find this sales aspect of your job search unsettling if—like many of us—you have the feeling you couldn't sell a glass of water to a wilting fern. But it needn't be. The sales job ahead is really only a matter of communication—communication of your abilities to employers. The most important instrument in your communications campaign will be a dignified sort of advertising flyer—a qualifications brief that does an effective job of convincing potential employers that it might pay them to commit X thousand a year to retain your services, and that, certainly, your qualifications are worth heavy consideration from here on out.

All right. Recognizing the importance of a good brief, what else does it do for you? Well, to be precise . . .

- It creates an instantly favorable impression of you.
- It immediately relates your availability to the needs of employers.
- It sharply focuses attention on your special abilities for the *specific* kind of job you want.
- It excites interest in you as a potential employee.
- It is attractive to the eye and yet dignified in appearance. In a pile of résumés, it stands a good chance of being among the first applications to be read and retained for further consideration.
- It fully covers the major strengths you will bring to the job you want and yet is not so long that employers will not find time to read it quickly.
- It creates the desire to meet you personally to find out more about you.

64

- It backs you up and helps to keep employers on the track during interviews.
- It greatly fortifies your prospects for obtaining a job offer in the shortest possible time at the highest possible pay.
- It saves you much time and labor in completing company applications. With it, you can reduce that task to filling in only those blanks regarding past experience not covered by your brief and insert "Please see the enclosed qualifications brief" for the rest. (Given this approach, hiring officials tend to ignore the official application and simply review your brief—a far more compelling statement of your qualifications than most applications allow.)

In short, your qualifications brief has one chief aim—to produce interviews with employers who are predisposed to look favorably on your qualifications. Or, if submitted after an interview, to bind up a job offer. *If you carefully prepare yours in line with the guides in this chapter, it will be among the most impressive qualifications statements ever seen by most employers who receive it.*

Creating such good impressions at the start strongly (even unduly) influences favorable consideration of your qualifications all along the line. Which is one more reason why we stress the need for so much care in preparing your presentation.

Still, submission of a good qualifications brief is not the *only* way to get interviews. Chapter 7 shows an approach to employers that starts with a letter alone. And Chapter 8 outlines techniques for obtaining highly productive interviews without advance written contact of *any* kind. But, in both cases, submission of a qualifications brief is almost always part of the process. You still need a carefully prepared brief—one that you can modify quickly in light of a particular job you have learned about for a fast follow-up to the employer.

Boost your morale with your brief

A good qualifications brief does one more thing: It will bolster your morale terrifically since it presents such a clear picture of just how capable you are. Even if you are not ready for a job switch now, having your brief on hand will strengthen your confidence in dealings with your present employer. It will keep you instantly ready for a persuasive presentation to your boss or, if necessary, to another employer in that fleeting moment when opportunity suddenly looms—or when necessity requires a quick change.

So, regardless of your immediate readiness to enter the job market, work up your qualifications brief now. Always keep an annually updated copy on hand. In addition to all the other benefits this will bring, you will avoid the need to take up the demanding task of writing it on short notice when you are least likely to do a good job. Because *every word* in your brief should be carefully chosen for its effect in arousing employer interest, it's not a job you will want to take up on a by-the-by basis.

Preparing your brief

Herewith, to guide you, are the briefs of Nancy Kramer, a high-school graduate, John S. Adams and Brenda Brigham, both right out of college, Albert Haynes Cross, a ten-year man, Ronald G. Kale, a skilled craftsman who has risen into the management ranks, and Lili Li Lu whose presentation more than likely will startle a number of women who have never "worked" (so the saying goes) a day in their lives. At the end of Chapter 3, you will find the brief for Jordan Pruitt who quit high school to go to work, and Chapter 4 shows the one for James Creed Kirby, the college dropout who thought he was a failure. You will find more at the end of this chapter—briefs that effectively reflect the abilities of men and women at all levels of experience.

So you will know what we are talking about in the rest of this chapter, please read them all right now. Yes, *all.*

2827 Scanda Street
Shepard, N. Y. 10046
June 20, 1979

Mr. John W. Brown, Vice President, Advertising
Teen Styles, Incorporated
516 West 47th Street
New York, N. Y. 10016

Dear Mr. Brown:

    Past experience in selling your most attractive styles, in advertising to the large teenage market, and recent most enjoyable employment as a secretary have given me a background which, I believe, would make me most effective with your firm.

    The trend-setting designs in which Teen Styles specializes made your ready-to-wear easily my best line during two summers' work as a sales clerk. I enjoyed selling them and bought many myself. Thus I am well acquainted with their moderate prices, durability, and strikingly casual flair . . . all so important to the young people of today.

    Because of my high interest in current style trends and advertising, I would very much like to talk with you about the possibility of secretarial work in your department as soon as a suitable opening occurs.

    May I call on Monday?

Sincerely yours,

Nancy Kramer

Nancy Kramer

P. S. I hope you find my qualifications brief, enclosed, interesting.
      It further explains my strong interest in working for you.

```
                    N A N C Y   K R A M E R

  2827 Scanda Street    Area Code 412, 362-4751    Shepard, N.Y. 10046
```

objective
Secretarial assistant - preferably with an advertising executive looking for high interest, a sense of humor, ideas, and the ability to cope accurately with vast amounts of detail.

rapid promotions
Won a high grade (98%) in civil service examination for secretaries. Moved from pool to much more responsible work (in public information office) after one month with IRS locally. Received two promotions since then. (1977-1979)

successful sales experience
Served as a sales clerk in Alton's Top-Teens Shop during summers. Learned to understand fashion tastes and buying sense of teenagers. Sold among the top three clerks with fewest returns--50% less than the department average. Store manager asked me to return permanently at a strong pay boost as soon as there was an opening. (1975-1976)

education
Graduate, Shepard High School, 1977. All A's in secretarial and business courses. Good Citizenship Award on graduation. Served as advertising manager for student newspaper. Designed ads for many of our accounts. Increased sales 40%.

personal
Born August 6, 1958 . . . single . . . often complimented on appearance . . . very healthy.

other facts
Type 80 words per minute. Shorthand: 110 wpm. Have earned my own clothing and spending money for past six years. Now attend dress-making classes as once-a-week recreation. Enjoy making my own clothes and keeping up with styles, materials, and techniques. Also enjoy people and, with them, sports, dancing, and music but am most fascinated when involved with problems of communication and advertising--particularly where the aim is to appeal to the interests of young people.

QUALIFICATIONS BRIEF
FOR A HIGH SCHOOL GRADUATE

Aiming your application at employers who can put your strongest abilities and experience to best use is bound to produce the best results. It definitely would be an "off" day for Brown if he failed to respond favorably to this covering letter and brief.

```
                                JOHN S. ADAMS


    2923 Clinker Street, Horton, Washington 44361      A.C. 718, Terminal 7-5777
```

objective	Editorial, research, or personnel assistant in an organization concerned with public affairs - especially where an analytical approach, broad writing ability, and a major interest in human factors are needed to assure reliable development of reports, studies, or programs.
education	Bachelor of Arts, University of Washington, 1976. Major: History and Government. English minor. Edited campus newspaper. German language facility. Graduated in top tenth.
practical experience with office operations and problems	Served as clerk for three months with the Gulf, Colorado & Santa Fe Railroad. Duties included all routine functions of a RR disbursing office - office machine operation, voucher recording and routing, etc. (Summer, 1976) Primary gain: Practical experience in handling large volumes of routine office work plus observation of the factors which contribute to high operating costs and resistance to improved methods.
successful work-crew supervision and public realtions	During previous summer vacations, served as counselor in a seashore camp for 100 children (up to 16). After the first year, acted as senior counselor with primary responsibility for directing the staff in all recreational activities. Also responsible for construction, maintenance, and deactivation of all camp and waterfront facilities. Directed ten-man crews (most of whom were senior in age) in this work. (Summers, 1972-1975) Primary gain: Valuable experience in supervision and dealing successfully with others (including an occasional irate parent) and in scheduling work crews for best results. According to the director, the success and strong reputation of the camp during these years was largely based on my performance of duty.
personal data	Born April 19, 1953 . . . single (but with designs) . . . height: six,one . . . 165 pounds . . . presentable . . . health excellent. Enjoy aircraft model designing, music, all aquatic sports . . . type 70 words per minute.
primary aims and assets	Aiming for employment which will enable me to create my own opportunities and accept responsibility for results . . . energy and drive . . . successful in relationships with others . . . wide interest in public administration and affairs.

BRIEF FOR A COLLEGE GRADUATE
WITHOUT PERTINENT EXPERIENCE

Adams shows that he has made the most of available opportunities despite the absence of experience directly related to his goal. However, avoid the "primary gain" approach shown in his brief if you have a number of years' experience behind you.

69

LILI LI LU
1536 Sierra Way
Piedmont, California 97435
Telephone: 436-3874

OBJECTIVE

Program development, coordination, and administration

. . . especially in a people-oriented organization where there is a need to
assure broad cooperative effort through the use of sound planning and strong
administrative and persuasive skills to achieve community goals.

MAJOR AREAS OF EXPERIENCE AND ABILITY

Budgeting and management for sound program development

With partner, established new association devoted to maximum personal development and self-realization for each of its members. Over a period of time,
administered budget totalling $285,000.00. Jointly planned growth of group
and related expenditures, investments, programs, and development of property
holdings to realize current and long-term goals. As a result, holdings increased twenty-fold over the period, reserves invested increased 1200%, and
all major goals for members have been achieved. (A number have been sharply
exceeded.)

Purchasing to assure smooth flow of needed supplies and services

Usually alone (but in strong give-and-take consultation with partner regarding
major acquisitions), made most purchasing decisions to assure maximum production from available funds. Maintained continuous stock inventory to determine
on-going needs, selected suppliers, and assured proper disbursements to achieve
a strong continuing line of credit while minimizing financing costs. Handled
occasional "crash" needs so that no significant project was ever adversely af-
fected by failure to mobilize necessary supplies, equipment, or services on
time.

Personnel development and motivation

From the beginning, developed resources to assure maximum progress in achieving potential for development among all members of our group. Frequently
engaged in intensive personnel counseling to achieve this. Sparked new community programs to help accomplish such results. Although arrangements with
my partner gave me no say in selecting new members (I took them as they came),
the results produced by this effort are a source of strong and continuing
satisfaction to me. (See "specific results" below.)

BRIEF FOR AN APPLICANT "WITH NO WORK EXPERIENCE"
Nonsense. Virtually everyone has work experience. The idea is to find out what
you have done that employers normally pay to have done for them. Despite

Transportation management

Jointly with partner, determined transportation needs of our group and, in consultation with members, assured specific transportation equipment acquisitions over a broad range of types (including seagoing). Contracted for additional transportation when necessary. Assured maximum utilization of limited motor pool to meet often-conflicting requirements demanding arrival of the same vehicle at widely divergent points at the same moment. Negotiated resolution of such conflicts in the best interest of all concerned. In addition, arranged four major moves of all facilities, furnishings, and equipment to new locations--two across country.

Other functions performed

Duties periodically require my action in the following additional functional areas: Crisis management . . . proposal preparation . . . political analysis . . . nutrition . . . recreation planning and administration . . . stock-market operations . . . taxes . . . building and grounds maintenance . . . community organization . . . social affairs administration (including VIP entertaining) . . . catering . . . landscaping (two awards for excellence) . . . contract negotiations . . . teaching . . . and more.

Some specific results

Above experience gained in 20 years devoted to family development and household management in partnership with my husband, Harvey Hwangchung Lu, who is equally responsible for results produced. Primary achievements: Son Lee, 19, honors student at Harvard majoring in physics, state forensics champion. Daughter Su, 18, leading candidate for the U.S. Olympics team in gymnastics, entering pre-law studies at the University of California, Berkeley, this Fall. Son Kwan, 16 a senior at Piedmont High School with 3.98 average, president of student council, organizer and leader of a highly successful rock band but heavily disposed toward future studies in oceanography. Secondary achievements: A lovely home in Piedmont (social center for area teenagers). Vacation homes at Newport, Oregon (on the beach) and a cabin in Big Sur. President of Piedmont High School PTA two years. Organized successful citizen protest to stop incursion of Oakland commercialism on Piedmont area. Appointed by Robert F. Kennedy as coordinator for his campaign in Oakland.

Personal data and other facts

Born in 1934. Often complimented on appearance. Bachelor of Arts (Asian History), Cody College, Cody, California. Highly active in community affairs. Have learned that there is a spark of genius in almost everyone which, when nurtured, can flare into dramatic achievement.

major differences in ultimate goals, Lu proved with her brief that she has a great deal of successful experience performing a wide variety of important management functions.

―――― BRENDA BRIGHAM ――――
Box 4425, Brown University, Providence, R. I. 02912 · 401/331-5270

objective

TEACHER OF ANTHROPOLOGY where ability to coordinate information from diverse areas into a single theme, to work closely with
individuals and groups, and to create three-dimensional projects to
intensify learning can be used in studies of anthropology, American
civilization, and/or literature with an anthropological perspective.

teaching experience

As teaching assistant at Phillips Academy, presented a series of lec-
ture-discussion classes on my thesis topic: Iroquois ethnology.
Became closely involved with my students' individual interests.
Worked actively with them at various digs and in their research.

As a museum aide, developed a wool project which became an exhibit
produced by neighborhood children under my guidance. We taught
visitors how to card, spin, dye, and weave wool by Indian methods.
Permanent staff warmly praised this work and asked that it be written up for continuation after my departure. Found the high interest
and excited response of the children involved most gratifying.

As senior counselor for a day camp, developed new nature and drama
programs for my group of 18 pre-teens. This stimulated creation of
similar drama programs camp-wide the following year.

work history

Teaching assistant, Anthropology and Archaeology, Phillips Academy,
summer, 1975 . . . Aide, Boston Children's Museum, summer, 1974
. . . senior counselor, Burgundy Farm Country Day Camp (Alexandria,
Va.), summers, 1972, 1973. Also resident counselor in my dormitory,
1974-1976, and part-time library assistant, Special Collections, Brown
University, 1972-1976.

education

Bachelor of Arts, Brown University, expected June, 1976. Major:
Anthropology and Archaeology. Now writing honors thesis. Major grade-
point average: 3.6. Creative writing minor. Adept in German.

other facts

Born 1956. Single. Excellent health. Very willing to live in dormitory
as resident fellow. Interested in sponsoring craft-related, literary, or
athletic activities. Draw deep satisfaction from observing the wide expansion of students' horizons under the influence of good teaching.

A CANDIDATE WITHOUT "REQUIRED" EDUCATION

With her brief, Brigham won appointment in a prestigious private school despite
heavy competition from other applicants—almost all of whom had Master's
degrees. She did it by emphasizing directly related experience and abilities first
while deliberately showing her education toward the end. With that approach,
72 school administrators were convinced of her strong qualifications even before
they learned of her "limited" education.

Because early
experience in the
various trades and
crafts offers
little variation from
job to job, Kale
got around that
limitation by
showing the
approach and
personality he
brought to his
work—both of
which assured
strong advancement.
Start with your
latest experience
and proceed back
to your school
days.

Make it interesting.
Let the success
in your record
speak for itself.

RONALD G. KALE

Tel: (202) 541-6451

3434 Hanover Avenue   Brigadoon, Maryland

JOB OBJECTIVE
ASSISTANT GENERAL FOREMAN - PRINTING

Composing Room Foreman, THE WASHINGTON GAZETTE
1976 - 1980

Currently Foreman of the main shift responsible for the production
of 60 men. (General Foreman leaves all responsibility to me.)
Promoted to this job after 18 months as Foreman of third shift
in ad room because of 30% increase in production, 27% decrease in
waste, and 40% lower crew turnover that occurred after my
assignment. Previously served eight months on linotype before
promotion to third-shift supervision. Awarded four-year college
scholarship by the GAZETTE--the first employee from the mechanical
department to be so honored.

Assistant Foreman, Burns Printing Company
Nashville, Tenn., 1974 - 1976

Started on linotype. After five months, during long illness of
the Foreman, was assigned full responsibility for the composing
room. Continued with this work after his return and was promoted to Assistant Foreman to ease his load. Moved to Washington,
D.C. a year later to broaden opportunity.

Tramp Printer, 1970 - 1974

Decided during apprenticeship that the best way to broaden skill
was to work in as many shops as possible. In this period, worked
in 32 cities in all sections of the U.S. - staying from one to
six months in each shop. Gained broad experience under all kinds
of conditions, with all types of equipment, and all sorts of men
- from the best to the worst. Soon learned how to cope with
print shop crises of every variety. Returned to Nashville for
permanent work after satisfying myself that I had gained about
all that was possible from this experience.

-more-

RONALD G. KALE

- 2 -

Apprentice & Journeyman, 1964 - 1970

Apprenticed at the Burns Printing Company in Nashville. Decided
at the beginning to make myself the best craftsman around.
Learned early in the game that the shop crew was glad to teach
me all they knew if I did most of the work. They seemed to enjoy
the teaching and I enjoyed the learning. As a result, became
proficient in hand composition, make-up, lock-up, and mark-up in
less time than normally required. Through mutual agreement between
the Shop Chairman and Foreman, was certified a fully-competent
journeyman in six months less time than the normal apprentice
period. After starting as a journeyman, took up learning linotype after hours. Began setting copy on the job in six months
and was considered fully competent within another six months.

Education

Had to begin earning my own living at 15 so quit school after
10th grade. Took the General Educational Development Test in
connection with the GAZETTE scholarship. Ranked in the 91st
percentile of high school graduates. Decided on mechanical
engineering as college major since I think too little attention
is paid to engineering aspects of the printing industry. Now
attending George Washington University evening classes. Expect
BS degree in 1983, if work permits continued studies.

Personal

Born 1943. Height: 5'9". Weight: 155. Married. One boy--
age 5. Another boy on the way. Excellent health. Enjoy golf
but gain greatest pleasure from real accomplishment on the job.

ALBERT HAYNES CROSS

1503 Rollingswells Avenue, Abounding, Arkansas 22431 · (202) 656-9681

objective

IMPROVEMENT OF PERSONNEL OPERATIONS: Assistant to executive concerned with improved personnel administration - especially where there is a need for development of policies and procedures to assure higher productivity and morale along with lower costs and turnover.

new personnel program development

For five years, served as Personnel Director for Project Blue Seas. Established a new personnel program for hiring, training, and motivating merchant seamen (10,000 on the payroll) using all of the techniques and tools of modern personnel administration. Despite their service under unusual and hazardous conditions, turnover declined 50%. Personnel production increased approximately 25% per payroll dollar. A new standard for safety at sea was established. The Blue Seas training program was broadly adopted throughout the maritime industry. Our crews became noted for discipline and high morale. According to one top-level observer, "The results achieved stand as a model for the maritime industry." (1975 to present)

improved personnel operations

As Personnel Officer of an Army unit employing 1,000 men, supervised testing, interviewing, and assignment of personnel on basis of intelligence, experience, and aptitudes. Analyzed educational and personal problems contributing to inefficiency and recommended steps to overcome them. Assured successful communications up and down the line. Unit commended for smartness, efficiency, and teamwork. (1972-1975)

education

Bachelor of Arts degree from Caramba University, 1971. Major: Psychology with emphasis on personnel administration. Graduated with highest honors. Phi Beta Kappa. President of Student Council. Entire course of instruction during evening hours and at my expense while working as personnel interviewer and later placement officer for a department store. Speak, read, and write German with facility.

personal

Born 1945. . . Married, 3 children . . . 6'2", 180 pounds . . . health excellent.

other facts

President of Citizens' Association . . . Scoutmaster . . . Private pilot - 1200 hours . . . Enjoy aviation, hunting, fishing, gardening, spectator sports . . . Considerable successful public speaking experience involving need to persuade to action and gain acceptance of new ideas . . . Several articles published in personnel journals . . . Program Director of local chapter, American Management Association.

BRIEF FOR AN EXECUTIVE (JUNIOR TYPE)

As with most briefs in this book, Cross has taken a reverse chronological approach. However, if a "functional" presentation (describing experience by its functional category such as "administration," "budgeting," "research," etc.) better serves to prove your qualifications for the job you want, by all means take it. See text and Lili Li Lu's brief.

These briefs are well done. They all present a clean, uncluttered, attractive appearance. More than that, the word pictures drawn show impressive individuals—well rounded, competent, excellently qualified for the job stated in each objective. This doesn't mean that these people had no failings. Kirby, for example, had failed with a rare consistency before he squared away and started (with his brief) to find a job that lined up with his abilities.

The point here is that your qualifications brief is supposed to show what you *can* do that will be valuable to an employer— not the countless things you can't do. If the latter were its purpose, it would fill a library. Literally. On this basis, it becomes clear that Kirby's brief is completely honest, factual, and very much to the point. It simply ignores those things he can't do (and at which he failed) while stressing his successes.

On the other hand, as you read Cross's presentation, you may conclude that the picture drawn is a shade godlike. We have included this example to provide a strong sampling of the various types of creditable information that can be included in your own statement.

As you study these briefs, you will see that Nancy Kramer and John Adams have concentrated on showing that they have made the most of available opportunities and have strong potential for further growth. This compensates for their lack of experience. Cross's record, on the other hand, reflects considerable success in his performance to date. Kale's, too. And, for that matter, even Kirby's.

There is little question that any employer with openings in line with these objectives would want to talk with the originators of these briefs. And don't think that the birth dates shown are a significant factor. Interest in Cross and Kale would be high even if age 45 were indicated.

The reason? These briefs reflect successful performance and high ability for the jobs designated. If employers can be sure of getting these general qualities under their direction, senior status becomes relatively unimportant. Moreover, employers who are really with it recognize that each year represents additional experience for which there is *no* substitute.

Should you take a "functional" approach?

Take another look at the brief for Lili Li Lu. Its emphasis is functional—that is, it spans a long period in work different from her current job goal while showing that she has performed a number of important management duties (functions) of different kinds that directly qualify her for the job she seeks.

Most of the rest of the samples in this book are chronological in their emphasis—that is, they describe experience in a more or less straight time frame starting with the latest (if best) experience first. They assume that the next job held will be in a logical line of progression from the last most pertinent employment or current job.

Should yours be "functional" in its approach? Yes, if you are planning a sharp career shift—as in Lu's case. No, if not. For example, a career diplomat aiming for work as an art gallery administrator would do best with a functional brief. So would a heavy-duty truck driver who wants to settle into work in inventory control or as head of a shipping and receiving department. And a functional brief is best if, for one reason or another, your career has lately been in reverse gear and you want to disguise that backward trend.

If you decide that a functional brief is best for you, be sure that it clearly shows where and when you gained the experience described. This can be accomplished in the body of your description much as Lu has handled it, or by adding a paragraph (see Brigham's brief) or page reflecting your precise "employment history" in reverse chronological order. If you add such a summary, show your job title, the name of the organization, its location, and the dates (in that order, usually)—perhaps with a line or two briefly describing your work—for each major assignment.

Beginning your brief

Getting down to specifics, and without going into detail on why all of these things are done this way, here is the formula for a qualifications brief that will greatly shorten your job search:

1. Show your name. If leaving military service, the church, academia, medicine, or any other highly specialized field,

delete any indication of rank, retired status, titles, etc. These usually have nothing to do with your qualifications for a job outside the primary field of your experience.

2. Then state your address and telephone number. Include your business number if that is where you can be safely reached during the day. Otherwise, let your spouse or someone else take the message at home. Or, if you have no phone, specify a number where a message can be left.

3. Next, state your "objective" or "job goal" using the term you feel most comfortable with.

We'll break off right here to go into this matter of your objective, since stating it properly is of major importance to the success of your entire campaign.

- **Your objective should be stated in terms of your highest abilities and accomplishments as proved by your experience to date.** It should clearly highlight the level and scope of the specific functions you can best perform for an employer. It need not cite a specific job title such as "Deputy Comptroller" if the level and function of the job you want are clear. In fact, at the upper levels, it is usually wise to generalize on this point since a job five or six echelons from the top in a very large company may provide you with the same financial and psychic returns as one near the top in a very small company. "Financial management" (in lieu of "Deputy Comptroller"), "Project engineering—electronic circuit development," and "Computer maintenance" are examples of good leads that don't name specific jobs but permit you to put the rest of your objective statement in the proper framework.

- **Equally important, your objective should be stated in terms likely to be identical with the employer's objectives.** Again, focus on stressing your strongest abilities as proved by the record of your experience to date. Cast your objective in terms of your ability and the employer's desire to expand operations, increase production, efficiency, quality, income, morale, sales, safety, etc.—anything that your past experience has already *proved* you can do to advance the interests of any new employer who takes you on.

As you do this, avoid citing overly generalized virtues that mean little. *Honesty, the desire to serve your employer's needs,* and *dedication* are examples of such generalizations. More important, do *not* include any indication of what you hope your employer can do for you. Avoid the very common "Middle-management-position-offering-opportunities-for-training-and-promotion" approach or the "Opportunity-to-put-ten-years-of-administrative-experience-to-full-use" gambit. Instead, as you write your objective, stress what you *offer* employers, not what you want from them.

Be sure to study the objective statements shown on the briefs in this chapter to see how they comply with the two key points made above. This will give you a good idea of how to write yours so that it:

1. Identifies the function and general level of the job you want,
2. Stresses your strongest abilities,
3. Shows what you can do for employers without specifying what you expect them to do for you.

Stating your objective in terms of the employer's interests in this way immediately takes your application out of the "routine" class. When you do this, employers react with the thought that you are offering exactly what *they* want. It causes them to identify with you as an applicant right at the start and to review the rest of your brief in the rosy glow of a highly favorable attitude.

Emphasize success

Once your objective is adequately stated, your next aim in writing your brief should be to *prove*—then and there—your strong qualifications to turn in an outstanding performance in the job you have specified. In doing this, show your best experience first—not necessarily your latest job or military tour of duty. DON'T simply recite your duties and responsibilities and let it go at that. That's résumé-style writing.

Instead, put yourself in a frame of mind to provide a bare-bones description of the level and duties of each position. Then focus your attention on writing it so that you can stress:

- The scope and effect of your work.
- Accomplishments, results produced, things changed for the better—all quantified whenever possible in terms of dollars

saved or gained or percentages of change up or down in desirable directions—up, of course, on such things as production, income, program expansion, etc., and down on costs, waste, or other problems. (Incidentally, don't be overly concerned as to whether such accomplishments are inscribed in gold with your previous employer. Include them if you *know* them to be true.)

- Brief words of praise—oral or written—you have received for jobs well done.
- Appealing aspects of your own personality, character, or attitudes. (For example, read Kale's description of the attitudes he brought to his apprenticeship.)

Do it all in a brief, staccato, telegraphic style.

Because this point is so important to your job search, it bears repeating for heavy emphasis: *Include specific examples of successful performance and the results produced whenever possible. Liven it with short quotations praising your work when you can. Include evidence of personal qualities that make it a pleasure to work with you.*

As you refine your presentation, keep in mind that the direct aim of your brief, after all, is to show just how good you are. *Never let modesty stand in the way of this!* Instead, lay out the facts on your accomplishments simply and directly and let them speak for themselves. On the other hand, avoid all lush adjectives, self-praise, and other résumé-style language that simply claims too much. (Example: "Accomplished administrator able to deal successfully with all management problems.")

Your close study of the briefs in this chapter and elsewhere will show how these things are done.

After describing your best experience supporting your objective, describe the next best, and the next. With each assignment, carefully follow the rules above. Give very brief treatment to experience unrelated to your objective. (Kirby, for example, said virtually nothing about the bulk of his Army duties.) And deemphasize experience over ten years old, but be sure to cover your whole career. In other words, leave no gaps in your account that may imply that you spent some time in Sing Sing but are not anxious to talk about it.

What to do about dates

Which brings us down to the matter of dates. How should
they be shown?

The résumé tradition is to specify dates prominently—out in
the left margin or in a headline over each paragraph where they
grab attention that should be drawn to more important facts.
The quality of your experience—*what* you did—is far more
important than *when* you gained it, particularly with experience
during the last ten years. Consequently, you will see that most
of the sample briefs with this chapter show dates very unob-
trusively at the *ends* of the paragraphs to which they relate.
Moreover, years only are shown. This puts dates in proper perspective. In addition to putting the focus on *what* you've done,
this approach reduces the possibility that employers will gain
the erroneous (or accurate) impression that you have been a
job jumper. (Incidentally, you will note that Kirby and Kale
chose to ignore this rule and elected the more traditional
approach.)

Showing your education

Your education should be first under your objective if it is
your *most* qualifying experience to date. Generally, it also
should be at the beginning where possession of the requisite
degree(s) is virtually a must requirement for a professional
job—for example, in medicine, law, and teaching. (Note the
exception in Brigham's case.) But, as your education recedes
in time, it also recedes as a factor in your current qualifications. This explains why most of the briefs in this book show
education toward the end.

As with the rest of your brief, put the facts on your education
in positive terms. If you completed 103 hours toward your
degree, state it but don't add that you did not graduate. Show
the highest level of your educational achievement. Where you
have more than one degree, specify them all with the highest
first. Be sure to show dates of graduation, unless more than
ten years ago. If you have attended numerous technical schools
while in uniform, select those that support your objective and
cover the others by a "plus others" statement. Generally, if
you have attended college, drop any reference to high school

unless there is some aspect of your high-school experience that particularly supports your objective (as in Cain's brief on page 96).

Special honors, pertinent activities, leadership positions, high class standing or grade-point average, foreign language ability, varsity sports, self-supported tuition, unique qualifying training, other accomplishments in school, and the types of courses in which you did best (if in line with your objective) are other factors to be considered for inclusion in your section on education.

Dealing with personal data

"Personal data," unfortunately, often involves small questions with big implications. Normally, such facts are best located in the next-to-last paragraph o your brief. Again, keep in mind that this information should also be designed to help prove your qualifications for the job you want. Here are clues on how to approach it:

- *Age.* Show it date-of-birth style. Otherwise, a passing birthday may outdate your brief. If over 55, "forget" to include it unless you have superior qualifications for a senior executive position. (The problem with leaving it out at, say, 40 to 55 is that employers are inclined then to assume that you are probably older than you are and may apply their own benighted prejudices to deny you a job regardless of what the law says to the contrary.)

- *Height and weight.* If your physical dimensions stated in print tend to conjure up a picture of a well-put-together human being, by all means include them. Also include them when they line up with the direct physical requirements of the job you want. For example, small stature and light weight are must requirements for a job as peak man or woman in a tumbling team and should be shown in that case. Otherwise, leave out this data. Your size has little to do with most openings and can be ignored in most cases if your dimensions are not impressive in print.

- *Marital status.* Should you specify it? Depends. Remember, you're writing a qualifications brief—not your autobiography or obituary. The answer is, include it when you think this will enhance your prospects for getting the job you want, leave it out when it won't. Unfortunately, some far-out prejudices have to be considered. For example, some stiffly starched establishmentarian types beam with benign approval on the male candidate who says he's happily married with three school-age young ones at home—especially if the offspring are boys. They frown heavily—however illegally—on female candidates who say the same thing. (This gal, they think, ought to be home taking care of the kids.) If you are a woman, one way to handle this problem is to say nothing about children in your brief while being prepared to come forward during interviews with assurance of arrangements for their continued loving care while you work.

Divorce is another touchy question although, happily, it is becoming less so as time lurches on. The best way to handle it is to say nothing, sort of as something you didn't think was important to employers (which it shouldn't be). Then, during interviews, when asked whether you are married, your honest answer can be "No," although you may want to add that you used to be. However, specifying that you are divorced can be an asset. Look, for example, at Dennis Cain's brief on page 96. The independence implied by his divorced status is a plus mark for an over-the-road trucker. It's a little bit like the ads they used to run for pony express riders that called for "young, skinny, wiry fellows not over 18 . . . must be expert riders willing to risk death daily . . . orphans preferred."

- *Health.*   The question to be answered here is not how your health is overall but how it is for the job you want—whether or not it will interfere in any significant way with the performance of your duties. For example, suppose that, without regular medication, gout would bring you down every now and then to the point of total and excruciating disability. Is that something to bring up in your brief? Of course not. Since the gout is under control and not a factor in the job you want, your health is "excellent." On that score, avoid stating that your health is "good." Putting it so cautiously immediately raises a question as to what's wrong with you. If you don't honestly feel that—in the normal course of things—your health won't interfere with your performance on the job (that is, if you can't say your health is "excellent"), say nothing. Incidentally, including word on vigorous activities under "other facts" at the end of your brief adds to the overall picture of physical vitality you convey and can compensate for silence on health under "personal data." Or, in the interest of total honesty, you can say (if true), "Some health problems but they are not allowed to interfere with superior performance on the job."

Skyrockets at the end

Résumés typically end with a yawn—usually with some dry facts about height, heft, and age and that's about it, sometimes with impertinent facts that may awe employers—but in the wrong way. (Examples: "Member, National Geographic Society," "like to boogie.") They usually conclude on a gray note that immediately inspires employers to put them in the discard pile where at least 95 percent go. Instead, aim to end your brief with a bang.

Under "other facts" (or some such heading), you have an opportunity to include information showing that you are a vital human being, a good citizen, an active person with broad interests. Here is where you should show *pertinent* professional memberships, publications, special honors, qualifying licenses, interests, civic activities, your security clearance, etc. Even more important, this is where you should incorporate brief information reflecting your personality and desirable attitudes you will bring to your work.

For good examples of such clues to personality, look at the concluding paragraphs in the griefs for Charles MacAllister (page 102), Janice Melton (page 99), and Juan Alvarez (on page 97). As you read them, you will see how such statements make these applicants come alive as interesting individuals—people you would like to meet. That thought, of course, is precisely the one you want to inspire among employers—especially when they are at the very moment of deciding whether to put your brief in the "to-be-interviewed" or "discard" pile. So pay close attention to the potential in this "final-bang" approach for greatly easing your job search.

Keep your brief brief

So those are the rules for putting together a qualifications brief that will get you vastly more favorable employer attention than almost all résumés that are considered along with it. But how long should it be?

As a general rule, limit your brief to one letter-size page for ten years of work experience or less, two pages for more than ten. Lists showing publications, technical equipment competence, special courses taken, your employment history (for functional briefs), and other back-up information can always be attached as an extra page with cross references to them in the brief itself.

But don't be too brief in your brief. Covering twenty or more years of experience on one page tends to discount its importance. On the other hand, if the body of your brief is more than two pages, it stands an excellent chance of being ignored altogether unless it comes on at the start like an Ian Fleming novel and builds from there. Busy employers simply do not have time to burrow through multi-page presentations.

You may have the feeling that such tight limits probably fit other people but they can't possibly apply to you. After all, much too much has gone on in your career to get it all into one or two pages. But they do apply, and it's only in highly exceptional circumstances that these rules regarding length should be put aside. Perhaps you will find comfort in the fact that virtually everybody feels the same way.

Be ruthless about cutting your brief down to size. First hew away at all useless paragraphs, then sentences, then words. Ask yourself whether each of these elements will play a significant role in causing an employer to invite you in. If not, cut it out. Keep only those paragraphs, sentences, and words that most effectively—and briefly—prove your superior qualifications for the job you want. And don't take refuge in having your brief cast in micro-filmy type so you can cram in more detail. Doing that will, all too frequently, impel it toward the paper shredder.

As you apply a red pencil to your first effort, cut out any of the following that may have crept into your presentation:

- Any *covering* sheet.
- Any statement near the beginning that summarizes your experience. (Such statements are usually weak for starters unless they deal solely with major accomplishments.)

- Details regarding employment more than ten years ago. (A line or two should suffice.)
- Statements such as "34 years of experience," which emphasize age.
- Reasons for leaving previous jobs.
- Pay data.
- Your own early history (unless particularly colorful or showing triumph over great odds) and personal histories of other family members. (Note exception in the case of Lili Li Lu.)
- Your date of availability, location preferences, pay desired. (These should be taken up in covering letters or interviews, as appropriate.)
- Your social security number.
- Names of references or mention of the availability of references. (Employers just naturally assume that you will supply references when needed.)
- Language lifted from official job descriptions.
- Official documents as attachments.

As you trim your initial effort, pay heavy attention to the *style* of your writing. Aim, as we said before, for pithy, tele-graphic, even staccato language to get your points across. Use short words, short sentences, short paragraphs. Start most sentences with action verbs like *conceived, directed, managed, sparked, accomplished, developed, achieved, saved, etc.* Be most sparing in the use of "I." Avoid passive verbs and never use the third-person approach as though someone else is describing you.

And add eye appeal

Even as you comply with the rules above, your brief must meet another important requirement: It should *look* better than the résumés that will be compared with it. If it does, employers will pick it up with a favorable first impression that just possibly can be the deciding factor in whether or not you get the job you want. Achieving that result is not hard to do. If you can make your brief look as good as any of the samples in this book, considering your experience, you will be *way* ahead. Most résumés have less eye appeal than a typical bill of lading. To avoid their failings, follow these rules:

- Keep your paragraphs short and your margins wide. Double space between paragraphs.

- Use marginal descriptions, underlining, capitalization, and centered headlines to stress information on your accomplishments that you most want employers to see.

- Whether your brief is one or two pages long, use all of the space available. That is, fill out the page(s) by introducing white space at the top and bottom, in the margins, and between paragraphs. But *don't* cram the space with print.

- If you are the right physical type, a photograph will help —especially if you are shown in a relaxed portrait-type pose, perhaps with a slight smile, and in clothing like that you would wear to work in the type of job you seek. But be sure your picture creates the impression of a friendly, capable, *youthful* individual. Ask your friends for their candid comment on these points before using it.

Finally, a word of caution.

Never let your brief be cast in the standard language and format of one of the widely advertised résumé-writing houses. Although such services often turn out handsome résumés, indeed, the problem is that major employers have seen so many examples of their product that they now spot them instantly and ignore them altogether. They have learned by repeated exposure that such résumés (1) are not the work of the applicants they describe, (2) contain wording (even whole paragraphs) identical to that in many other résumés turned out by the same organization, and (3) simply cannot be believed. So what you are paying for in almost all such cases is an ineffective résumé—certainly not a qualifications brief.

But what if writing simply is not one of your abilities? In that case, get the help of a friend whom you consider both wise and good with words. Have your friend study this chapter and then, together, work out a brief that meets the requirements we have been talking about. Or find a good professional writer to help you—one who specializes in career-development questions. (They are rare birds. Chapter 12 provides clues on what to look for in engaging a professional.) But be prepared to pay more than $100.00 for such help. The reason is that an outsider will have to spend at least ten hours applying a high level of analytical and writing ability to accomplish good results for you. (Hopefully, someday, public employment offices will be able to make such expert help available to *all* job seekers.)

When it comes to reproducing your brief, good, *clean* Xerography is appropriate for openings at the lower ranks—up to supervisory jobs. When using this method, have 25 copies run off at a time. If your aim—immediate or long range—is for professional work or the upper ranks, have it reproduced by multilith or photo offset on good quality paper. The results will be more than worth the small additional expense involved. Print on only one side of the page and, if your photo is to be included, have it reproduced directly on your brief. This will save money. When using this method, print 100 or 200 copies since the cost of additional copies after the first one is low indeed. And going back to press for additional copies is unnecessarily expensive.

But don't follow our formula blindly. It's foolhardy to straitjacket your qualifications in somebody else's list of specifications. Even ours. Where you have good, strong reasons for taking a different approach, by all means take it—just as has been done with some of the samples in this book.

How to proceed

Now, knowing all this, what's the easiest way to proceed? Here are our suggestions:

1. Go back and *study* all of the briefs in this book, beginning with the one for Jordan Pruitt in Chapter 3. Take a red pen and underline the kinds of presentation that you like and that most fit your situation.
2. Rough out your initial draft in light of the rules above, reviewing the rules as you go along, and adapting aspects you like in the sample briefs to your own use.
3. Trim the content of your first efforts so that it hits only the strongest elements of your qualifications for the job stated in your objective and fits the formula of one page

for ten years' experience or less, two pages for more than ten—all without appearing crowded on the page.

4. Then cast your brief in the format of one of the samples in this chapter that you like, keeping in mind that the more sophisticated your aim, the more sophisticated the format should be. Make yours look at least as good as the samples we have shown.

5. Finally, check it all out.

At this stage, you will be normal if you conclude that anything requiring so much time, thought, and effort *must* be good. With so much work already poured into it, you may be inclined to shunt aside any nagging second thoughts about your brief's effectiveness. However, because very small considerations can have a very large bearing on the outcome of your application, it is critically important that you give your brief a detailed and dispassionate review before putting it to work for you.

The *QualBrief Checklist* at the end of this chapter enables you to perform your own critical review. Use it. When you do, you will discover whether or not your brief requires more work, and if so, what you need to do to put it in the "outstanding" category. Certainly, you should not waste your time, money, effort, hope, and opportunities with anything less than a top quality brief.

To back you up, you may want a conscientious professional review showing any areas in which your presentation should be improved and how your brief compares with most others at your experience level. If so, the National Center for Job-Market Studies can provide it for you. You will find brief facts on its services in Chapter 12.

Putting it to work for you

We will go into these matters at greater length in later chapters, but right now you should know that there are four main ways to use your qualifications brief to produce hiring action. As you will see, the most usual use of the brief is to open doors to interviews. The happier way to go is to use your brief to bind up a job offer *after* an interview.

■ **Responding to an advertised opening** with a mailed or personally delivered copy of your brief is one way to go.

However, don't expect too much action here. It is down this track that your brief will run into the heaviest going, simply because openings that are publicized in these ways attract the greatest number of applicants. One study of companies that advertise heavily for applicants shows that, *on the average,* 245 résumés are received for every interview granted.[11] (Note: That's interviews given, *not* jobs offered.) Although your carefully prepared qualifications brief will beat out most résumés, those are still heavy odds to overcome.

Because of such heavy odds running against you, it is far better to aim your application in the direction of the great majority of openings that are *not* publicized. (Remember, the unpublicized openings run at a rate of four to one over those that are advertised, and, in the main, represent the most desirable opportunities.)

■ **Mailing your brief** to a very carefully developed list of hiring officials is one way to aim for such unpublicized openings. Taking this tack starts with substantial library research into directories of companies and their officials in order to develop a list of 100 or more organizations that you know —or strongly suspect—employ people with your qualifications. Your librarian can lead you to the directories that are locally available. *Poor's Register of Corporations, Directors, and Executives* and *Thomas's Register of American Manufacturers* are the ones most likely to be on hand. The index to the *Yellow Pages* is another great source of information on employers who have people like you working for them —one often used by employment agencies. Incidentally, if you are looking for likely employers in another town, call your library or telephone company business office to learn where you can get access to the *Yellow Pages* for that town. In both cases, when you take down employers' addresses, also record their telephone numbers so you can call to get the name and title of the official responsible for work in your area of qualifications.

This mass mailing technique is most likely to work if you are at the management-trainee, supervisory, professional, or higher level. And it's about the only way to go if you are seeking employment on a long-distance basis.

11. See Appendix A: Footnotes, page 259.

To be worth the effort and expense involved, you must meet three critically important requirements: (1) Your qualifications brief must be very carefully prepared in line with the rules above so that it will be clearly superior to almost all résumés compared with it; (2) it must be sent under a commanding covering letter (see Chapter 7) which clearly sets your submission apart from most others; and (3) you must follow up with a call to the individuals addressed asking when you might come see them. This can be impractical on a long-distance basis, but if your mailing (asking when—not if—you might come see the employer) produces one invitation, call the other employers contacted in that area after you get there to ask when you might stop by.

The state of the economy has much to do with the kind of results you will get. On balance, however, you should expect about 12 interviews from every 200 employers contacted. That's so much better than the 1 in 245 odds for advertised openings as to warrant breaking out bronze gongs and tambourines in celebration. Still, if your mailing is long distance without a telephone follow-up, there is an effective way to *double* the interest produced without too much extra effort. To do that, simply mail the *same* letter and qualifications brief to the same list of employers a month later—except, of course, to those who have already asked you to come see them. When you do, don't mention your previous submission. Because of the peculiar ways in which the job market operates, your second mailing will produce results just as good as the first.

- **Direct personal contact** with people who supervise personnel with qualifications similar to yours is easily one of the most effective ways to obtain job offers—especially if a friend, relative, or acquaintance has recommended it. As indicated in Chapter 3, don't ask if there are any openings. Instead, aim to prove that you should be hired for the *next* job in your line that opens up. When making the rounds, have copies of your brief with you. If applying for a job below the supervisory, management trainee, or professional level, lead off the discussion by presenting it. At higher levels, hold it back if you can until you have learned as much as possible about the employer's problems and needs. Then, if your brief is reasonably close to the mark, offer it. If not, you can answer the inevitable question, "Do you have a résumé," by saying, "Yes, but it's at the printer's," and then add that you will be glad to have a copy there the next day. That way you can deliver a modified copy of your brief—one that zeroes in on the employer's needs as discovered during your discussion.

- **Delivering your brief after a job offer** is easily the best way to go. This rare happening can occur when you see an employer and have been so highly recommended by a mutual friend that, after a cordial discussion of your needs and theirs, you are offered a job on the spot. Or it can occur when you conduct an exploratory interview (like that described in Chapter 8 under *Get advice—and job offers—from experts*) and the employer says, "Truth is, we would like to have you working for *us*." Or it can happen when you send only a letter, something like that on page 141, asking for an interview, and it works. Then all you need to do is modify your brief so it focuses precisely on the employer's specific problems and submit it as part of the appointment process—something to keep in their files.

Brief your friends and references

There are two important collateral uses for your brief. The first is to give a copy to every friend, relative, or acquaintance who might be in a position to uncover the job you want. (This, of course, includes counselors in public or private employment agencies whom you contact along the way.) This way, they will get a better idea than they had before of your strongest abilities and the kind of job you are best suited for so they can talk you up to people *they* contact. When you rely on your friends in this way, they get the feeling that they really *should* do something to help you if they can. Just as you would for them.

The second collateral use for your brief is to give a copy to each of your references. Be sure to ask for consent to use their names before listing them. Then send them your brief under a covering note thanking them for this help. The brief will fortify them with information to give to inquiring employers regarding your background. It just may add that additional note of enthusiasm to their comments that will cause an employer to conclude that the tiresome search for a good employee has just come to an end.

We'll have more to say about each of these major techniques for using your brief in later chapters. But, before that, one last thought: As you prepare your brief, remember that it should be an attractive, broad-brush, factual account of your personal assets as they relate to the work you want. Its aim is to excite enough interest in your abilities to cause an employer to want to talk with you, or, if submitted after an interview, to impel a job offer. It's that important. Consequently, your qualifications brief merits your heavy attention—even more than may seem reasonable as you undertake its development.

The reason is simple enough: Doing it right can change your life.

Remember that.

QUALIFICATIONS BRIEFS—
MORE OUTSTANDING EXAMPLES

On the following pages, you will find qualifications briefs for applicants ranging from high-school graduates to senior executives. *Study* each one. Mark the kinds of presentation that you find impressive and that best fit your experience. Do the same with the preceding briefs in this chapter and those for Jordan Pruitt in Chapter 3 and James Creed Kirby in Chapter 4.

As you study these briefs, you will note that it is not the quality of the experience described (most of it is quite ordinary) but the *quality of presentation* that makes these people seem exceptionally well qualified. To achieve this result, note how:

- Objective statements are cast in terms of strongest abilities and the needs of employers while highlighting the type and level of job sought.

- Important aspects of experience are emphasized through various visual techniques—spacing, marginal descriptions, centered headlines, underlining, and all-caps treatment—all in an attractive, uncrowded format.

- Dates have been deemphasized by locating them at the ends of the paragraphs to which they relate.

- Short words, sentences, and paragraphs are used in a brief, pithy, almost breezy writing style that concentrates on facts while avoiding superlatives, self-praise, and "canned" résumé language.

- The most qualifying experience is described first, and earlier or unrelated experience is very briefly treated.

- Examples of specific accomplishments (interesting problems overcome, results produced) are cited to show how well each of these applicants has performed in the past and to prove qualification for the job indicated in the objective statement.

- Brief quotations from supervisors or others are often used to liven the presentation and provide proof of strong qualifications.

- Appealing aspects of personality and attitudes toward work are introduced wherever possible and particularly at the end in a "final bang" approach designed to impel the brief into the "invite-for-an-interview" pile.

Once you have noted these aspects and marked the sample briefs, review once more the rules in this chapter for preparing your brief. Follow them carefully as you develop your own presentation. Then check it all out. Use the *QualBrief Checklist* at the end of this chapter to do it.

LeRoy Greene
    2247 East 17th Street, Memphis, Tennessee · 962-0516

Applying for: Assistant to auto spare-parts manager
    Especially where the job requires a knowledge of inventory and ordering
    methods, and ability to improve service for mechanics and customers.

* *

Graduated in top 10% of industrial arts class at Robert Moton High School, 1978.
    Concentrated on business and mechanics courses. Most enjoyed accounting,
    auto shop, and gym. In auto shop, offered to help keep records of tools
    and parts used. After three months, began filling out forms to be signed
    by the teacher and sending for materials. No student had ever done this
    before. In a note to my foster parents, the teacher said, "Your boy is
    the best student-mechanic I've ever seen. His knowledge of our materials
    and catalogs makes him like a second teacher."

Part-time job--suggested changes to increase sales.
    After school hours, worked for two years as a stripper for Key's Auto
    Wreckers. Suggested several ways to arrange stock to make it easier to
    get at and better for customers. Mr. Key said these changes increased
    his sales. They also gave me more room and handier tools so I could
    strip faster and get parts into stock quicker. This past year, Mr. Key
    had me classifying, testing, and renovating parts in addition to stripping.

Worked two summers as a mechanic's helper at Gray's Exxon Servicenter.
    Also learned how to pump gas, inventory, order stock, and keep customers
    happy. Beginning last summer, customers began asking for me by name to
    work on their cars. After hours, used my good will with Key's Auto
    Wreckers to get parts at low cost to build my own stock racer. Put the
    car together from scratch during spare time and weekends. Finished in
    five months. Began winning medals and money in six months.

Born May 9, 1960.
    Excellent health--never missed a day from work . . . 5' 10", 165 lbs. . .
    single, but not for long.

Want to learn as much as possible about the automobile business
    . . . while continuing auto mechanic work in spare time. Some day hope to
    run a dealership or an auto service department. Also, want to help less
    fortunate folks get some skills. Like contact sports but have the most fun
    tinkering around with cars. Have been earning money at different jobs since
    age 8.

94

ANNETTE BOURJAILY

436-8686

1670 Mountainview Avenue   Denver, Colorado 80603

OBJECTIVE

Office assistant where typing skills, a strong sense of responsibility, accuracy in handling detail, energy, and a cheerful outlook will be assets.

EDUCATION

Graduated in the top third from Monroe High School in June, 1977. Best grades in and most enjoyed language courses (English, Latin, French). Also remained in the upper half on most other courses-- including Advanced Algebra-Trigonometry. Learned to type 50 words per minute accurately. Now working to increase speed through daily home practice. Speak and read French.

SUMMER EMPLOYMENT

In 1975, served as a proofreader for the County Gazette. Last summer, worked as a clerk for Woolworth's. In both cases my supervisors were expecially complimentary with regard to the speed and accuracy of my work as well as my general helpfulness. Both asked me to come back.

RELATED EXPERIENCE

Worked on editorial staff of the Monroe High newspaper and yearbook. Member of the girls cheerleaders. Assisted with the production of all plays and musicals during my four years at Monroe. Had full responsibility for all arrangements for props and costumes for "The King and I"--the most lavishly staged (and successful) musical in Monroe's history.

PERSONAL DATA

Born 1960 . . . single . . . medium height . . . excellent health . . . enjoy good books, outdoor activities, and church drama group.

PRIMARY AIMS AND ASSETS

Considered a fast learner . . . most enjoy myself when very busy . . . like to take on new tasks and complete them successfully . . . have always made friends of others working with me . . . hope to continue my education through evening studies as work permits.

DENNIS CAIN

4424 Bannockburn Drive, Bethesda, Maryland 20034 * 301/229-6946

CURRENT GOAL: <u>Over-the-road trucker</u> for a company seeking a safe,
efficient driver who is able to increase customer satisfaction
and good will through outstanding service to both shippers and
receivers.

<u>Over 180,000 miles' safe heavy-duty driving</u> during four years
over all kinds of roads and terrain. Broad experience with most
major types of tractors and trailers. (See attached list.)
Frequently praised by customers for careful, on-time delivery
and friendly dealing. My employer (Corland Company, Tysons
Corner, Va.) has asked me to stay on at a good pay increase
but my aim now is to find an interstate opening. (1974-present)

<u>Worked two years in shipping and receiving</u> with Brown Brothers,
Oakland, Calif. Learned much about what carriers must do to
please their major customers and how ridiculously small things
can make or break an account. This inspired my interest in
trucking. Obtained basic skills through the A.W. Training
Service in tractor-trailer handling. (1972-1974)

<u>Served as Flight Crew Chief aboard USS ENTERPRISE</u>. Moved up to
E-5 in much shorter time than it usually takes. Cited for valor.
After four-year Navy hitch, organized and led San Francisco rock
band for 14 months. (1966-1972)

<u>Safe driver since age 15</u>. Learned early how to cope with hazard-
ous driving conditions. Took part in sanctioned drag racing when
15 and 16. Later took part in personal sports car races and
rallies. Began flying single-engine aircraft at age 16. Bug on
highway and traffic safety. Totally clean accident record.

<u>Education</u>. Nearly two years toward Associate's degree completed
at Merit College, Oakland, Calif. (1970-1972) High school letters
in track, basketball, football. Co-captained football team to
state championships.

<u>Other facts</u>. Born in 1948 . . . 6'1", 190 pounds . . . 20/20
vision . . . well coordinated with unusually fast reflexes.
Divorced (no family responsibilities) . . . Totally turned on by
trucking as an occupational field . . . Believe in maintaining
equipment and self in top condition . . . Member, Virginia
Trucking Association . . . Believe much can be done to improve
the industry's image and that it starts with the individual
driver.

JUAN   ALVAREZ

Box 333, Dranesville, Mississippi 39437   601/470-8459

objective	COMMUNICATIONS-ELECTRONICS TECHNICIAN: Responsible for maintaining complex electronic equipment where improved procedures and performance are needed to assure more efficient operations at lower cost.
improved maintenance procedures	For three years had sole responsibility as head of a five-man team for the electronic maintenance of a multi-million dollar Air Force radio receiver station. Revised and improved the quality of preventive maintenance tests. <u>Result</u>: Cut the outage time of several important communications circuits in half. Based on our performance, my crew won the coveted Air Force Outstanding Unit Award for ". . . sustained superior performance by all members over an extended period of time." (1973-1977)
set up communications network	During the same period, also set up, checked out, and maintained a command-post communications network in support of a nuclear test in the Pacific. Officially commended for providing "<u>flawless performance</u> on an exceptionally complex task."
related achievements	Conducted on-the-job training of four radio repairmen. All were promptly up-graded to the skilled level. As a Team Chief for the Air Force Ground Electronic Engineering-Installation Agency, devised and accomplished maintenance evaluations for single-sideband radio receivers and aircraft control tower consoles (1977 to present).
education	High school graduate. Strongest subjects: Physics and Mathematics. Currently pursuing, at my own expense, a correspondence course in Advanced Electronics Theory given by the Capital Radio Engineering Institute.
other training	Completed a one-year course in Ground Radio Communications Equipment at Keesler Air Force Base. Also three correspondence courses in communications theory. Graduated from transistor theory course at Hickam Air Force Base, Hawaii. <u>First in my class</u> at Leadership School, Langley Air Force Base.
personal	Born April 24, 1951, San Juan, Puerto Rico . . . married, one son . . . 5'10", 160 pounds . . . health excellent . . . presentable . . . enjoy hunting and fishing . . . like to be assigned challenging jobs involving important results and requiring imaginative solutions.

ROBERT P. KOVALESKI
1654 Shawano Road
Sioux City, Iowa 51103

Telephone
Home: (712) 323-4502
Work: (712) 365-5500

FIELD ENGINEERING REPRESENTATIVE (ELECTRONICS)

Aiming for employment where complete technical reliability,
the ability to produce practical on-the-spot solutions to
problems of efficient equipment use, and development of
strong customer relations are required.

* *

* Installation and progressive maintenance program development
for better results.

Developed programs for maintenance and efficient use of airborne and
ground-support electronic equipment. Kept ahead of new theory, technical
innovation, and changes in installation methods. Modified equipment to
meet the special needs of the Air Force or the personnel using it. Motivated crews in my radio, radar, and electric shops to produce results which
they themselves thought impossible. As a result, my crews were consistently singled out and praised for the high level of equipment readiness
and ingenuity in meeting new and unusual problems--often under extremely
negative circumstances. (1978 to the present)

* Earlier experience in electronics.

Started as a radioman. Advanced through progressively more responsible
jobs to positions requiring on-the-spot modification of equipment. Developed
new progressive maintenance programs including required forms and records
to assure continuous high performance. Frequent promotions led to current
assignment as Master Chief Technician. (1970-1978)

* Education

Courses in physics, transistors, algebra, English, and Spanish at San Jose
State (Calif.), differential calculus at William and Mary (Va.). Extensive
classroom technical training. (See attached list.) Consistently graduated
at the top of the class. Sixteen USAFI correspondence courses in electronics.
Speak Spanish well enough to have served as technical translator with U.S.
mission touring South America.

* Personal data

Hold First Class Radio Telephone and Amateur Radio licenses. Top secret
clearance. Born in 1952. 6'3", 230 pounds, single and very healthy.
Fixing motorcycles, photography, and travel are my spare-time interests.
Especially like work which involves helping others in ways which benefit them
and produce results of permanent value.

98

JANICE F. MELTON

4513 Washtenaw Road   (414) 687-2948   Milwaukee, Wis. 53201

ASSISTANT TO PROGRAM DIRECTOR - PUBLIC HEALTH

where there is a need to combine medical knowledge with good humor and
perseverance in organizing community energies to develop or expand health
programs and services to meet major community problems.

New programs in public health

As a volunteer health worker in rural South Carolina, assisted a local doctor
in planning and establishing the first maternity, child-care, and first aid
clinic that poor people could use in the county. Discussed health needs with
most of the local people, discovered early child death and lack of nutritious
meals were two major problems. Gathering community help, secured a building,
repaired and renovated it for our needs, and worked out regular examination
schedules for county residents. Met initial discouragement from two officials
with frank and open discussion. Calmed several "touch and go" situations
which threatened the project with violent disaster. During this time, also
trained 5 young women in basic health care so they could continue to assist
the doctor after I left. In a community meeting, one old lady drew strong
applause by saying, "...without her pushing them officials, we'd sure still
be sick and dying today. God bless her." By the end of 1978, the clinic was
serving 40 people a day. (1976-1978)

Quick grasp of nursing duties

After school hours during both high school and college, volunteered part time
as nurses' aide ("candy striper") at Clark Memorial Hospital. Learned all the
fundamentals of health care and was able to perform some bedside functions, by
the grace of the nursing supervisor, after one year. Supervisor warmly
praised me for adaptability and a cool head in emergencies. (1973-1975)

Red Cross fund raising at school

Graduated from Manatoc Junior College, Milwaukee, Wis. 1975. Major: Medical
Technology. Took over Red Cross fund drives. Involved more students in these
activities and increased gifts by 50% each year.

Other facts

Born November, 1957...5'6", 125 lbs...single...enjoy popular music, dancing
and traveling. Have a strong feeling that much needs to be done...and can
be through the simple application of well-directed energy.

──── CLAUDIA HAEBERLE ───

1453 Westpath Way, Cobalt, California 91250 ˙ 432-6504

* Objective

ASSISTANT TO EXECUTIVE--especially where there is a need to keep operations
under firmer control and where communications skills, a pleasant manner in
dealing with people, and strong typing ability would be assets.

* Operated successful secretarial and mailing service

Between times coping with household chores, developed my own secretarial and
mailing service operating from my home in Boston. Started by teaching myself
touch typing during children's nap times. After developing reasonable competence, solicited envelope typing jobs from local mailers. Soon found
myself swamped with work. Had to enclose a large side porch to accommodate
stocks, install automatic equipment, and provide room for two permanent employees plus swarms of neighborhood high schoolers during frequent peak
periods. Later found that clients wanted help with composition and production
of sales pieces and letters and we were only too glad to accommodate them.
It was hectic, but most enjoyable--especially the relationships with business-
men in our area and keeping things moving ahead. The increased workload was
beginning to tax our space again when move to California necessitated selling
the service to my assistant. (1971-77)

* Developed new sales technique

Previously undertook home telephone sales for magazine subscription agency.
Worked at it for six months. Experimented with various forms of presentation
that sharply deviated from the company standard. Found one that worked much
better even though it involved less "hard-sell" and no sham. Company adopted
my approach as standard for all of its sales people. Although I thoroughly
disliked this work, my performance prompted the agency manager to offer me a
job as his assistant recruiting and training new sales people. Decided that
staying with the children was more important and soon terminated the telephone
work. Bought an IBM Electric with some of my earnings to start the secretarial
operation. (1971)

* Other facts

High school graduate--all A's in English, History, Public Speaking, and similar
courses. Read Gesell during high school and opened a nursery school for
toddlers during summer vacations. Attendance doubled each year.

* Personal

Born 1938. Married. Three children--two in college, one about to be. Strong
belief in good personal grooming and the value of a sense of humor in tense
situations.

100

Winston C. Howell

964 Lehigh Ave., Apt. 6D, Philadelphia, Penna. 19115 (215) 634-9288

OBJECTIVE

DATA COMMUNICATIONS TRAINING--where there is a need for better course organization, reduced administrative costs, and the introduction of new ideas and techniques to graduate more effective and enthusiastic students.

EXPERIENCE

TELECOMMUNICATIONS INSTRUCTOR - Responsible for training and placement of 30 persons per 6 month cycle. (Have consistently met this quota.) Developed the basic course of study as well as trainee unit guide which simplified the program . . . wrote a proposal for an inter-organization teletype system to coordinate data and on-line training. Continuously achieved lowest dropout rates and highest placement within the organization. Cut training hours by 10% and costs by 23% in performing preventive maintenance on the equipment. Initiated numerous industrial contacts with resulting donations of instructional supplies and equipment. (Opportunities Industrialization Center, 1975-present)

AUTOMATIC OPERATOR - Graduated as top trainee from Western Union Automatic Training School. Became proficient in the operation of numerous types of communications equipment and learned the overall branch office operations quickly. Enjoyed this work . . . attained a perfect record for attendance and punctuality. After six months, was recommended by the Regional Manager for the position I now hold. (Western Union Telegraph Co., 1973-1975)

JUSTOWRITER OPERATOR - Learned many phases of newspaper work including layout, proofreading, and preparing rough copy into justified finished pieces. Adapted to equipment rapidly (according to my supervisor) and cut down on preparation time. Initiated a training program for high school students to work part time for the newspaper. Received an award from the school for implementing this program. Promoted to junior reporter prior to relocating. (Gainesville, Fla. Newspaper Co., 1971-1973)

EDUCATION

Finished three courses in Electronics Technology at Drexel Institute, 1976. Completed Office Automation Course from International Correspondence School. Also completed, with very high averages, courses in communications operations, management, and journalism through USAFE while in the Army. (1969-1971)

OTHER FACTS

Born April 4, 1950, married with a young son. Health excellent - 5'11", 145 lbs. Derive personal satisfaction from seeing young people I've trained stick to meaningful employment. Hobbies include playing jazz saxophone, table tennis, reading.

CHARLES J. MacALLISTER

7701 Dalroy Road, Bethesda, Md. 20034 · 301/638-4084

objective

SYSTEMS SOFTWARE PROGRAMMER/ANALYST - for an organization involved in the development of third-generation software--from conception through implementation--with strong emphasis on improved data communication, assembly/machine language programming and individual creativity.

Instructor-Programmer for the Air Force

Three years' diversified experience covering all phases of data processing from problem definition and system design to final programming and implementation. Spent numerous off-duty nights and early mornings attending technical schools in order to broaden and increase my technical knowledge and flexibility. Specialized in assembly and machine language programming and software analysis on the Univac 1050-II, Burroughs B263 and B3500 systems. Became an authority on the organization, operation, and utilization of the Burroughs B3500 Master Control Program.   (1973-1977)

equipment experience

Designed and wrote production programs and software for the Univac 1050-II, Burroughs B263 and B3500 systems; utilizing 6 tape drives, 90 million byte disk storage and 66 million character drum storage peripherals. Experienced in multi-processing on the B3500 and real-time processing on both the 1050-II and B3500; utilizing Teletype 35 and Friden 7511 Communication Terminals.

language proficiency

Extensive experience in COBOL, FORTRAN IV, RPG, Advanced Assembly and machine languages on the Univac 1050-II, Burroughs B263 and B3500. Additional training in JOVIAL and 360/35-45 COBOL & RPG.

education and training

Over 60 weeks of specialized USAF data processing training from basic and advanced PGAM to third-generation multi-processing and data communications, in addition to 170 hours of EDP management training through Air University. Stayed in top 5% of all classes. 3.4 average in electronic engineering courses during 1 year at UCLA.

other facts

Born May, 1952 . . . Married . . . Excellent health . . . 6'4", 215 lbs. Experienced public speaker and technical writer . . . Ability to address large groups and "get across" highly technical material . . . Enjoy fine music, competitive marksmanship, and amateur radio. Member: Data Processing Management Association, Institute of Electrical and Electronic Engineers. TOP SECRET clearance.

areas of greatest interest

Software . . . R&D, analysis and programming. Any application unique to data communications, assembly or machine languages. I am happiest when challenged by the job that "can't be done" . . . that fights back . . . that no one wants. Meeting the challenges of the "impossible" program is the source of my greatest personal satisfaction!

Suzanne L. McCullogh

65 Tripletree Road, Malden, Massachusetts 02135 · 531-5741

objective   ADMINISTRATIVE ASSISTANT to an executive looking for an
                 imaginative alter ego to take over detail, improve pro-
                 cedures, and increase office productivity.

Increased club interest and membership

. After one year's membership in the local chapter of the American
   Association of University Women, campaigned for and won the position
   of Program Chairman and Secretary. Scheduled more interesting (and
   controversial) speakers...increased study group participation and
   projects...installed new member recruiting techniques...enlivened the
   monthly newsletter...doubled local news coverage of our activities.
   Result: Increased membership by 50%. Typical comments from members:
   "the most exciting two years we've ever had...her energy, know-how,
   and imagination have brought us new self respect and community
   attention." (1975-1977)

Developed teacher-support program

. During PTA meetings, suggested to the principal that student learning
   would improve if teacher taught more and "bookkept" less. Volunteered
   to assist a sixth-grade teacher as an experimental project for one
   term. Assumed responsibility for maintaining order, record keeping,
   and recess activities. Grade levels improved almost immediately. My
   report of results and later recommendations to school officials produced a county-wide program of teacher support with paid part-time
   assistants. At the end of three years, test scores are up 20%, failure
   down 80% because of increased teacher attention to the individual needs
   of students. (1973-1976)

Assisted college professor

. As an undergraduate served two years in Economics Department.
   Administered and graded tests, prepared correspondence, and handled
   office matters. His comment: "the best assistant I ever had...your
   ability to take over doubled my time for research and writing."
   (1963-1965)

Education and other facts

. B.A., Economics, Western Michigan University, 1965. Honors student
   three years. President, Economics Club. Secretary, Student Council.
   Other activities. Graduated in top tenth from both high school and
   college. Facility in French. Type 70 wpm. Urban League, AAUW, PTA
   (President, one year). Like reading, politics, good music (Bach to
   Beatles), gourmet cooking. Enjoy bringing order out of seeming chaos.

personal   Born 1943...married...two school-age children at
                 home in the loving care of their grandmother.

ANTHONY B. HARRIS

Until July, 1981: MOQ 29-04, N.A.S., Bel Air, Texas 78416 (512) TE7-4323
Thereafter: 1558 Clinton St., Bridgeport, Conn. 06606 (203) 736-1980

job objective

ADMINISTRATIVE SPECIALIST to provide effective <u>coordination of technical and administrative functions</u> for increased efficiency--es-
pecially where there is a need for trouble-shooting, problem analysis,
higher personnel production, and lower operating costs.

****

experience

PERSONNEL RECRUITMENT, TRAINING, AND MOTIVATION

• For the past four years, acted to improve performance among
eleven units of the Naval Reserve in the Bel Air Area. Acted as
trouble-shooter to analyze causes of poor productivity. Initiated
measures to reduce duplication of effort, improve procedures and
production. Established a new system for recruiting highly qualified technical personnel by innovative visual presentations on
"talk show" programs, at technical schools, etc. (Applications
increased 87%). Motivated personnel to improve performance through
clearer guidelines and closer coordination of operations--pur-
chasing, payroll, plant and equipment maintenance, personnel training, recruitment, etc.

• <u>Results</u>: Five of these units achieved national recognition
for their excellence with very broad improvement noted in the
remaining six. According to official record, they all "...dis-
played outstanding resourcefulness, ingenuity, and devotion to
duty...under extremely trying circumstances" under my direction
during rescue and salvage operations in the worst hurricane ever
to hit the Texas coast. (1969-present)

PLANT ADMINISTRATION FOR IMPROVED OPERATIONS

Served as primary engineering executive in various ships.
Provided technical and administrative direction to five engineering divisions with responsibility for maintenance and operation
of large geared turbine systems plus direction of electrical power-
plant operations, damage control, purchasing, personnel training,
supervision of machine, carpenter, electrical, and paint shops, etc.

• <u>Results</u>: As an example, assumed direction of a badly demoral-
ized department characterized by a terrible state of equipment dis-
repair and personnel inefficiency. Despite openly expressed racial
contempt at the outset, raised morale and production to a level suf-
ficient to win recognition by the Navy Department for outstanding
performance in our class. (Only one other unit among two hundred
received the same award.) My superior said that "...this is the

experience   first time that the outstanding success of <u>any</u> of my operations has
continued   rested solely with the accomplishments of the engineering depart-
              ment." (1970-1976)

COST REDUCTION IN PERSONNEL RECRUITMENT

● For two years beginning in 1968, directed thirty recruiting
offices with heavy emphasis on attracting technically oriented
candidates. Supervised a large staff (initially 110) in this effort. <u>Established new procedures which eliminated the need for
30 people and cut the annual budget 50% while increasing total
production by ten percent</u>. Effective performance required strong
public relations and sales contacts--especially with civic officials and at high schools and colleges.

EARLIER EXPERIENCE

● Previous duties similar in type and accomplishment but of
less scope and responsibility. Entered the Navy as a machinist
and rose through the ranks to positions of responsibility in
machinery maintenance and repair. Effective performance often
required round-the-clock work under the most hazardous conditions
conceivable.

● Non-Navy experience including profitable business operations
of my own (gasoline service station and tobacco farm) plus successful employment as a passenger agent with the Santa Fe Rail-
road and as a salesman for the Magnificent Natural Products Co.

education   ● Graduate of Amistad High School, Laurenburg, N.C. Additional
training in public speaking. Numerous professional and technical
courses in plant engineering.

personal   ● Five feet, nine inches, 165 pounds. Married, six children
from toddler to teenager. Excellent health with no physical limitations. Born 1938.

Active in civic affairs - N.A.A.C.P., United Givers Fund, Naval
Affairs Committee. Enjoy woodworking, small boating, and fishing
as hobbies. Gain greatest pleasure from producing new solutions
to old problems and succeeding where others have failed.

─────MALCOLM D. FORRESTER─────────────────────────

3915 West Truro Lane, Pendleton, Oregon 97264 * (503) 267-5166

O b j e c t i v e   CITY PLANNING ASSISTANT to develop substantially
                      improved sociological and ecological data plus
                      related plans to assure sound urban renewal
                      while achieving strong citizen support.

Urban Planning to improve living condition in multi-racial communities.

*   Served as primary coordinator of civic improvement programs for
     the Umatilla-Pendleton Municipal Association. Brought together
     representatives of the various government agencies, business and
     civic groups on different occasions to discuss mutual concerns
     of public safety, vocational education, transportation, sanita-
     tion, and employment opportunities.
     Aim: To reduce major duplication of services while solving
     long-standing problems with newly released energies.

     After reorganizing my staff, convinced the groups to meet reg-
     ularly and adopt a short range schedule for implementing deci-
     sions. . . collected data on economic potentialities and popular
     feelings in the region. By appealing to civic pride, persuaded
     volunteers and part time professionals to do all the surveying
     and basic analysis within eight weeks at very low cost.

     RESULTS: Initiated programs to consolidate police work, use
     school buildings for year-round education, overhaul and stengthen
     water supply and sewage systems (incorporating pollution controls).
     Gained active cooperation and participation of representatives of
     all major groups - including several Indian tribes. (Restoration
     of their dignity and pride produced increased respect from the
     community generally as well as health and happiness which "old
     timers" say they have never seen before.) Accomplished all of
     these improvements with lower tax drain than any other area of
     comparable size, according to the American Society of Public
     Administration. (1977-present)

Statistical and fiscal experience.

*   Staff executive for an Army unit that processed nearly 500
     individuals per month to and from overseas locations. Projected
     workload requirements, transportation usage, and logistical
     support factors. With budget fixed in advance, kept operations
     within limits by quickly identifying trends which might add
     costs and devising procedures to avoid them. (1975-1977)

- more -

106

Malcolm D. Forrester

<u>Supervised construction of community facilities overseas.</u>

*   Formulated the policies and directives to speed construction
    of housing for American personnel in the suburbs of Kayseri,
    Turkey. Negotiated with local landowners. . . approved archi-
    tectural plans. . .contracted laborers and supervisors from
    surrounding area. Directed the procurement and distribution
    of materiel to virtually eliminate pilferage and resulting
    expense. Also advised the local vocational school principal
    during the construction of buildings. Later, because of my
    own interest in training methods, supervised curriculum
    development and scheduled training programs to include local
    students. My Army superior noted at the time: "Not only has
    his skill as a bargainer provided us with quality supplies at
    low cost, but his fine spirit of generosity has given us a
    solid link with the local people." (1973-1975)

<u>Earlier experience.</u>

*   Made surveys, analyzed policy objectives and procedures, and
    provided advice in administration and organization to Turkish
    officers in charge of ammunition procurement for their entire
    army. . .worked my way up through the Quartermaster Corps after
    starting as a supply clerk. (1956-1972)

<u>Education</u>

*   Studied International Relations, Logistics, Procurement, and
    Economics at the University of Maryland. Engineering and
    Geography at the University of Nebraska. . . numerous corre-
    spondence courses through Army Command and Staff College.
    Normally completed all courses in the top 15%.

P e r s o n a l

Six feet, one inch, 170 pounds. Happily
married, two children (no longer dependent).
Health excellent. Born 1938 in Crete,
Nebraska. Like "roughing it"--camping and
fishing. Most enjoy bringing widely divergent
individuals and groups together so they will
work creatively.

TELECOMMUNICATIONS ENGINEERING AND MANAGEMENT
where the prime requirement is the highest
technical reliability and operational effectiveness at the lowest cost.

objective

In Defense Communications Agency, managed the
DOD world-wide, direct-dial telephone network
--a combined, government-owned and leased system of over 24,000 access line and trunk circuits.
Directed annual expenditures of well over $30
million. (1976--1980)

telephone
network
management

Produced significant innovations in the processing
and routing of calls as a result of my studies of
traffic loads and computer simulation. Lowered
costs by more than $8 million over a two-year
period. Conceived and executed a system to
reduce network traffic load by rearrangement
of terminal access circuits through application
of unique traffic engineering techniques. Improved
the network call-completion rate 10% and further
cut costs by over $3.5 million a year.

higher
productivity
at a much
lower cost

Developed a concept and supporting procedures for
real-time network control of telephone traffic on
a world-wide basis. (Teaching this concept is now
standard in Army training courses on the subject.)
Adapted latest commercially proven techniques to
unique electronic switching centers overseas and
identified specific requirements for design modifica-
tions to improve traffic management capability.
Guided development of other highly effective
operational procedures for overseas switching
equipment.

new
conceptual
development

Evolved operational parameters for a Centralized
Alarm System for overseas portions of the network
to telemeter selected data to control centers.
Result: Improved responsiveness of network traffic
control decisions under degraded performance
conditions. Designed display arrangement for real-
time, telemetered data.

systems
design

installation
and testing

Managed and supervised installation and testing of
complex Army communications, electronics, and
navigation equipment. Organized and directed large
work forces in this effort. (1971--1976)

system
saved

Identified specific design deficiencies for
correction when supervising the installation
and testing of a prototype automatic secure-
voice electronic switching system--deficiencies
not known to the manufacturer. This saved the
system.

increased
productivity

Reorganized work force management system to
increase job productivity 30%, cut staff 10%,
and improve morale.

earlier
experience

Previously performed duties similar to those above
but at lower management and engineering levels
(12 years)

education
and
training

Bachelor of Science, magna cum laude--telecommunications
engineering--UCLA, 1974. Army Signal School, Commercial
Communications, one year, 1970. Communications Officer
Course, 10 months, 1965. Ranked in top 5% in each of
these.

personal

Born 1940. Not married. now obtaining voluntary
release (in the rank of Colonel) to devote myself
to civilian work. Top Secret clearance. Light,
trim appearance. Particularly enjoy tennis and
equitation. (Better than most at both). Excellent
health.

other
facts

Honored by Army Chief of Staff and Secretary of
Defense for my role in expanding military communications capabilities. . . Helped persuade the Army
that full use of available female talents would lead
to better utilization of all personnel. . . Gain
great satisfaction from watching men and women bloom
under leadership which deliberately attempts to
inspire each individual to perform at the peak of
ability.

for
details

Anna Maria Bonelli, 4027 O Street, N.W., Washington
D.C. 20007. Telephone: 202/337-4857 or (in DOD)
543-7866.

THOR A. DOLPHIN

607 Mira Drive, Key West, Fla. 33040   *   305/534-6471

objective

ASW RESEARCH, DEVELOPMENT, AND PRODUCTION
Assistant to senior executive concerned with defense sys-
tems--especially where major ASW program development is
needed to meet current military requirements.

summary

Twelve years' experience in all phases of antisubmarine
warfare with emphasis on research, development, and program management. Won official recognition for ". . . significant contributions toward solution of the Navy's ASW
problem." Record of numerous inventions, original ideas,
and studies resulting in improved sonar, detection systems,
ordnance, fire control, electronic equipment, radar navigation, training techniques, and fleet operating procedures.

major research
and development
in ASW
techniques

Served as primary executive of the Navy's ASW base at Key
West. Completed 22 major R&D projects to produce basic
innovations in ASW equipment, procedures, and tactics in all
areas of this field of operations from mechanical to psycho-
logical. (See the attached list for personal contributions,
inventions, and concepts produced during this period.) Official
note of this performance included such terms as these: ". . .
outstanding qualifications in ASW material design, tactics, and
planning . . . maintains a high state of enthusiasm and morale
. . . improved the Navy's readiness in all aspects of antisubmarine warfare." (1978-present)

Pentagon
coordination
of ASW
development

At the Pentagon level, coordinated submarine and antisubmarine
programs. Succeeded in obtaining greater emphasis on development
projects and speeded up production in many areas. Screened bud-
gets and contract proposals . . . assured technical assistance to
contractors to reduce costs 10%. Saving in one year:
$18 million. (1975-1977)

                                                . . . more

110

Thor A. Dolphin - page 2

substantially
improved
administra-
tive
operations

As chief executive of a large organization of 86 naval
units operating in the Western Pacific, introduced a new
concept for overhauling major shipboard equipment which
cut repair time 20%, reduced costs 5%, and noticeably raised
morale. According to official record, these efforts ". . .
streamlined and improved considerably on past methods through
the display of administrative abilities of the highest caliber."
(1972-1975)

additional
achievements

international
negotiations

personnel
training

improved
public
relations

As the primary U.S. naval representative in the Netherlands,
negotiated at the highest levels to modernize existing forces,
train personnel, and accomplish major improvements in antisubmarine forces - all with a saving of several million dollars
in U.S. aid funds . . . In Japan, instituted a personnel rotation
system which strengthened the economy, improved international
relations, and reduced total operating costs 15 per cent . . .
On the West Coast, won various plaques and trophies for exceptional performance in training large groups of personnel (2.5
to 5 thousand at a time) in the most technical phases of the
Navy's operations . . . In the Midwest, executed programs
to produce a significant improvement in relationships between
naval activities and civic and industrial leaders as evidenced
by a substantial increase (500%) in favorable editorial and
news coverage. (1958-1971)

education

Bachelor of Science degree - engineering - Naval Academy,
1957. Postgraduate studies in oceanographic electronics,
international relations, world history, etc. Fair ability in
Japanese language.

personal

Born June 7, 1935 . . . 5'7", 150 pounds . . . married,
3 children . . . excellent health . . . achieved top status at
Academy in track, boxing, and handball . . . now active in
tennis, golf, water skiing, and other aquatic sports.

other facts

Commended by the Secretary of the Navy, Chief of Naval
Operations, and the Commander in Chief Atlantic Fleet for
inventions in ASW and navigation . . . Obtaining release
from active service in the rank of Rear Admiral . . . Top
secret clearance.

ROBERT T. IRELAND

3254 Wrightsboro Road, Dallas, Texas 75240 · 214/839-5467

OBJECTIVE

MANAGEMENT ASSISTANT--MARKETING RESEARCH AND ADMINISTRATION particularly where there is a need to expand markets and develop new marketing concepts, products, and services of a technical nature.

EDUCATION

Master of Business Administration--Management, University of Texas, 1978. Bachelor of Business Administration--Marketing, University of Texas, 1975. (Minor in electronic engineering.) Distinguished student, graduated in top tenth. Student Council. Letterman - Varsity Baseball. Vice President, Marketing Association. Graduate Assistant to Vice President, Business Affairs --a position providing valuable experience and insight into top management problems. All college expenses financed by summer employment.

RELATED EXPERIENCE

Served as Research Assistant at University of Texas Institute of Human Resources. Supervised two researchers and office staff. Expanded thesis and spear-headed research which established early stages of model for economic impact of water impoundment in arid areas. Result: $60,000 grant to the University from Department of the Interior for further development.

SUMMER EMPLOYMENT

As a junior in high school, observed that lack of summer employment for students was due to inadequate organization, information, and marketing of their abilities. Established an organization called STUDENT MANPOWER ASSOCIATES. Spent $20.00 on professional-looking flyers of my design seeking both jobs and student applicants. Distribution door-to-door produced a flood of applicants and requests for help in lawn maintenance, window washing, child care, office work, equipment repair, etc. Coordinated available student talents with work demands. Provided close supervison of students to assure high performance. Eventually able to charge as much as $30.00 per man day for student help with many students earning $110.00 to $140.00 per week. Expanded area of program and numbers of employers and students served each year with particular emphasis on ghetto areas in last two years. During last three summers, State Employment Office called on US to find jobs for students. Gross income in Summer, 1977 was $23,533.00.

OTHER FACTS

Born 1953 . . . 5'10", 170 lbs. . . . Excellent health . . . Married . . . Spend spare time with cabinet making, reading, golf, baseball, civic activities, and--especially --working with young people. Have learned that decisiveness and leadership are just about synonymous.

TOPICS TO COVER
IN YOUR BRIEF

Here are some of the
topics you will be
thinking about as you
prepare your
qualifications brief.
They may also appear
in your own presenta-
tion. Incidentally,
you can use these
headlines to sharpen
the appearance of your
brief, if it is to be
reproduced by a
photographic process
(offset or Xerox).
Take a look at the briefs
for Annette Bourjaily
on page 95, Robert T.
Ireland, page 112;
and Winston C. Howell,
page 101 to see how
this is done. Simply
cut out the headlines
you need from this page
and paste them where
you want them to
appear. Be sure the
lines of type are perfectly
straight. Cover the edges
of the clipped headlines
with "white-out,"
available at office supply
stores or ask your
printer to do it for you.

OBJECTIVE

PRIMARY EXPERIENCE

RELATED ACHIEVEMENTS

EARLIER EXPERIENCE

SUMMER EMPLOYMENT

**OBSERVATIONS OF
SUPERIORS**

EDUCATION

AFFILIATIONS

SPECIAL TRAINING

PUBLICATIONS

PERSONAL DATA

PHYSICAL DIMENSIONS

**PRIMARY AIMS
AND ASSETS**

OTHER FACTS

113

Rules for the Office

1. Godliness, Cleanliness and Punctuality are the necessities of a good business.

2. This firm has reduced the hours of work, and the Clerical Staff will now only have to be present between the hours of 7 a.m. and 6 p.m. on weekdays.

3. Daily prayers will be held each morning in the main office. The Clerical Staff will be present.

4. Clothing must be of a sober nature. The Clerical Staff will not disport themselves in raiment of bright colours, nor will they wear hose unless in good repair.

5. Overcoats and topcoats may not be worn in the office, but neck scarves and headwear may be worn in inclement weather.

6. A stove is provided for the benefit of the Clerical Staff. Coal and Wood must be kept in the locker. It is recommended that each member of the Clerical Staff bring four pounds of coal each day during cold weather.

7. No member of the Clerical Staff may leave the room without permission from Mr. Rogers. The calls of Nature are permitted and Clerical Staff may use the garden below the second gate. This area must be kept in good order.

8. No talking is allowed during business hours.

9. The craving of tobacco, wines or spirits is a human weakness and, as such, is forbidden to all members of the Clerical Staff.

10. Now that the hours of business have been drastically reduced, the partaking of food is allowed between 11:30 a.m. and noon, but work will not, on any account, cease.

11. Members of the Clerical Staff will provide their own pens. A new sharpener is available, on application to Mr. Rogers.

12. Mr. Rogers will nominate a Senior Clerk to be responsible for the cleanliness of the Main Office, and the Private Office, and Boys and Juniors will report to him 40 minutes before Prayers, and will remain after closing hours for similar work. Brushes, Brooms, Scrubbers and Soap are provided by the owners.

13. The New Increased Weekly Wages are as here under detailed.

Junior Boys (to 11 years)	1s. 4d.
Boys (to 14 years)	2s. 1d.
Juniors	4s. 8d.
Junior Clerks	8s. 7d.
Clerks	10s. 9d.
Senior Clerks (after 15 years with owners)	21s. 0d.

The owners recognise the generosity of the new Labour Laws but will expect a great rise in output of work to compensate for these near Utopian conditions.

SHADES OF EBENEZER SCROOGE (1843)
Translated into dollars, the new "near Utopian" pay provided the office staff ranged from 32¢ per week for Junior Boys to $5.04 for Senior Clerks.

QUALBRIEF CHECKLIST

Check your qualifications brief against the questions on the following pages in order to determine whether it needs more work, and, if so, where and how much. Because these questions leave little room for escape based on pride of authorship, don't be surprised if some of the answers point to a need for further revision. If so, take the results to heart and go at it again before you encounter the far more serious consequences of wasted time, energy, money, and opportunities that come from use of an inadequate brief.

How to proceed

Review your brief carefully in light of each question below. Think about the implications of each question before answering it. Mark your answers with a check (✓) in the appropriate box. When you reach the end you will know whether or not more work is needed on your brief.

Appearance and format

YES NO

- Is your brief neatly typed or machine printed and not a carbon copy?* ☐ ☐
- Is the typography good with no errors, strikeovers, obvious erasures, etc.?* ☐ ☐
- Does it appear on only one side of each page?* ☐ ☐
- Is the copy neatly centered or nicely balanced on the page? ☐ ☐
- Is the paper of good quality? ☐ ☐
- Is the paper no larger than 8½ by 11 inches?* ☐ ☐
- If reproduced, is the type sharp and clean and the paper spotless?* ☐ ☐
- Have you used an attractive, businesslike type style (but not script type)? ☐ ☐
- Is the print of typewriter size, avoiding a fine-print appearance? ☐ ☐
- Is there plenty of white space on each page with wide margins and good space between paragraphs?* ☐ ☐
- Is your best experience highlighted by marginal leads, centered headlines, underlines, or other emphatic treatment?* ☐ ☐
- Does any photograph with your brief create the impression of a capable, pleasant, vigorous, well-groomed, youthful individual?* ☐ ☐

- Is the photograph no larger (and not much smaller) than passport size?

- Does it show you in civilian dress?

- Is the pose and background reasonably formal?

- Is the photo printed on your brief?

- Is your brief in a format of your own selection and *not* in a form that identifies it as the work of a professional résumé writer (or on any presupplied résumé form)?*

- Does it conform with the general (but not ironclad) rule of one page for ten years' experience or less, two pages for more than ten?

- If bound with a backing sheet, is there a French fold at the top hiding the staples and a thin margin of color on the sides and at the bottom?

- If a backing sheet is used, is its color distinctive and conservative but not French blue?

- Have you avoided adding a cover that hides your brief?*

- Is the general appearance at least equal to that of the samples in this chapter of WHW?

Organization

- Is your name, address, and telephone number included, preferably at the top of the first page?*

- Is your name at the top of each page?

- Have you omitted your business address unless compelling reasons exist for including it?

- Have you included your business phone number, if any, if such inclusion would not involve risk for you?

- Does your objective appear immediately under your identification?*

- If your brief includes a summarizing first paragraph on your experience, is the summary limited to significant accomplishments related to your objective rather than to positions held or duties performed?*

- Have you avoided writing your brief as a one-page synopsis plus a detailed account that runs to three pages or more?*

- Is your strongest qualifying experience described immediately under your objective, followed by the next strongest and so on?*

- If you are the recent recipient of a degree that lends major support to your objective, is your education shown close to your objective?* ☐ ☐

- If your education is less qualifying for the job you want than your experience or was obtained years ago, does it appear toward the end? ☐ ☐

- Is your highest education shown first in the education paragraph? ☐ ☐

- If you have completed college, have you omitted or lightly stated the facts regarding your high school education unless it is especially significant in your case? ☐ ☐

- If your age, marital status, or physical characteristics are important qualifiers for the job you want, does this information appear close to your objective? ☐ ☐

- Is *pertinent* data on your age, height, weight, marital status, and state of health (see Chapter 5 text regarding personal data) included—usually near the end? ☐ ☐

- Have you included an "Other Facts" or similar paragraph at the end to highlight additional information reflecting credit on you as an applicant and citizen and showing desirable traits or attitudes you will bring to the job?* ☐ ☐

- Are any lengthy lists of pertinent courses taken, equipment handled, publications, etc. attached as a separate sheet with a cross reference from your brief? ☐ ☐

- Have you omitted official documents?* ☐ ☐

Your objective

- Does your objective statement visually emphasize (through underlining, all-caps, etc.) the functional area in which you seek employment and the general level of the job you want?* ☐ ☐

- Does it avoid designating a specific job title (like "Personnel Manager") when a more general designation (like "Personnel Management") would permit consideration for a wider variety of openings at your level? ☐ ☐

- Is your objective stated in terms of your primary abilities as proved by your past performance?* ☐ ☐

- Does your objective show what you can accomplish for your employer (increased production, sales, efficiency, or whatever)?* ☐ ☐

- Is it cast at a level consistent with your record to date—not too low or too high in its aim?* ☐ ☐

- Does it avoid emphasis on what *you* want from your employer in terms of opportunities or conditions of employment?* ☐ ☐

- Is it reasonably short—not exceeding the length of the samples in this chapter? ☐ ☐

- Does it avoid offering overgeneralized virtues such as "maturity," "integrity," "conscientiousness," etc. on which the decision to hire seldom depends? ☐ ☐

- Are all abilities and assets indicated in your objective (except those of minor importance such as "sense of humor") *proved* by the rest of your brief? ☐ ☐

Content

- Are marginal leads, underlined statements, or other attention getters stated in terms of your accomplishments or primary functions you have performed?* ☐ ☐

- Have you avoided visually stressing dates or names of employers (both relatively meaningless information) in favor of emphatic treatment of your most qualifying experience? ☐ ☐

- Does the content, wherever possible, emphasize results produced, interesting problems overcome, significant achievements, etc.?* ☐ ☐

- Have you avoided a straight recitation of duties and responsibilities that fails to show *how well* you did your job?* ☐ ☐

- Where possible, have you livened your brief with very short quotations from others that reflect credit on your performance?* ☐ ☐

- Does your experience description cover your whole career, even if very briefly, with regard to early or unrelated experience?* ☐ ☐

- Are dates of experience in the last ten years included but generally deemphasized?* ☐ ☐

- Have you deemphasized experience not related to your objective (even if very strong) and experience that is more than ten years old? ☐ ☐

- Does your paragraph on education cover all important aspects of your schooling that add merit to your application—honors, high class standing, activities, leadership displayed, language facility, self-supported tuition, etc.?* ☐ ☐

- Have you generalized regarding courses taken that do not contribute directly to your objective? ☐ ☐

- Have you given due emphasis to awards, accomplishments, or activities in school, your community, or elsewhere that reflect ability, energy, versatility, wide interests, etc.?* ☐ ☐

- Are any pertinent publications, professional associations, licenses, etc. covered? ☐ ☐

- Where possible, does the final paragraph ("other facts") cover attitudes or personal attributes that show energy, competence, a constructive outlook, good citizenship, or—most important— personal traits indicating a pleasant personality who will turn in a strong performance?* ☐ ☐

- Have you avoided indicating frivolous or controversial activities or associations? ☐ ☐

- Have you avoided indicating conflicts in previous employment or other negative factors?* ☐ ☐

- Have you couched all references to military citations in civilian language and included only those that reflect significantly on your personally? ☐ ☐

- Have you left out references to military rank unless especially significant, or to military retired status?* ☐ ☐

- Have you eliminated such data as your social security number, religion, or race? ☐ ☐

- Have you left out location preferences, pay, or pay require- ments? ☐ ☐

- Have you excluded names of references? ☐ ☐

- Have you avoided summarizing the qualifications of other family members? ☐ ☐

- Have you shown your age date-of-birth style only? ☐ ☐

- If over 55, have you left out your birthdate? ☐ ☐

- Does your brief include any light touches or mild humor? ☐ ☐

- Have you omitted the date your brief was prepared and your availability date?* ☐ ☐

- Have you included every major significant factor that supports favorable consideration for the job you seek? YES NO

- Have you carefully phrased your brief to *prove* your ability to perform successfully on the job cited in your objective or to otherwise reflect merit on you as a potential employee?* ☐ ☐

Writing style

- Have you used short, pithy sentences in short paragraphs?* □ □
- Is the grammar and punctuation correct?* □ □
- Do all statements appear in proper syntax? □ □
- Is the spelling correct?* □ □
- Is all detail unnecessary to a broad appreciation of your abilities and assets eliminated?* □ □
- Have you avoided big words, lush adjectives, and superlative statements?* □ □
- Are you comfortable with everything your brief says and sure it is not exaggerated (even if a glowing account that accents the positive)?* □ □
- Are all laudatory quotations extremely brief and in smooth reading context? □ □
- Have you avoided technical or parochial jargon to the maximum extent possible? □ □
- Have you eliminated all unnecessary military terminology and substituted equivalent civilian terms?* □ □
- Do most of the sentences in your brief start with action verbs such as "directed," "supervised," "wrote," "developed," "planned," "produced," "achieved," etc.?* □ □
- Have you avoided the third-person approach and passive voice?* □ □
- Is "I" used sparingly if at all?* □ □
- Have you avoided picking up text for your brief from official descriptions?* □ □
- Have you avoided an unduly modest approach and let the facts on your accomplishment speak clearly for themselves? □ □
- Does your brief avoid the use of "canned" résumé language (e.g., "Distinguished military career," "experience in all phases of administration," etc.) that seems to claim too much?* □ □
- Have you avoided emphasizing senior age through the manner of describing your experience (e.g., "Thirty years' experience in...," etc.)?* □ □
- Does your brief avoid general statements regarding your performance in lieu of specific facts (for example, "Commended for exemplary achievement in this assignment" vs. "Fifty percent increase in production and 5 percent decrease in costs produced this official comment: 'extremely impressive performance...an example for all members of the Division.'")?* □ □

- Where possible, do you cite specific examples of successful performance supporting your objective?* ☐ ☐

- Do such examples quantity results (e.g., "increased effective placements of chronically unemployed by 52 percent.")? ☐ ☐

Overview

- Is your brief an attractive, interesting, quick-reading, broad-brush, factual account that *proves* that your experience and personal assets qualify you for the job you want (your job objective)?* ☐ ☐

Evaluation and action

So much for questions to be asked about your qualifications brief. They indicate the many factors that should be kept in mind if you are to produce a brief that puts you well ahead of competing applicants and causes employers to think about hiring you as quickly as possible—at the highest possible pay. These questions also indicate the many factors that must be kept in mind by fee-paid writers operating at the professional level. They help to explain why such professional writers fully earn their fees (which normally exceed $100) for turning out good work.

Now that you have rated your presentation, here's how to proceed: If it is in the draft stage, correct all items where you indicated a "no" answer. Be sure you have compelling reasons before letting any "no"-rated item stand as is. If you have already had copies produced at some expense, discard them only if any item marked with an asterisk (*) above rated a "no" or if *any* five questions produced "no" for an answer.

If you talk in military jargon when looking for a job,
many civilian employers will fail to understand you.
Here's how to translate your military experience
into "civilianese."
And how anyone who wants to move
from a highly specialized field—religion, for example—
into a more general, or different, line of work
should approach this communications problem.

6
Make the most
of your
military
experience

Men and women leaving military service often confound themselves by describing strong experience in military terms that few
civilians understand. More than that, they often tend to underrate the value of their experience when looking for civilian
employment. On this score, two points should be made clear
right here at the outset:

- There are few functions performed in military service that
  are not also performed in civilian employment.
- *Most* civilian employers can look to military standards and
  systems for direct guides on how to improve their own
  operations.

In other words, when properly presented to the right employers,
your military experience is a decided asset.

Sure, you have seen many examples of waste and inefficiency
in military operations—maybe even some that seemed beyond
belief. But keep in mind that most of this stems from the fact
that the armed services must be immediately prepared to meet
enormous and highly unpredictable contingencies. The need
to maintain an overpowering stance when there is no immediate use for even a small fraction of its potential is alone
enough to explain almost all appearances of waste you have
encountered. On the other hand, when the military services
are called upon to operate at the peak of their capacity, few
private concerns can match them for sheer awe-inspiring
efficiency.

It will help you to keep your military experience in perspective if you think about the general level of efficiency with
which private enterprise performs *its* job. No doubt you have
frequently been frustrated by junior-grade performance, poor
service, shoddy products, and outright failure to meet commitments—despite the vaunted reputation of private business

and the far more manageable problems facing it. These failings apply even to the nation's industrial giants, although less frequently than to the bulk of private enterprise which is composed of small-to-middling organizations. (Recall, for example, the costly recalls of automobiles to put them in safe operating condition.) Many civilian organizations can use your military training and experience to great advantage to improve their own operations.

So be proud of your experience. And let that pride show.

Pin down its value

Analyzing your military experience to determine which aspects of it are most useful to civilian employers is the first step to take. Chapter 4 gives you the guides you need to do this. When you have completed that chapter, you will know much more about the strong points you offer employers than most civilian job seekers know about theirs.

As you go through this self-analysis, an important thing to remember is that military service tends to generate a highly developed sense of modesty regarding performance on the job. No doubt this stems from a system that automatically assumes that assigned duties *will* be performed—presumably to perfection. But don't let such modesty stand in your way now.

As a military member you are very likely to think of your experience in terms of the tasks performed—not in terms of the results produced. Because of this, you may lose sight of the true value of what you have done. Consequently, as you explore your experience, concentrate on digging out *accomplishments*—things changed for the better, money saved, more efficient operations—all of the things that show *how well* you did your job. And, where you can, try to quantify the changes you produced.

After you have discovered your strongest abilities and experience, it is critically important to *translate* them into terms that civilians will immediately understand. Keep in mind that your aim from here on out is to *communicate* your qualifications to employers—orally and in writing—not to hide them in "insider" military terms that few civilians fully comprehend. Do it right and you'll create the impression that you always were a true civilian at heart despite your uniform.

How to do it

Here are two good examples:

- If you tell civilian employers that you led long-range recon patrols in search and destroy missions involving frequent fire fights deploying ARVN personnel, they will amost certainly wonder why you have come to them. They usually don't have anything to do with recon (long or short-range), ARVN people (whoever they are), fire fights (barring occasional battles with smoldering cigarettes in trash cans), or searching and destroying (except when it's time to clean out the files or fumigate the stockroom).

  On the other hand, if you talk about your experience in logistics planning, leading field teams, organizing effort, gathering and analyzing information, directing foreign nationals, assuring proper safety measures, maintaining equipment, communicating, building morale, and fully and completely executing your assignments—all under extremely bad conditions—they will hear you. Some will even need your abilities as a marksman. Or they may need your experience in demolition, explosive disposal, crowd control, or interviewing. Not to mention physical endurance, strength, and courage—all required to do your job.

- Or if you lead off your contacts with employers with the word that you were Commanding Officer of the USS *Enterprise,* you may well get the civilian reaction that we don't need any CO's around here and we certainly don't have any aircraft carriers that need skippering. Yet, virtually all of the important duties performed as CO of the *Enterprise* have their direct civilian equivalents in operations ashore. The idea is to cover those duties and stress the abilities needed to perform them while breaking the news of where and how the experience was gained as an incidental matter.

So the key point here is to show how much *like* civilian employment your military service has been, not how different. To do it, take the following steps:

- **Study the qualifications briefs included in this book that reflect military experience.** Look, for example, at the briefs for James Creed Kirby (page 50), Albert Haynes Cross (page 74), Juan Alvarez (page 97), Robert P. Kovaleski (page 98), Charles J. MacAllister (page 102), Malcolm D. Forrester (pages 106-107), Anthony B. Harris (pages 104-105), Thor A. Dolphin (pages 110-111), and A. M. Bonelli (pages 108-109). And take another look at the brief for Lili Li Lu (pages 70-71). While hers is not concerned with military experience, it is another good example of translation of one kind of experience (household and family management) to another field (project or program management).

■ **Find civilian substitutes for all military terms that come to mind.** If you have never heard a non-service-connected civilian use a term (for example, *quartermaster, adjutant,* etc.) that applies to your experience, don't use it. So you will know what we are talking about, the following examples show the types of substitutions to make.

"Served as chief project officer (not Force Embarkation Officer) responsible for providing sea transportation for (not outmounting in troop transports) 45,000 passengers (not officers, enlisted men, and DAC) plus 125,000 tons of cargo (not ordnance, supplies, and military equipment) from Viet Nam to the U.S. (not ZI)."

As a further guide, these additional examples will show you the approach to take to substitute "civilianese" for "militarese":

Militarese	Civilianese
Commander, Commandant, Commanding Officer, Chief of Staff, First Lieutenant, Company Commander, Petty Officer, ranking NCO, etc.	Senior line executive, operating executive, executive assistant, department head, senior line officer of field unit, administrator, manager, supervisor, group leader, etc.
Commanded, ordered	Directed, administered, managed, coordinated, planned and executed, supervised, etc.
Civilian, military, commissioned, noncommissioned, officer, enlisted, etc. (used as adjectives)	Drop altogether. Such differentiation of people partially on the basis of the clothes they wear seldom occurs in civilian work situations.
Civilians, officers, enlisted personnel (or "men"), soldiers, sailors, airmen, troops, etc.	Personnel, staff, crew, team, clerical force, technicians, task force, etc., as appropriate (but not "employees" when referring to military personnel).

DAC, G-4, NROTC, GySgt, JAG, BuPers, E4, etc.	Spell out, drop, or substitute civilian terms. For example, use "supply operations" or "logistics," not "G-4."
Combat, combat-ready, fighting men	Highly hazardous conditions, highly trained personnel
Retired, retiring, retirement, discharge, honorable service	Talk in terms of your voluntary (if true) separation or release. Or say nothing.
Your military rank or rating	Avoid using it except under unusual circumstances where it will be a clear asset in the job you are applying for.

- **Don't scare civilians with the size of your fiscal responsibility** if that is part of your qualifications. If it is a factor in your qualifications brief, tone down fiscal responsibility by discrete terminology designed to fit the size of the job you are aiming for. For example, if you were responsible for a $25 million annual budget and are aiming your application for an operation that is happy to get by on $2 million a year, they may be concerned that you will spend them to death if they hire you or that you are terrifically over-qualified for their little business. State it this way (if you can without being absurd): "Administered expenditures in excess of $2 million annually. Introduced economies that produced a 20 percent reduction in costs while raising production levels 5 percent. Did this by changing . . . "etc. As another common error, avoid putting a monetary value on the equipment or real estate you were responsible for. Don't say "As a fighter pilot, assumed direct responsibility for the efficient and safe utilization of equipment costing $1,947,000.00." or something like that. This technique, often used by fee-charging résumé writers, is usually looked upon by employers as an attempt to puff up your qualifications.

- **When it comes to decorations,** bear in mind that civilian employers don't "decorate" their personnel. They may give them a letter of praise, a promotion, a bigger bonus, a vacation in Pago Pago, or some other recognition. But not a decoration. Hence, avoid the term in your contacts with employers. And shy away from the names of citations— especially those that are more or less routinely awarded like theater decorations, the good conduct medal, etc. On

the other hand, if you have been singled out for exceptional performance, describe your accomplishment and
then say something like "Performance described by superiors as . . . " (and quote a very brief phrase or two from
the citation, picking whatever most aptly sums up the
quality of your accomplishment). But don't say you got
a commendation medal for it.

- **Citations for personal valor are something else again.** They
add interest to your qualifications brief, appeal to the pa-
triotism of employers, encourage a desire to meet you, and
might even produce an invitation to dinner so that the
employer's spaced-out son can be exposed to a different
system of values for a change. Say "Awarded (name of
decoration) for . . . " and describe what you did to win it
in a flat, factual, modest style of writing. Avoid such terms
as "personal heroism," "conspicuous gallantry above and
beyond the call of duty," etc. Also, put such information
—modestly—at the end of your brief under "other facts"
where it will have its greatest impact. If the award was the
Purple Heart, don't go into detail. Just say "Purple Heart"
under "other facts" and leave it to the employer to ask
about it.

- **Nonroutine promotions** are best handled by saying something like this: "Selected for special promotion three years
ahead of normal date for . . . " and describe the accomplishment that produced it. Avoid such commonly overworked
terms as "advanced in rank ahead of contemporaries,"
which do not adequately convey the importance of your
special promotion to civilians who are unfamiliar with
military operations.

Show pride in your experience

On the other hand, don't hide the military source of your
experience and don't *strain* to get it into civilian terms come
hell or high water. If any particular aspect of your duties won't
translate without looking ridiculous, let it stand. But be sure
you have given it a strong try. In any event, be sure that what
you say in your brief and interviews carries a strong undertone
of pride regarding your accomplishments and the valuable
experience gained while in uniform. The sample briefs cited
above will provide clues on how to do this. Study them carefully.

As you check out in the final stages of your separation, take full advantage of the help and guidance offered at the separation center by your branch of service. But keep in mind that staff and funds are not available to provide more than a quick steer in the direction of getting started with your job hunt. In the final analysis, success in your transition to civilian life will depend almost entirely on *your* efforts—not those of others. Be sure you have fully studied the other provisions of this book so that you will know the strange ways the job market operates and the things you must do to succeed in it.

A word of caution. Because of the inadequacy of employment programs for veterans, many released military personnel engage the services of various types of employment specialists with advance fees involved (sometimes running to four—even five—figures). Some of these services offer extremely valuable help—help that can assure transition into employment close to the peak of your abilities and pay potential. Others closely resemble rackets. They deliberately play on your lack of experience with the job market and your concern about the future to lead you through a time-wasting, wheel-spinning, ineffectual routine that can crush your morale, all with only one aim in mind—their enrichment at your heavy expense. Veterans are often victimized by such services. Check the guides in Chapter 12 to determine what kinds of services are available, whether you need them, and how you can tell the good from the bad.

Finally, remember that there is a vast difference between serving your country and serving a company. Your military service has been oriented to pursuit of national goals. In the future, your efforts may be oriented to pursuit of dollars. If service to others has been an important source of satisfaction for you to date, aim for employment that includes such service as an important element.

If you prepare adequately for your job search, you will find that it is an exciting and interesting challenge—a game of strategy designed to produce the opening you want at the highest possible pay. But if you fail to do your homework, you may find yourself at age 38 cleaning up ketchup spills as a "management trainee" for a fast food chain, despite extremely valuable experience gained in uniform.

It has happened to others. *Don't* let it happen to you.

The letter covering your qualifications brief
gives employers that all-important first impression.
A routine approach to writing it
will produce a routine result for your application
—a quick trip to the confetti maker.
Write a letter that makes employers
want to buzz buzzers,
reach for the telephone,
or dictate a prompt reply.

Write a letter that *demands* attention

A high percentage of résumés are sent to employers under covering letters that seem almost deliberately designed to kill off any enthusiasm that the résumé itself might arouse. Since you plan to break with the résumé tradition and send a qualifications brief instead, now is a good time to break with the deadening covering letter approach as well.

The primary limitations of most covering letters we see are these: they use the wrong form; they say the same things the great majority of covering letters say (and therefore are not even read beyond the first line or two); they often emphasize negative factors, and—worst of all—they are as dull as dust.

Fate of the average letter

Keep this in mind. The average employer who has a job opening you may want is likely to be swamped with applications of one kind or another. Put yourself in the place of employers and you can picture them thumbing through huge stacks of paper hoping for something that excites their interest enough to cause them to reach for the telephone. Letter after letter disappoints them—and they would disappoint you, too. Such letters, of course, are headed for oblivion in the wastebasket —and the résumés with them.

Let's take an example. And, because some people operate under the misconception that military experience has little application in private enterprise, we'll take a hard example —that of a retiring naval officer.

Now, in this case, our man realized that typing individual letters takes either time or money. So he had his letter preprinted to save substantial expense. Here's what it said:

Dear Sir:

I will retire from the Navy early next month.

Because my experience has been heavy in contract administration, I will be available for the position of Contract Officer and would like to be considered by your organization at that time. My goal is to become employed with a firm which provides good opportunities for training and promotion based on merit alone.

Needless to say, I have heard many favorable things about your company and would like very much to be associated with it. Hence, my résumé is enclosed for your consideration.

I will look forward to hearing from you if there should be an opening in line with my experience.

Then came the usual cordial close and signature.

It sounds like a great letter, doesn't it? Well, maybe not great, but certainly okay. Nevertheless, it was destined to fail in its job the day it was mailed. Utterly.

Why is this?

Read the letter once more. One thing stands out above all else. The writer (let's call him Joe Jones) is talking exclusively about what *he* wants—not what the employer (whom we'll call Smith) needs.

Because there's much to be learned from it, let's examine this letter in some detail.

First of all, it's printed—not typed. "Obviously," Smith thinks the moment the letter comes to hand, "this guy has nothing to say to *me*" but the impulse to put the letter on the discard pile is nevertheless quelled.

"Dear Sir," the letter says, and the temptation to give it a short flight to the wastebasket is heavily reinforced. Smith is deeply affronted by the sex change just imposed on her. Moreover, she likes to read letters addressed to *her,* not some impersonal "Sir" (or "Madame," if you will). However, she reads on, negatively.

"I will retire . . . ," the letter says. To the average civilian, and Susan Smith is one of them, retirees are largely used-up dodderers, not people who are approaching their prime years of productivity as Joe is. (Joe is 43). After this misleading piece of advice, Smith will continue reading only if she has nothing better to do.

How not to win friends

Fortunately, time is heavy on Smith's hands and she next learns that Joe wants the job of Contract Officer. The sad thing about this is that Smith is already the Contract Officer. Joe Jones has made the awful mistake of applying for Smith's job—one that she likes very much.

No application, of course, can survive that blow. Smith's impulse is to tear Joe's letter and résumé into little bits and take a quick trip down the hall where the pieces can be flushed away forever.

But Joe is the type who always gets the breaks. His letter has aroused a morbid curiosity in Smith and she continues to read on. Grimly.

As the next item, Joe asks Smith (or whoever) to give him a job that will lead to training and promotional opportunities —undoubtedly in an attempt to convey the idea that he is energetic, ambitious, and going places.

Unfortunately, up to now, Smith has been given no clue as to why such expensive largess should be bestowed on Joe. Moreover, all that follows in the letter smacks of bold insincerity since Joe can't possibly mean his printed statement (designed to flatter the employer) that he has heard many favorable things, etc.

There's no doubt about it. Joe's application is dead. A glance at the final paragraph satisfies Smith that she will not have to tell Joe this to his face and she turns to the next application. She never even looked at Joe's résumé. Too bad, too, since Joe had paid a professional résumé writer $150.00 to help him put it together. And it wasn't bad, as résumés go.

Basic rules for good covering letters

All of this brings us down to the basic rules for letters of application:

1. Type each letter individually.
2. Address each employer by name and title.
3. Open your letter with a strong sentence that would make you take your feet off the desk if you were sitting in the employer's chair.

4. Devote the center of your letter to brief facts about your experience and accomplishments that will arouse the employer's curiosity. Use such facts to impel attention to your qualifications brief.

5. Appeal in your letter to the self-interest of the person to whom you are writing. Include clues that indicate that hiring you will lead to higher production, greater efficiency, reduced waste, better sales, higher profits, etc.—that is, things that will help solve the employer's problems and increase his/her own prospects for advancement.

6. If at all possible, include some challenging thoughts that will cause employers to feel that discussion with you would be worthwhile even if they really hadn't been planning to hire anybody right now.

7. Where possible (in letters to nearby employers), bid directly for an interview and indicate that you will call to arrange a suitable time. Softly imply in your letter that they will be dogs if they don't grant your request. Or, better still, make them feel that declining your request would be an act of sheer irresponsibility simply because you obviously have so much to offer them.

8. Keep your letter short to hold interest and save yourself substantial typing expense or time.

Now what happens when we rewrite Joe Jones' letter with these guides in mind? The result is on the next page. Take a look at it.

If you were Smith, would you give Joe the interview he wants? Of course you would. You'd probably even invite him out to lunch.

Joe's rewritten letter is the standard you should aim for whenever you can. But, obviously, you can't always have this kind of familiarity with the specific problems of employers who are likely to be interested in your application. Where you don't, your stress should be on your ability to help solve problems common to virtually all employers who hire people in your line of work.

1446 Crouton Place
George Town, Ill. 45432
June 16, 1981

Ms. Susan R. Smith, Contract Officer
The Ansonia Company
Ansonia, North Dakota 58760

Dear Ms. Smith:

While serving as a contract administrator for the Navy, I
uncovered information about defense contracting procedures which
I believe will interest you a great deal. Briefly, I learned that
almost all contractors can substantially improve their competitive
position through minor changes in approach which will align them
more directly with the requirements of military agencies. I am
sure that adopting such changes will prove most profitable for
Ansonia.

This discovery was made during ten years spent in military
procurement operations. You will find that experience described in
my qualifications brief enclosed. The experience gained has given
me a very thorough appreciation of the hurdles facing defense
contractors plus many ideas on how they can be reduced when pursuing major government business. I would very much appreciate
the opportunity to discuss these ideas with you.

I will be in Ansonia next week - on Wednesday - and will
call you before then to learn when we might get together. If you are
due to be away at that time, please let me know.

Very truly yours,

Joseph A. Jones

Joseph A. Jones

JOE JONES'S LETTER *(See text)* This is the kind of letter most
likely to arouse a favorable response—one that zeroes in on the interest of
the official to whom it is addressed. Even so, this same letter probably
would be equally effective with any military manufacturer's contracting
officer.

103 Long Sound Road
Hasselfield, N.Y. 117.
November 19, 1979

Mr. William Poliachic, Vice President
Field Operations
The International Development Corporation
2120 North Wabash Avenue
Chicago, Illinois 60651

Dear Mr. Poliachic:

In view of International's plans for expansion in South America,
I believe you will be interested in the following experience:

> Successful establishment and administration of major over-
> seas organizations . . . ability to develop local resources
> and use them effectively . . . broad experience in obtaining
> productive cooperation from foreign officials and employees
> . . . full knowledge of the logistics required for efficient and
> low-cost overseas operations . . . "native" fluency in English,
> Spanish, and German.

My qualifications brief enclosed provides details.

Whether or not IDC has an immediate need for experience of this
kind, I do hope to have the opportunity to meet you briefly during
my forthcoming trip to Chicago. There have been some important
(and as yet unannounced) developments with regard to Argentina's
transport system which I believe will interest you. And, in any
event, I would appreciate the opportunity to obtain your views
regarding the general situation in Latin America.

I will be in Chicago during the week of December 5 and will call
before then to learn when a meeting can be arranged.

Sincerely,

Greta Schuller

Greta Schuller

, John J. Green, Vice President
Operations and Engineering
Telectronics, Incorporated
427 Farrel Street
San Francisco, CA 92414

Dear Mr. Green:

By far the greatest satisfaction in my electronic and communications engineering assignments to date has come from coaxing
superior performance from the personnel and equipment assigned
to me--and from finding new ways to get the job done at less cost
than is usually the case. I have learned that some remarkable and
highly rewarding results are produced when an energetic drive to
find a better way is coupled with due concern for costs and the needs
of the people who work with me.

The enclosed qualifications brief provides brief examples of
these results.

Because of your broad experience in this field, I would greatly
appreciate your advice on where experience of this kind might be put
to best use either with Telectronics or elsewhere in the Bay area.
Since I will be down there during the week of May 2, I will call you
then to learn when we might get together for a brief meeting.

Sincerely yours,

Anton Degoray

Anton Degoray

**Aim for
an interview
every time.**

If you have
uncovered
information that
you know will
interest employers,
use it as an
effective means
to generate a
strong urge to
see you. You
should try,
where possible,
to arouse the
feeling among
employers you
contact that
failure to see you
would be a gross
dereliction of
duty.

Ask for help.

When you do,
the first question
likely to come
to the employer's
mind is,
"Where can we
use this candidate
here?" especially
if the rest of
your presentation
is interesting.
And every such
contact can be
a rich source
of new leads
even if it fails
to uncover
the immediate
opening
you want.

Things to remember as you write your letter

While the rules for writing your letter are simple enough, there are some other things you should keep in mind as you do it, if you are to do a good job. For example:

- **Remember, you are an applicant, not a supplicant.** In your letter, you are proposing a mutually beneficial association with another human being. You are *not* seeking the benefaction of a king. In a highly self-respecting way, you are offering to put your energy, experience, and abilities to work in that person's interest in return for pay and other benefits. It is essentially a business proposition. As with any such proposal, your emphasis at the outset should be on how the association you are proposing will advance the aims of the employer.

- **Address the president of the firm** if distance or other factors prevents your learning the name of the official directly responsible for employees in your category. Do it even if you want an entry-level job. When received, such letters normally take one of two routes: (1) They get sent directly to the official most likely to be interested in your qualifications, or (2) they end up in the personnel officer's lap. Most frequently, it's the latter—especially in large organizations. Either way, you're still ahead. Correspondence from the front office almost always gets special consideration and handling. And the people who get it for action never know whether the president just might follow up on it— especially if your presentation is impressive and the president has recently been growling about jacking up staffing standards.

- **Stress accomplishment.** Regardless of your experience level, if you have ever done anything well or out of the ordinary, you have something to bring out in your letter. Find such examples that support your qualifications for the job you want. Point to them briefly in your letter while calling attention to your qualifications brief for the full facts.

- **Always bid directly for an interview.** But avoid using the term *interview.* Instead, ask for a brief meeting. Or ask when you might get together. Or when you might come to see the employer. Be direct about it. Write your letter as though you *expect* the meeting to occur. Indicate that you will follow up with a call to arrange a suitable time. If that is impractical because you are applying on a long distance basis, say something like, "Could you please let me know when I might see you briefly to discuss these possibilities. I can be in your office on short notice and will appreciate a collect call indicating a time convenient for you. My number is . . ."

- **Address your letters on a regional basis** to avoid spreading yourself too thin with excessive travel time and demands. Send them out area by area at phased intervals. If one employer at a distance responds with an interview bid, ask whether they will pay expenses before committing yourself to come. Whether or not they will, call the others in the same area saying you plan to be out there and would like to see them briefly while in the area. (Or call them when you arrive.)

- **See that your letters are neatly typed.** The letter for Greta Schuller shows a good, business-like style and how to set it up. If you can't do the typing, perhaps your spouse or a good friend can. If that's impractical, look under "letter writers" in the Yellow Pages Index for services that will do it for you. Where large mailings are involved (25 or more) check out the cost of automatic typing. It's usually cheaper. And less prone to error.

- **When responding to advertised openings,** follow the rules above to write a letter that responds directly to the needs specified in the ad. In addition, the ad may ask for your pay requirement and salary history. If it does, state your pay expectations in a *range,* something like this: "My pay requirement is in the $15,000 to $18,000 range depending on the challenge and opportunity offered." To determine your pay range, put the lower level at about ten percent above your last pay level. If this is impractical because your pay has not been well related to the level of your performance (as in the clergy, military service, voluntary organizations, etc.) put the minimum ten percent higher than the least you would accept. (See Chapter 10 for more on this.) If reciting your salary history would handicap your application, say that your salary has been commensurate with the experience reflected in your brief *without* being specific. In any event, you don't need to cover more than five years back.

- **Aim for interviews even though no openings exist.** You have several good reasons for doing this: (1) You want the opportunity to persuade the employer that you should be the first hired as soon as the need for new personnel *does* occur (perhaps a day or two later, to everybody's great surprise). (2) You want the opportunity to convince the employer that an opening should be created for you to take advantage of the unique problem-solving abilities you offer. (Keep in mind that this happens all the time.) Or (3) if neither of those works out, you still want the opportunity to get the employer's advice and help and to ask that he/she keep your brief on hand for referral to others who may indicate a need for someone with your special abilities. At the very least, each interview gives you the opportunity to make an influential friend in the job market and such friends are *most* likely to produce the opening you want.

- **But expect rebuffs in your follow-up calls.** They are inevitable—especially from secretarial guardians at the gate. Such rebuffs, even rude ones, are a "go-to-jail-do-not-pass-go" aspect of the job-hunt game. Try to take a tough-hided attitude toward them. Don't let them get you down. The thought to keep uppermost in your mind is that your follow-up calls will produce many more interviews and prospects for the job you want than if you don't make them. And apply as much strategy as you can to avoid being cut off. When you call to arrange the meeting and get the employer's secretary, say, "This is Joe Jones (using your nickname). Is he (she) there?" to convey the impression that you are an old friend of the boss. This often works. Or you might even take it a step further by opening up with, "Hi, Joe Jones calling. Is Sam in?" as though you have a game of golf in mind. But some secretaries are canny, indeed, and you may well get the response, "Oh, Mr. Jones, Mr. Smith asked me to tell you that he's sorry but we have no openings now." In that case, don't fold up. Not yet anyway. Instead, say, "I can appreciate that. However, I would still very much like to get his advice on current developments in this field. I am sure he could be most helpful to me. Could I talk with him for just a moment, please?" Then when Smith gets on the line ask him if you might meet him briefly to get his advice and suggestions regarding the current outlook especially in view of his broad experience. More than likely, he will be hard put to turn you down.

But if he tells you he's right in the middle of the annual inventory and just can't see you now, ask if he can suggest other officials in his or other organizations whom you should contact. If that proves productive, you can proceed with such contacts, saying that Sam Smith of ABC Company suggested that you see them. And you're on your way.

Letter without a brief

Sending a high powered brief under a commanding covering letter is undoubtedly the best way for most applicants to go when initially contacting employers by mail. However, if you can *briefly* point to a series of more or less thundering accomplishments in your letter, then it's best *not* to send a brief. The letter for Fernando Hernandez on the following page is a good example of what we mean. And you'll find others at the end of this chapter. A compelling letter without a brief offers one major advantage. It permits you to adjust all of your later communications (including your brief when you finally submit it) so that they zero in on the employers' problems as disclosed in the interviews that your letter generates. This way, you are in the strongest possible position to command the best possible pay and working conditions. For example, Hernandez parlayed the numerous interview opportunities opened up by his letter into a position as staff assistant to the president of the organization he finally found most suitable—a job that, incidentally, did not exist until Hernandez inspired his new boss to create it.

So the thing to do now is *study* all of the letters with this text and at the end of the chapter. As with the sample qualifications briefs, underline those passages that most fit your situation and style. Use them as a guide to preparation of your own letter, aiming for similar impact but including a large element of your own personality and attitudes. Get the help of a word-wise friend if converting your thoughts to ink is a chemical process at which you never felt particularly adept. Or consult a professional in the career field. But be sure he/she has read this chapter before making a commitment.

When you are finished, check your letter out against the rules for good covering letters on page 133. Remember, the test of your letter is not whether it gets the message across that you

489 Laredo Canyon Rd.
San Antonio, Texas 77506
Telephone: 536-6492
May 15, 1978

Mr. Claude Doagy, President
Prairie National Bank
329 Travis Avenue
San Antonio, Texas 77500

Dear Mr. Doagy:

I thrive on challenge and most enjoy myself when getting things done. Perhaps you will be interested in my record:

. Student Council President, Crocket High School

. Junior Achievement company president.

. Boy's State's Outstanding Mayor

. Distinguished Military Graduate, University of Texas

. Unusually rapid advancement as an Air Force officer

. Honors MBA Graduate, University of Texas (next month)

In the belief that you will soon need abilities of this kind in operations or financial management, I would like very much to discuss employment possibilities with you. I hope you won't mind a call on Thursday to arrange a time convenient for you.

Yours, truly

Fernando Hernandez

Fernando Hernandez

Letter without a brief enclosed:

If you can briefly point to resounding accomplishments of a kind bound to interest most employers you address, then send a letter alone without a qualifications brief. This alone is likely to get you interviews leading to job offers. Then you can follow up with a modified brief to cinch the job offer—a brief that deals specifically with important areas of the employer's interest uncovered in the interview.

are applying for a job. All letters of application do that. For the most part, letters so limited represent a burden—not a challenge and opportunity—to the employers who get them. Instead, ask yourself, "Is it interesting? Does it convincingly convey the point that I offer abilities that can help solve the employer's problems?" If not, discard your first try and go at it again.

Is it worth all that effort?

You bet it is. Good letters of application are received so rarely by employers that they tend to tingle with excitement when they get one. Certainly, you want that to happen with yours.

MORE GOOD
COVERING LETTERS

The following pages show the body content of more good covering letters. Study them all. Underline the kinds of expression that appeal to you and that best fit your experience. Use such expressions as guides to development of your own letters but try to choose different words to the greatest extent possible. Otherwise, your letter may have a familiar ring to employers who get it.

Most of these letters were written to employers who could conveniently be reached by telephone to arrange an interview. Some (specifically samples 12, 15, 19, 23, 31, and 33) ask employers to initiate interview action because a telephone follow-up is impractical due to distance or other factors.

Samples 17, 30, and 31 are **"advance scouting"** letters written within three months of availability date to uncover employers who may be interested when the time comes. While worthwhile, such letters produce a relatively low response. A slightly modified second letter making no reference to the original should be sent to the same employers (except those who responded earlier with an interview invitation) as your date of availability draws closer.

Blind ad responses (where the employer cannot be identified) are shown in samples 7 and 16.

Samples 12 and 13 are examples of **letters without a qualifications brief** enclosed. Sample 23 probably would have worked as well even if a brief had not been enclosed.

Military experience is covered in samples 2, 3, 11, 17, 19, 20, and 22 through 28.

①

How often have equipment breakdowns in your overseas facilities unnecessarily delayed construction and created costly headaches?

I can prevent that.

You will see from my qualifications brief enclosed that I know how to maintain, repair, and operate most kinds of heavy-duty equipment. If it goes out and can be fixed, my experience has shown me how to get it operating in the shortest time and at the least cost.

Because it is likely that you will soon need experience of this kind, I hope you won't mind a call in the next few days to arrange to see you. I will be able to supply all the details you need at that time.

②

If you are looking for an aircraft maintenance technician who sets unusually high standards for himself, then I believe you will be interested in the enclosed qualifications brief. I get a kick out of doing a better job for the sheer pleasure of doing good work. And I've noticed that this attitude sometimes rubs off on others working with me. All of the crews I've worked with ended up with top ratings.

May I come see you? I hope you won't mind a call on Thursday to set a time convenient for you.

3

My Air Force training and experience have
given me a strong background in the maintenance
and repair of electronic navigation equipment and
search radar--good enough, in fact, to teach these
subjects with an exceptionally high pass rate among
my students. The result has been less aircraft
down time at less cost for the work.

On the assumption that (name of company) will
soon need experience of this kind, I will call in
the next few days to determine when I might come
see you.

4

In view of your continuing need for flight
stewards, it may interest you to know that I advanced from apprentice to steward in full charge of
dining operations in two years at the Hilton Hotel
in Amsterdam. My performance frequently drew
strong praise from customers and my superiors
(along with an extra raise).

As for personal attributes--I am multi-
lingual (English, Dutch, and Indonesian) and
blessed with a great liking for people--one to
which they usually respond in kind. I am presentable, hard-working, like responsibility, have
a good sense of humor, and am totally dependable.
My qualifications brief enclosed lays out the
full facts.

May I discuss employment with you? I'll
call later this week to learn when might be
convenient for you.

(5)

While technical writers are not usually considered the money-makers of a corporation, I saved
(name of previous employer) $15,000.00 simply by
raising some questions about one contract I was
working on. In addition, I have received five
merit promotions in three years based on the outstanding clarity of my writing.

Will (name of company) need a technical
writer with this kind of initiative and ability in
the near future? Since I will be in San Francisco
next week, I hope you won't mind a call then to set
a time to discuss that possibility.

(6)

I like what I hear about your company. Although it's a long shot that you personally need
a staff assistant with my capabilities at this very
moment, it seems reasonable--in view of your
growth--that you soon will. Please read my qualifications brief enclosed and see.

If not, perhaps a member of your executive
staff will find my background . . . in sales,
finance, operations, and as a crackerjack Presi-
dential Aide . . . of unusual appeal.

If you think--as I do--that I can make a
contribution to your company, I hope you won't
mind a call on Friday to set a time to see you.

7

As a recent 4.0 graduate in Accounting due to receive an MBA degree in June, I have produced recommendations for my employer that resulted in major cost reductions and increased profitability. For example, in one instance, marketing economies that I introduced cut costs 38 percent without reducing sales volume.

My qualifications brief enclosed provides the facts. I think you will find it interesting in connection with your opening advertised in the Times today.

Depending on the nature of the opportunity offered, my pay requirement is in the $11.5 to $13.5 range.

When may I come see you?

8

I have always had a keen interest in buying and merchandising and have always been tremendously impressed with the way (name of employer) does it. I would like to work for you.

As a current graduate in marketing, my qualifications brief enclosed shows a record of success in this field that I believe you will find most interesting.

May I come see you? I hope you won't mind a call on Wednesday to arrange a good time.

9

My background is in industrial and business administration (MBA, Cornell). Skiing and the industry behind it is a consuming interest of mine. In view of your current expansion, I believe you will be interested in my qualifications brief enclosed.

This year's trade shows pointed to new challenges in the marketing and distribution of your products that I would very much like to discuss with you. In addition, I have investigated Alpyne Ski's slide into oblivion and learned some lessons from their mistakes that might be put to good use by your company.

I will be coming west the second week of July and will call you then to learn when we might get together. Please let me know if that time will be inconvenient for you.

10

Because of my background in the scientific use of color to promote maximum eye appeal, safety, and sales, I have examined several items in your product line with a great deal of interest. I am quite sure that nominal alterations in coloring techniques in your products and packaging will significantly increase the desire to buy among your customers.

My qualifications brief enclosed describes the experience that brings me to that conclusion. I think you will find it interesting.

I hope you won't mind a call in the next few days to arrange a time during which we might discuss the possibility of my joining your staff.

(11)

Coping with the crisis building around the need
to educate the culturally deprived has particularly
interested me. For example, at Shemya AFB (located
at the tip of the Alaskan Chain), I attracted seriously undertrained personnel into strong involvement
with major social issues. As a direct result, many
of these men gained the opportunity to enter college.
In addition, the University of Alaska asked me to
become a permanent member of its teaching staff.

My qualifications brief reflects other similar
experience that I believe will interest you.

May I come see you to discuss the possibility
of joining your faculty? I will be in Seattle next
week and will call in advance to determine when a
meeting might be arranged.

(12)

Applying new ideas to convert foreign oilfield
drilling, supply, and service operations from loss
to profit is the kind of work that turns me on.
Also, multiplying the productivity of currently
profitable operations. For example:

- In Brazil, I was responsible for negotiating
  a union contract and bargaining for equipment
  purchase to initiate the company's first off-
  shore drilling. This turned operations from
  a $35,000 loss to a $90,000 profit.

- For a new company in Ecuador, I introduced
  novel drilling techniques and equipment that
  resulted in progress from a $120,000 loss
  to $124,000 profit.

- I originated surplus material purchasing and
  resale programs in Mexico, Brazil, and
  Argentina that netted $230,000 profit in
  one assignment.

Could we talk about the possibility of applying this kind of ability to your operations? Since
I will be returning to South America in mid-June, I
will appreciate a collect call to arrange a time
suitable for you.

As a Senior Engineer engaged in test planning, I conceived and implemented programs that produced significant savings for my employer. Because it is possible that this experience can be applied with equally good results in your technical or administrative staff, you may be interested in some of the things that I have done:

- I planned and designed an automatic test system that reduced test time 98 percent. The final cost of the test equipment was 13 percent less than estimated.

- In another instance, I produced an automatic check-out procedure and auxiliary equipment that reduced test time from 240 man hours to 16.

- In a third example, I developed a test program requiring more than $1,000,000 in special equipment without having one item disallowed during the pre-award audit by government examiners.

All of this work took advantage of available equipment with massive savings in capital expenditures. It required coordinating the efforts of highly diverse groups to set up production testing lines. All on tight schedules. _All_ on time.

My record contains other accomplishments like these which I believe will interest you. May I see you to discuss application of these abilities to your needs? I hope you won't mind a call to set a good time.

(14)

Can you use a mechanical engineer with the ability to . . .

- Maintain tight control over a dozen development programs simultaneously?
- Analyze thorny problems to arrive quickly at sound solutions?
- Obtain the willing cooperation and increase the productivity of staff?
- Provide clear and concise documentation of these activities for the guidance of others?
- Produce significant production economies?

I have these talents, as highlighted in the enclosed qualifications brief. I would like to put them to work for (name of company).

On the assumption that you may soon need abilities of this kind, I will call in a few days to learn when we might meet to discuss that possibility.

(15)

Under my direction, (name of previous employer) narrowed down an extensive R&D program to develop fluidic systems so that we could identify commercial (as well as government) uses and go after the broader sales that this reorientation of goals promised. Not to mention saving major R&D costs. Result? We developed a fluidic stability system for helicopters that, according to customer's engineers, "worked first crack out of the box and continued to work as advertised throughout the program."

The immediate sale in prospect is $200,000 with $6 million more strongly in prospect over the next ten years. Most of it in the stable civilian market.

150

You will find this and similar experience described in my qualifications brief enclosed.

On the assumption that you may soon need abilities of this kind, I will appreciate a collect call indicating when we might get together.

(16)

Not long ago, I initiated procurement innovations that shortened allotted production time 25 percent. The concepts I developed then have since become standard throughout the industry. In view of your need for a Manager of Purchasing, I believe you will find the enclosed qualifications brief describing that and similar accomplishments unusually interesting.

My pay requirement is in the area of $22,500-$25,500, subject to further consideration of your needs and mine.

When may I come see you?

(17)

As you know, the Navy looks _very_ carefully before assigning any man to serve as an officer aboard nuclear subs. I had the good (my wife says "ill") fortune to be selected for that kind of assignment under Admiral Rickover's close scrutiny.

The experience has been invaluable. It taught me how to mold highly disparate characters into a smoothly operating technical and engineering team working under just about the most negative circumstances imaginable. My qualifications brief enclosed contains facts on this experience that I think will interest you.

On the assumption that (name of company) may need this kind of ability soon after my release in May, may I come see you then to discuss possible employment? Please let me know.

(18)   In the belief that (name of company) is always
on the lookout for management assistants with a
record of strong accomplishment, I think you may
be interested in some of the things I have done:

- I established a new department in a new organization and administered it to the point where
  it produced, by far, the strongest favorable
  public recognition of all of our activities.

- I recruited, trained, and motivated individuals
  to turn in performance as members of a team
  that they themselves frequently thought impossible.

- I mobilized community, business, and press
  support previously unmatched in that area, resulting in strong recognition for our efforts
  throughout the region.

- I supervised the administration of these developments, in all of their detail, to assure
  steady progress toward the goals I had set for
  us.

    In doing these things, I drew heavily on my
MBA background and experience in varsity basketball
at the University of Pennsylvania.

    As you will see from my qualifications brief,
this experience was gained as head of the business
and physical education departments of Notre Dame
High School in Troy and as coach of its basketball
team--a team which I established and brought to
championship status in three seasons.

    Now I am looking for a new challenge. In the
belief that abilities of this kind probably can be
put to profitable use in your operations, I hope
you won't mind a call later this week to arrange
a meeting in which we can discuss that possibility.

    With my best wishes,

19

I have learned that astonishing results in
terms of cost cutting and increased profitability
can be achieved through more attention to management problems, improved procedures, and closer
supervision of individual programs--especially where
top executives simply have too little time to devote
to such details.

My qualifications brief (enclosed) shows the
abilities I can bring to your operations and the
kinds of results I can achieve. If some aspects
of (name of company's) operations are not quite as
fully controlled as you would like them to be, I
would like the opportunity to show you how I would
approach the problem.

Could you let me know when I might come see
you?

20

After visiting an isolated Arctic Station
under my management at Barter Island, Alaska, the
Assistant Secretary of the Air Force called it "one
of the smoothest operations of its kind I have ever
seen" and took note of the high morale and productivity of the 150 men and women under my direction
who made it go.

As reflected in my qualifications brief, my
abilities sum up in strong management experience on
a variety of problems, a high degree of initiative,
the ability to communicate effectively at all levels,
and a good sense of how to plan and organize operations for maximum efficiency.

In the belief that you may soon need abilities
of this kind (or, if not, may know of others who do),
I would greatly appreciate the opportunity to discuss my experience with you. To that end, I will
call early next week to determine when a brief
meeting may be arranged.

21

In my present job on the Controller's staff
with another manufacturer of quality food, I con-
solidated over $200 million in annual cash dis-
bursements into a single system to cut costs by
$50,000 per year while greatly improving manage-
ment's information and control. You will find a
number of similar accomplishments described in my
enclosed qualifications brief. I hope you find it
interesting.

In the belief that (name of company) may soon
need experience of this kind, I will greatly appreciate the opportunity to discuss my qualifications
with you and hope you won't mind a call on Wednesday to set a time convenient for you.

22

Data processing management leading to higher
production is my area of specialization. Here are
some of the things I have done:

- Developed and implemented four new computer
  applications in two years--one of which has
  been accepted for worldwide application by
  the Army and the other of which is under
  consideration for such acceptance.
- Produced new inventory control procedures
  that reduced customer back orders 35 percent.
- Reduced equipment maintenance costs 18 percent while increasing utilization 10 percent based on new failure-analysis procedures of my design.

You will find more experience of this kind
covered in the enclosed qualifications brief.

On the assumption that you may soon need
abilities like these in your operations, I will
call next week to set a time when we might discuss
that possibility.

In these days when every dollar in personnel management must do the work of two, I am sure I can make a contribution to your operations. Working both with very small and very large operations, I have . . .

- Reduced personnel costs 27 percent (saving $1,375,000) while raising productivity—by the available measures—17 percent.

- Clarified and simplified lines of communication and responsibility so that management could maintain much closer control in a newly responsive organization.

- Produced a unified approach among highly divergent functions to achieve greater cost effectiveness, morale, and operating capability.

My qualifications brief enclosed outlines those and other achievements of this kind. I believe you will find it interesting.

On the assumption that you do, I will greatly appreciate a collect call indicating when I might come see you.

24

While serving as a personnel officer for the Air Force, I achieved a 65.9 percent reenlistment rate in Iceland—27 percent above the national average. This stemmed from my conviction that most people like to take pride in their work and that they will stick with you even when the Artic freezes over if you give them a base on which to build that pride.

My qualifications brief (enclosed) contains more information on the productivity achieved and money saved as a result of this approach.

Whether or not you have an immediate need for abilities of this kind, I do hope to meet you briefly during my forthcoming trip to Denver. I have some ideas on motivation programs that I would like to discuss with you and on which I would value your views.

I will be out there during the last week of this month and will call you then to learn when we might get together.

25

I am convinced that air-freight operations are figuratively on the pad for a moon launch. When they blast off, opportunities will probably be limited only by the capabilities of staff to meet the challenges ahead.

My qualifications brief enclosed reflects considerable experience in solving air shipping and terminal problems—sometimes under extremely heavy conditions. I am sure (name of company) can put these abilities to good and profitable use as it moves to claim a larger share of the expanding market ahead.

May I come see you to discuss these prospects? I will be in Minneapolis during the week of July 12 and will call beforehand to set a time. Please let me know if another time would be more convenient for you.

26

Cutting the incidence and heavy costs of accidents—both in ground and flight operations—is the area of my special ability and experience. I would like to put it to work for (name of airline).

You will see from my qualifications brief enclosed that I have established major safety programs that produced as much as a 30 percent drop in claims. In my view, my ability as a pilot was a major factor in assuring that these programs were realistic, practical, and effective.

On the assumption that (name of airline) will soon need experience of this kind, I would very much like to talk with you. In any event, I am sure you could give me good advice on where my experience can be put to best use. I hope you won't mind a call later this week to arrange a brief meeting.

27

A prominent executive claims that "all organizations are at least 50 percent waste." I can't defend his arithmetic but I have a firm conviction that most organizations can substantially improve their systems--particularly in telecommunications management. That's one major area of operations that often fails to get the management scrutiny it should have.

In my previous assignments, that conviction--combined with due concern for costs and organizational needs--has produced some very rewarding results. The enclosed qualifications brief includes brief examples.

I will be in Moline next week and will call then to determine when we might meet to explore application of my experience to your operations.

28

As Housing Officer for officers at Fort Holabird, it was my task to provide first-class accommodations and dining facilities for a group of customers notorious for prompt, loud, pointed--and often lewd--complaints when all did not go well. I kept them very happy. Despite a severely limited staff and pinchpenny budget.

My qualifications brief describes this and related experience. I hope you find it interesting.

In the belief that (name of motel chain) may soon need abilities of this kind, I will call next week to learn when I might come see you.

(29) Within six months of joining my present employer as director of manufacturing, I converted a 30 percent loss situation to a 17 percent profit. Increasing shipments by as much as 40 percent per quarter, cutting inventory over $1,000,000 (27 percent), and reducing manufacturing costs 18 percent ($650,000) all contributed to this successful outcome.

My qualifications brief enclosed describes this experience and similar previous performance. I think you will find it interesting.

On the assumption that you may soon need abilities of this kind, I will call later this week to arrange a brief meeting in which we can discuss the contributions I can offer (name of company).

(30) Do you have a unit in your organization that just seems to "be" there? A group that should be a definite asset but instead is barely holding its own? My experience in the Navy and with civic groups has shown me that this situation exists to a certain degree in almost every organization. In most cases I have been able to solve this problem with a few minor organizational changes and by motivating the people concerned to take new pride in the importance of their work.

The enclosed qualifications brief provides additional facts on my accomplishments in improving the production of established organizations and setting up new ones.

I am being released from service on 1 July and hope we can explore the possibility of achieving similar results in your organization at that time. May I come see you then? Please let me know.

31

While with the Air Force, I was able to produce a quantum leap in the productivity of highly trained but poorly motivated and careless personnel. In another instance, I analyzed serious problems connected with heavy materials handling and developed a new approach that moved official evaluation reports on these operations from the bottom of the well to unprecedented new highs. Not only that, but my training syllabus and procedures manual have been adopted for use throughout the Air Force in the U.S. and overseas.

My qualifications brief enclosed provides the facts.

In these days when personnel productivity is the critical question for business and industry, I feel sure that my ability to cope with a wide variety of problems of that kind can be put to constructive use by (name of company) in the areas of production management, quality control, or sales. May I come see you to discuss that possibility? I can be there on short notice and will appreciate word from you indicating a good time.

32

As one who has risen from the bench as a tool and die maker to top production-management positions, I think "recession" is too much on everybody's lips. The current economy, I believe, requires people who know how to appraise, inspire, and, if necessary, even create performance.

My product knowledge ranges from high-volume competitive consumer products to sophisticated state-of-the-art, high reliability military and NASA items requiring the widest application of the most advanced assembly and processing techniques.

I am the short-sleeve type who is not afraid to get his hands dirty to solve production problems. I thrive under pressure and most enjoy applying

creative imagination to find new and better ways
to get the job done.

My qualifications brief enclosed shows the
kind of results this approach has produced.

In the belief that your company may soon
need an executive with my training, experience,
and controlled impatience, I hope you won't mind
a call on Tuesday to determine when we might meet
to discuss that possibility.

33 By selecting, training, guiding, and motivating
superior sales staffs, I have expanded sales (and
profits) on every assignment held in the last ten
years. And by as much as 40 percent. Chances are,
I can do it for you, too.

Considered to be a "take-charge" sales executive comfortable with full profit-center responsibility, I have conducted market evaluations, originated new products and packaging, created high-
impact promotional materials, administered distribution operations, and instituted profit-making
cost control systems. All with award-winning results.

My qualifications brief enclosed summarizes
this experience. I believe your review will show
marked potential for increased sales and profits
through use of these abilities. May I come see you
to discuss that possibility?

Please let me know when would be convenient
for you.

With mounting organized protests, I am sure the problems of veterans are a source of concern to you as State Governor. As shown by the enclosed brief statement of my experience, much can be done to bring such problems under firm control while relieving top officials of the heavy pressures that often stem from this source.

I feel sure I can help with the management of your veterans program in a way that will serve to defuse the current issues and allay future ones.

May I come see you or a member of your staff to discuss the approach I have in mind? I will call your secretary this week to determine the time best for you.

Some final notes on your letters

Monday is a heavy mail day. Post your letters to arrive on Tuesday (normally a very light day) or later in the week. They will get more attention.

Try to call within two days of your letter's arrival to arrange an interview. If more time is allowed to elapse, chances are that receipt of your letter (and its disposition) will have been forgotten.

When bidding for a job from out of town, send your letters before traveling and call after you get there. But keep the elapsed time between receipt of your letter and the call as short as possible.

Mondays tend to be hectic. You will have better luck if you try for interviews later in the week.

*Most people
like to give advice and help where they can.
By seeking such help,
you get others personally interested in your success.
Maybe it will suddenly dawn on some of your advisers
that you have exactly the experience they need
—with appealing job offers following close behind.
It has happened many times before.*

162

8
All of your contacts will help

Let's assume that you've developed a high impact qualifications brief plus a covering letter that makes employers feel that it is their *duty* to talk with you but that the results of your first mailing are not in yet. So now where do you turn?

Since you are in the middle of one of the great campaigns of your life and its object is to leave no stone unturned until you find work that holds strong promise for long-term satisfaction for you, obviously this is no time to sit back and wait. There are many more things to do.

As we pointed out earlier in this book, research shows that the odds are nearly 50-50 that you will find your job through people who know you. The odds are about 1 in 4 for "cold" contacts with employers, 1 in 20 through help-wanted ads, and 1 in 25 through employment agencies. At least, those are the odds for most job seekers—the ones who use castabout, trial-and-error approaches. With your informed and highly organized job-finding methods, these odds will be sharply improved all along the line. The idea is to know just how to use each of these techniques to produce the best possible results for you.

Clearly, the thing to do is to make your talents and availability known to as many people as possible who may produce job leads. The best place to start is among people who know you.

Do you cringe at the thought? Some people—especially those who are fairly well along in their careers—feel compelled to keep their need for new employment a deep and rankling secret. Some even keep word of it from their mates like some mind-boggling disgrace that is corroding their souls.

Nothing could be more foolish in these days when explosive change is forcing highly competent people into periods of unemployment.

Think about it. Have you ever thought less of friends who asked you to let them know if you should hear of any openings they might consider? Weren't you, as a matter of fact, a shade flattered that you were sought out in this critically important business? And if you were able to produce the lead that produced a job, didn't you have a feeling of positive accomplishment?

Your friends will feel the same way.

A good topic for talk

Knowing that there is a huge reservoir of good will and potential help out there, you should not hesitate to use your job-finding campaign as a topic of conversation among friends, relatives, acquaintances, former business associates—everybody you meet. Among other things, your search is a far less mundane topic for talk than the weather—both for them and for you. Since practically every meeting begins with "How are you?" or something similar, you can easily bring up the topic of your job hunt then and there. Your answer, with a broad grin on your face, might well be, "Looking for a job. And you?" This puts it in a nutshell and offers the prospect for every important progress toward your goals in the following discussion.

The people you talk with will be interested to learn how thoroughly you have organized your campaign and how vigorously you are carrying it out. For most of them, the approach you are taking will be noteworthy and they'll admire you for it. They'll be interested in your special insights into the job market, your specific aims, your progress, and the problems you've encountered because, after all, they might profit from your experience. And, in almost every case, they will offer suggestions, evaluation, or direct leads if you give them a chance.

Talk about your job campaign among your instructors (if you are leaving school), at the local pub, at parties, at the club, at church socials, during breaks at PTA meetings, while the kids are warming up for the Little League game, at the bowling alley—in fact, wherever you can get an ear. Liven the topic with examples of some of the painfully funny things that seem to afflict everybody in the job market and ask your friends how they would handle such situations.

Practically always, you will be able to close the topic by urging your friends to let you know if they hear of a suitable opening or have other suggestions. And you might add: "Let me send you a copy of my qualifications brief in case you run across someone who needs the kind of abilities I offer." Then send it under a short note expressing warm thanks for this help. Every copy delivered in that way will stand as a potential source of leads to that ideal job.

But don't stop there.

If you were laid off, ask everyone you know at your former place of work to please call if they hear of any plans for new hiring. And keep in touch with them periodically.

Next, go out to get the help of others who know you—especially those who have many contacts themselves. Your clergyman, insurance agent, physician, banker, barber, bartender, mortgage holder—all can be of great help. Moreover, they have a vested interest in your success. Willy-nilly, they may lose a customer if they don't help you solve this problem. We know of one worried wife of a laid-off turret-lathe operator who told her egg man. Sure enough, three blocks down his route he found the lead that produced the needed job. (Incidentally, he also sold more eggs.)

The key to this whole approach is this: Never ask personal contacts for a job. Doing so tends to kill interest in your campaign. But always encourage suggestions, advice, and evaluation of your approach. People like to give counsel and, once they have, they become personally interested in your success.

Form a club

In truth, you have more friends than you know in the job market. For example, as you make the rounds of employers and agencies, you are likely to find yourself exchanging glum looks with other applicants in various reception areas or compensation lines. Yet they're your natural allies. They know exactly what your problems are at the moment. They have them, too. They need all the help they can get just as much as you do.

So offer it.

Don't just sit there. Strike up a conversation. Open it up by lightly asking the applicants next to you what kind of luck they're having, what problems they've encountered, etc. Tell them that you are seeing a lot of employers who may have openings that interest them. Ask them if they would like you to let them know if you hear of any that line up with their needs.

They are likely to leap at the chance.

When they do, pull out a blank 3 x 5 card and take down names, telephones, kinds of jobs sought, and anything else they want to tell you about their needs. One card per person.

Then give them cards that you have already prepared to show your requirements. Or, better still, give them a copy of your qualifications brief. Ask them to let you know if they hear of anything suitable and to call you if they find a job themselves so you won't be scouting for them after they are happily at work.

Seize every reasonable opportunity at the conclusion of your own interviews with employers and agencies to tell them that you are also scouting for other applicants. Ask them directly whether they need people in any of the categories shown on your cards. If they do, note it on the back of the right card so you can call the applicant concerned with the good news.

One more thought along this line.

The group represented by your cards have strong mutual concerns and interests. Call them and ask whether they wouldn't like to get together every week or so to exchange ideas, suggestions, and information on the best ways to cope with the problems that you all face. Or just to let it all hang out. If they take you up on it, you and they will find that the group is a powerful source of useful information and a great morale builder. Maybe "Club Jobfinder" won't offer dancing girls (or boys?) but you will find it highly stimulating in other ways. Your job search will profit mightily from it. So will theirs.

Do it.

Get advice — and job offers — from experts

Because people like to give others the benefit of their experience and wisdom—especially to receptive listeners—this opens the door to ways to make new and highly influential friends in the job market through exploratory discussions with experts in sessions that are normally tremendously enjoyable affairs. They involve none of the heavy pressures on both sides that exist in most job interviews and this path is open to all career-minded applicants, from entry to executive levels.

So that we can give this highly productive career-development method a name, let's call it *Career Opportunity Research* or, more briefly, the CORE approach.

The CORE method involves talking with high level people in a business or industrial field or a specific organization—*NOT to apply for a job*—but simply to explore the question of (1) whether your qualifications adequately fit employment in that business, industry, or organization, (2) if so, whether such employment offers good prospects for a rewarding future for people of your type, and (3) where such prospects are likely to be best.

If there is magic in any system of job finding, there is in this one. So pay close attention to what follows because we are approaching highly unfamiliar territory for most people. Because of that, let's set some ground rules right here at the start:

1. To succeed with the CORE approach you should have completed the exercise covered in the *Career Analysis Guidelines* at the end of Chapter 4. Or you should at least know where your strongest abilities lie, where your interests are, and what kind of work turns you on. (It's unsafe to assume that you *do* know these things unless you have completed the CAG exercise.)

2. You should have prepared your qualifications brief outlining your strongest abilities, but be ready to modify it quickly in line with what you learn about specific employers' needs while taking the CORE approach.

3. You should accept the fact (and it *is* a fact) that most people in responsible positions—from section heads to presidents and directors of major organizations—are highly receptive to men and women who come in with a strong interest in

167

their field of work, activities, and problems and with some good ideas about them.

4. You should have informed yourself in advance about the functions, products, or services with which the officials you are contacting are most immediately concerned. You should do this so that you have more than a passing familiarity with the kinds of problems they face along with ideas about those problems appropriate for applicants at your experience level.

5. Paradoxically, you should take the CORE approach with the firm personal conviction that you are *not* looking for a job offer. Instead, for the moment, you are only seeking to explore that field of work or organization as one that may offer the kind of opportunity you are looking for. (Sure, you will consider any job offers that come along—and they are likely to when you take the CORE approach—but that is not your *immediate* aim.)

6. You should have enough confidence in yourself and your ability to serve your contact's needs to simply show up at the office of the man or woman you want to talk with and ask to see him or her if it is not practical to arrange an introduction through a mutual friend. (In every case, this should be a person who can immediately make the decision to hire you or greatly influence that decision.) Completing the CAG exercise at the end of Chapter 4 should help to give you that confidence.

How the CORE approach goes

All right. Those are the ground rules. Now, let's take an example to see how it might go.

First, as a result of the CAG exercise, you've decided that resort hotel operations (they like to call it the "hospitality industry") offer the greatest prospect for the kind of life you are looking for from here on out. Preliminary reading in the library, you found, confirmed the thought. The next question is "Where?" So you look around, write for brochures from those hotels in areas that most interest you, and settle on one in particular that appears extremely promising—the Mountainaire, managed by Craig Gladhander.

Next you go to the Mountainaire to look at its facilities, grounds, and activities—perhaps you even register for two or three days—to get a good idea of what's going on. At every opportunity possible, you talk with the staff, probe operations behind the scenes, listen to what guests and employees are saying, and evaluate what you observe. Because *every* organization has problems that are more or less out of control, you look particularly for those on which you might offer a solution. In Craig Gladhander's case, these might include (1) getting the spots off the water glasses, (2) inspiring much more friendly treatment of guests by the snarling staff at the front desk, (3) far more compelling publicity regarding the Elysian comforts offered by the Mountainaire, (4) reorientation of the housekeeping department to get the wrinkles out of the sheets and the dust cloths from under the beds, (5) relocating the horse stables so they are downwind from the dining room, and (6) greatly increasing use of the Mountainaire's facilities during off-seasons.

When you have a pretty good appreciation of what's going on, you show up at Craig's office and ask to see Mr. Gladhander.

As the first bat out of the box (the furry, leathery, beady-eyed kind), the secretarial sentry at the door may say, "Miss Jones, if you are looking for employment, we don't have any..." Your immediate response is to interrupt to say, "Not at all. I am *not* looking for a job offer. I would like to see Mr. Gladhander to get his critical judgement regarding some of the problems of resort hotel operations and my ideas on them." Or, perhaps more simply, "I am thinking about entering resort operations as a career field and want to get his expert views on requirements and opportunities in that field before making a move in that direction." Then you add, "I am sure he would want to offer that help. May I see him for a moment, please?" —all in a very friendly but very firm way that implies that granting your request is the only decent, patriotic, and industry-minded thing for the sentineling secretary, and him, to do.

Even with all that, the secretary may next say he's tied up at the moment. If so, ask to arrange an appointment with him, saying that you have some thoughts about the Mountainaire's operations that you feel sure would interest him—still smiling broadly. And, if *that* fails, ask who else on the staff might be able to help you. At that point, the sentry is likely to decide that Gladhander is the best one for you to see after all.

(We've dwelt here and elsewhere in this book on the road-blocks thrown up by secretarial guardians-at-the-gate because they represent one of the heaviest obstacles to effective communication among many in the job market and it is important to know how to get around them. Friendly persistence backed by the assumption that granting your request is the only reasonable thing to do in the *employer's interest,* as indicated above, is the best way to go.)

So when you get to see Gladhander (or his deputy), you go in expressing tremendous interest in his operation and due appreciation for the good results he has achieved. (No insincere flattery permitted here.) You tell him that you are thinking about entering resort-hotel operations as a career field and wonder out loud how he accomplishes the results he does.

Invite evaluation and advice

As Gladhander warms to your strong interest in this subject closest to his heart, you ask him what the heaviest headaches are that face people in his position and gently lead him into discussion of some of the problems you've observed, along with some of your own ideas for handling them. Throughout, you avoid flat assertions, but, instead, state your thoughts as questions, inviting his evaluation and guidance.

During the discussion, you discover areas of real concern to Gladhander in which you feel you can make a positive contribution. You ask him for his views on your ideas and what qualifications he looks for among people handling such problems and the pay range normally applicable to them. Finally, you ask whether he can recommend other resort hotel officials you should see for further guidance—either at the Mountainaire or elsewhere.

During all of this, you are lending a warmly receptive and appreciative ear while Gladhander is talking about things that intensely interest him. As you do, you are casually and indirectly touching on your own abilities, attitudes, and experience that would make you an outstanding employee in that kind of operation. Through it all, Gladhander is likely to be wondering whether he can use you on his own staff. He may even be thinking about creating a new job for you—one precisely structured to take advantage of the abilities he observes in you—in short, that ideal job. He may offer it then and there.

In the context of a CORE discussion, your lack of direct experience in resort-hotel operations becomes very unimportant to Craig Gladhander. Instead, he sees strong potential in you as a friend who will relieve him of some of the excruciating headaches that have been bothering him for a long, long time. But it may be that there simply is *no* way for Gladhander to take on new people right now. Still, he is likely to give you the names of others in his field whom you should see. He may even call them to tell them what tremendous potential you have and to arrange appointments for you. Meanwhile, there is the likelihood that he will keep your name at the top of his own list of "most wanted" candidates for the first suitable job that opens up.

Whatever the outcome, call or simply show up in the offices of the people named by Gladhander. Say he suggested a meeting. Go through essentially the same process as described above as you focus more and more sharply on the job you want. And do one more thing. Deliver a copy of your qualifications brief to Gladhander the next day—one modified to focus specifically on the kinds of opportunities the Mountainaire offers. In your covering letter, thank him warmly for his great help and ask him to let you know if he hears of any openings that you should know about. Or, if you are really excited about the prospect of working at the Mountainaire, tell him you have been giving a great deal of thought to the problems discussed in your meeting with him. Add that you will be back in a few days with a specific proposal on how they might be handled. Then send him an outline of the approach you would take. Arrange to see him again to discuss it.

If you take that same approach with a number of employers, you may well end up with the problem of more highly productive job leads—and more exciting job offers—than you can comfortably handle. A very nice kind of problem to have. Aim for it.

One final important point: In all of your contacts, look for an organization that is just getting started and that appears to be headed for strong growth. Get in on the ground floor. The sheer volume of people coming in after you will push you higher and higher.

Then, as growth stabilizes, find another that is about to take off. Enter it at the level you have already achieved. You will be in a rocket to the top of your career potential.

If you are well prepared,
you will find that most interviews
are highly pleasant and stimulating discussions.
Your aim?
To get the employer to like you personally
in the context of the job you want.
Here's how an applicant at age 42 might handle it.
Even so, these ideas apply
regardless of your experience level.

172

9

For a major payoff —
prepare for
interviews

Interviews—that is, face-to-face sessions with hiring officials when there is a definite job opening at stake—can be extremely tense affairs. And no wonder. Chances are that all of the time, skill, and effort you have poured into getting to that point will be wasted if such sessions are not properly handled. The opportunity you have sought will be cinched or sunk by what you do now.

But, even with all that at stake, high tension need not be part of it. Fact is, interviews can be just as pleasant and rewarding as the CORE (Career Opportunity Research) discussions we talked about in the last chapter. Preparation is the key. Because so few applicants *do* prepare adequately, this gives you a chance to walk through the interview door knowing you are already well ahead of the game.

As you lay your plans, keep in mind that most employers don't know how to conduct interviews in order to relate your abilities to their needs. Most are just as uneasy about the situation as the average applicant. And most have a highly frustrating problem on their hands—the need to fill a job so they can get on with their regular work.

If you show them how that can be done, they'll count you as a friend from the start.

To lead up to your interview, you wrote the employer a letter enclosing your qualifications brief. Both were well done. Now, most people would chalk this up as a job completed and sit back and wait. And wait. Not you.

It's a good thing, too. The employer (we're back to Smith again) liked your qualifications. But not your age. He would have put your brief in the discard pile but he noted your plan to call to set a time to see him. This caused him to create a special "maybe" category with your brief the only one in it.

It's certain, given all this, that Smith would *not* have called you. But now he has to decide whether to be plain negative or not. After all, he feels in his bones that age really is not a valid question. Moreover, your letter and brief *are* exceptional. He's wavering.

Your call comes at a moment when Smith is leaning your way. It gets results. Appointment Friday.

Now, again, most applicants would call this a day and go off to the ball park. But not you. You're determined to stay ahead of the game. Remember?
So you get busy. First stop, the library. There's a broad picture of Smith's particular line of work in the encyclopedia. You study it for background.

Next you ask the librarian to lead you to the primary business periodicals in Smith's field. These give you a good idea of what's going on in his line these days, who his competition is, how they're doing, and quite a bit more. You scour these for specific word on Smith's company—looking both at the ads and the editorial content.

Now, Smith himself. Nothing on him in *Who's Who,* but the librarian takes you by the hand to another massive work, and, lo, there's a brief biography of Smith. Having taken this in, you note that Smith maintains a summer residence in the same resort town that your good friend Henry does and you call Henry to see if he knows Smith. You were right. Now you have a good picture of Smith as a man along with some of his foibles.

(If Henry didn't know Smith after all, you might get the word at the local chamber of commerce or by calling on the executive secretary of a trade or professional society Smith is likely to belong to, or maybe Henry knows someone who knows someone who knows Smith. And, barring any of those leads, the employment officer at Smith's company would probably be willing to give you a brief, even if flattering, rundown on him.)

Next, you put your hands on as much material as you can get regarding the products and services of Smith's company. You stop by the sales office to pick up brochures. Among other things, you conclude that *they* certainly could be better done and that Smith probably feels the same way. You also get a copy of the annual report from the Treasurer's office.

At home, you study all of it.

But here it is Thursday noon. Interview tomorrow morning and you're still uneasy about it.

Time to plan

You organize all of the material you have gathered, reflect on it, analyze it. You want to go in ready to convince Smith that it would serve *his* interests to take you on. How to do it?

You analyze your own experience in light of all you have learned to determine the most effective ways you could be useful to Smith. But, among other things, you have learned that Smith prefers younger people in his office. Disconcerting.

You go over your list of past accomplishments, duties exceedingly well done, those things that gave you that full, round feeling of success. (See Chapter 4.) As you do, you decide that you have a great deal to offer Smith. And you deliberately plan to convert the age barrier into an asset.

After all, each year of your age represents a year of experience and there's *no* substitute for that. Luckily, you had met one of Smith's clients who complained about the rash commitments made by some of the younger members of his staff. And you know for a fact, *as a direct result of your years of experience,* that they have overlooked some highly profitable aspects of their market. You figure out ways to make this clear to Smith.

Your interview plan is taking shape.

Friday morning comes. After the routine amenities, Smith opens up with this one, "Now tell me, Mr. Jones, just why are you interested in joining our company?"

You are well prepared.

So well prepared, in fact, that you know that Smith's opening question isn't one you need to answer. Not directly and not right away, at any rate.

You know that chances are excellent that Smith hopes you will take the initiative and that this will give you an opportunity to guide the discussion to bring out the full facts on your qualifications.

It's good that you do know this. If you had not prepared in advance, you might have heard yourself replying, "Well, I have heard many good things about your company's personnel policy and I, of course, want to join an expanding organization."

And as the echoes from those remarks folded themselves into the carpet, you probably would have realized with a certain sinking feeling that what you were talking about was what *you* wanted—not what Smith needs to gain his goals. In an instinctual flash you might have decided that *that's* the biggest question in Smith's mind as he talks with you. So you might have added weakly, "And I thought my experience might have a valuable contribution to the company's effort."

Time to go.

Take the initiative

Instead, you reply like this: "Mr. Smith, may I ask you a question first?" (He nods, of course.) "It seems to me that the company's operation has been . . . ," and then you draw on some facts and conclusions regarding his company that you know will interest Smith.

This touches it off. Smith is delighted—even a little astonished —to be talking with an applicant who knows something about *his* problems. He evaluates your conclusions and their implied recommendations, gets a little deeper into the situation, wonders what you think, asks your opinion, and weighs your suggestions. *Through it all, you are demonstrating your experience in action rather than telling Smith about it.*

Then the opportunity comes to ask Smith a question something like this: "Mr. Smith, if you had to define the biggest headache facing your office today, what would it be?" The response to this one is likely to initiate even more discussion regarding Smith's operations in terms of your own usefulness to him.

Here is where the opportunity may crop up to say, "We had a similar problem at Henderson. It looked for a while like curly-haired chaos was in our corner. This is what we did."

Then you tell Smith about it and indicate any changes in approach that you would take now in light of what you learned then.

Smith is fascinated. In fact, a shade beside himself. He had been concerned about the age question (natural enough at his age of 33) but now example after example of successful performance on similar problems has him thinking that the bright young candidates he's been considering would probably be groping around for a solution weeks after your experience had already told you what it is.

Demolishing the age question

But you don't leave it there. Instead, you decide that a frontal attack may be in order. Knowing from your advance research that age is a problem with Smith, you add: "Time and again, I have seen contracts lost by young representatives who were inclined to promise more than their companies could deliver.

The assets I offer add up to mature judgement seasoned by experience that points to *new* ways in which such problems can be handled."

Result? The age question is demolished. Or, at least, badly bent.

Now you are at a critical point. Smith clearly is impressed. Still, if you say nothing more, he's likely to come through with a "let you know" type of close. Now is the time to bring him to a decision even before he has formulated any such thought. So you say, "Mr. Smith,"—by now, incidentally, you may be calling him "Sam" if he has led off in this direction—"don't you think I could make a strong contribution to your operations?"

It is at that immediate juncture that he will be most inclined to say "yes"—perhaps with a profound sense of relief that *that* problem is settled. Your next move, after settling on salary, is to ask him when you should start work.

Suppose he says "no"

But let's suppose all does not come off quite so neatly. Despite your bid for a commitment then and there, Smith says he has other candidates to consider. He asks you to call on Wednesday.

Instead, when Wednesday comes, try to arrange to see him. Tell him that you have an appointment close by and would like to stop in briefly.

If the final answer is "no," tell him how much you have appreciated his consideration. Ask him whether he knows of others who might be able to use your qualifications and whether he would be willing to keep your qualifications brief on hand for referral to others who may need your talents. If he does give you the name of others to see, call them to arrange a meeting saying that Sam Smith suggested it. (Unless, of course, he does it for you.)

Then follow up with a cordial note to Smith again thanking him for his consideration and telling him you would appreciate a call if he should hear of other openings in line with your experience.

Successful or not, such might be the scenario of an interview that you (and Smith) handled quite well, indeed.

Be prepared for rough terrain

But, if you are ill prepared, you will find that many interviews can be exotically random affairs. Unless you assert control, they often tend to wander far afield as the employer, not really knowing what else to talk about, takes you county by county through last month's bike hike through old Eire with interminable stopovers at Kilkee, Dingle Bay, and Ballybunion. Then, when the allotted time is spent, you find yourself out the door —with thatch in your hair—after a couple of superficial remarks about the job and cordial thanks for coming in. With no hope, really, that anything will come of it except a new peak in your frustration chart.

Keeping *why* you are there strongly in mind will help you avoid such bewildering excursions through Wonderland.

- You're there to convey information regarding your accomplishments, abilities, and personality that will convince the employer that *you* are the one to hire.

- You're there to uncover as much information as possible about the opening and the person you would be working for so you can determine whether this is the right job for you supervised by the kind of person you can work with happily and productively.

- And, finally, you're there to provide a resounding answer to the one question dominating the employer's view of the discussion—however foggily formulated it may be. That is, "How will hiring this applicant best serve *my* interests?" Note that it's not the company's interest that's overriding the thinking of most employing officials who talk with you. Not the country's. Not society's. Above all, unfortunately, not yours. It's *their* interests. In short, they want to know how hiring you will help *their* advancement. So, up to the point of a commitment to hire you, talk about what *they* want—not what you need to realize your goals.

Adequate preparation in light of the three key factors above will leave you considerably better able to cope with interviews than most employers you talk with. Since they are often painfully aware of their own general ineptitude in this important area of their responsibilities, it's your job to settle them down and make them as happy as possible with the situation as you help them solve this major problem of the moment.

A smiling, friendly, not-too-heavy approach will help assure that.

As for the rest of it, be sure your statements in interviews are completely honest—even if strongly accenting the positive. Always aim to stress your strongest qualifications for the job in question. Use "for example" freely to cite specific instances of successful past performance. Try to use each question as a springboard toward discussion that will enable you to uncover more information on why you are the one to hire. Lighten the discussion with easy humor, where possible. But don't oversell yourself or filibuster your interviewer with endless talk. If you spot the employer checking the time, vacantly shuffling papers, or unsuccessfully trying to get a word in, it's past time to be quiet.

Master the tactful dodge

Also, be ready to use a tactful dodge if the interviewer asks a question you need to think about or are unprepared to answer at that point. Something like this: "Mr. Smith, do you mind if I ask you a question first?" or "Before we get down to specifics, could you tell me...?" and then come back to the original question later after you have formulated a good answer. Or "forget" to come back to it if you can't think of one.

And remember this important point: Because filling job openings is such a tough, time-consuming, important, and unfamiliar task for most hiring officials, your interviewers are likely to be aching to be sold on your qualifications so they can hire you and go back to their regular work. Understanding this motivation should do much to put you at ease in the situation.

So, it's clear. Successful interviews are give as well as take affairs—on both sides. That's why we've included a list of questions at the end of this chapter that you should consider asking, along with many you can expect to hear as you make the rounds. If you prepare answers to these questions, you should be ready to deal with almost anything that comes up without hesitation. But it's wise to expect an occasional curve ball as well—one probably intended to rattle you. Don't let it.

When *asking* questions, use them to dig out facts about the job itself and the employer's needs so you can bring out information about yourself that fills those needs. Use them to get the employer back on the track when the interview goes astray. And use them to show that you have gone to some trouble to learn about their operations, problems, and needs, and have given thought to how you can make a positive contribution. Such preparation happens so rarely that it, more than almost anything else, will heavily impress your interviewers.

Of course, tact and respect are essential. Avoid flat questions. Precede your queries with gentling modifiers like, "Do you mind if I ask a question?" or "With regard to that, could you tell me..." or "In connection with that, I had wondered...," etc. But avoid pressing too hard. Proceed as long as the interview is producing a strong interchange on the job and your qualifications. After the facts are out, prepare to bring it to a courteous and positive close with a strong bid for the job.

When you get home, send a cordial letter thanking your interviewer for the time and consideration shown. Stress high interest in the job and confidence in your ability to produce strong results. Add anything of importance that may have been overlooked or inadequately emphasized in the interview. Or, if you have already been told "no," reiterate your continuing interest in the employer's operations—perhaps in another capacity. This letter alone may be the clincher that produces the job you want.

Ten key considerations

From all that we have just said, it should be clear
that despite all that has gone on in the years of great
change just past, establishmentarian attitudes still
heavily dominate most employment situations.
Consequently, these are the key considerations in
a successful interview (male or female):

1.   Appropriate clothing.

2.   Good grooming.

3.   A firm handshake.

4.   The appearance of controlled energy.

5.   Pertinent humor and a readiness to smile.

6.   A genuine interest in the employer's
     operations and alert attention when the
     interviewer speaks.

7.   Pride in past performance.

8.   An understanding of the employer's
     needs and a desire to serve them.

9.   The display of sound ideas.

10. Ability to take control when employers
     fall down on the interviewing job.

All are important.
Your success can turn on any one of them.

CHECKLIST FOR INTERVIEWS

With every interview, drive for a job offer as though it were the ideal opening. Forget, for the moment, about any misgivings you may have about the position under consideration. Leave these to be considered along with other job offers after all the facts are in. And keep in mind that the impression you create in interviews will determine your success in landing the job. Regardless of the type of work you want, give attention to each of these important points before you go. Check each off this list as you prepare. Then try a "dry run" with your spouse or a good friend.

☐ Learn as much as possible about the work being done by the organization and person you will be talking with.

☐ Decide in advance what you can do to serve the interests of the individual who will interview you. Remember that such interests usually center on quality work, increased production, greater efficiency, lower waste in time, effort, and/or materials, and reliable and likeable people to help get the job done. Keep these uppermost in mind as you prepare.

☐ Be prepared to ask about the duties of the job and the qualities wanted in the person to be hired. Be ready to show how you can match or exceed those requirements. Leave questions regarding pay, vacations, and other benefits until after hiring interest is shown in you.

☐ Be prepared to lead your interviewers into discussion of work problems facing their staffs or crews. This will give you strong clues to the kinds of information about your qualifications that you should stress.

☐ Wear clean, well pressed clothing of a kind suitable to reporting for work in the job you seek (the best you have of that kind). Avoid heavy perfume or "high" styles of hair or clothing. Arrive well groomed from head to heels.

☐ Have extra copies of your qualifications brief with you. Also the names, addresses, and telephone numbers of references. Bring samples of your best work if design or writing is involved.

☐ Double check the time of appointment. Arrange to be there five minutes before the scheduled time.

☐ Give the appearance of energy and self-confidence as you walk through the door. Smile. Shake hands firmly but don't crush bones. Be genuinely glad to meet the interviewer as a person who can play an important role in your life. Be relaxed. Maintain eye contact. Recognize that interviewing is a game at which you will occasionally lose.

After every several interviews, review the preceding chapter in light of your experience to see what can be done to improve your approach. Also, check the following *Interview Questions* before each meeting so that you will have pertinent questions and answers well in mind. *Above all, exercise just as much care in selecting your next job as interviewers do in selecting applicants.* The person you decide to work for will play a major role in your future. Do all you can in interviews to determine whether that person is well qualified for that role.

INTERVIEW QUESTIONS

Review these lists before each interview so you will have your answers and pertinent questions for the employer freshly in mind when you go. In addition, you should anticipate numerous questions from employers regarding specific aspects of your experience.

QUESTIONS FROM THE EMPLOYER

Openers

- May I see your résumé?
- What can I do for you?
- Why are you interested in joining our company?
- Why do you feel qualified for this job?
- What do you think you can do for us?
- What attracts you to us?
- Tell me about your experience.
- What pay do you have in mind? (Try tactfully to avoid answering this one early in the interview.)

Regarding motivation

- Is your present employer aware of your interest in a job change?
- Why do you want to change jobs?
- What caused you to enter your job field?
- Why do you want to change your field of work?
- Why are you leaving military service at this point?
- What would you like to be doing five years from now? When you retire?
- What is the ideal job for you?
- If you had complete freedom of choice to be a great success in any job field, which would you choose? Why?

Regarding education

- Describe your education for me.
- Why did you pick your major?

- What was your class standing?
- What were your activities?
- What honors did you earn?
- What were your average grades?
- Did your grades adequately reflect your full capability? Why not?
- What courses did you like best/least and why?
- Have you had any special training for this job?

Regarding experience

- Why should I hire you?
- How do you fit the requirements for this job?
- What did you do in military service?
- What would you do to improve our operations?
- Who has exercised the greatest influence on you? How?
- What duties performed in the past have you liked best/least and why?
- What are your three greatest strengths/limitations for this job?
- What are the strongest limitations you have found in past supervisors?
- Which supervisor did you like best and why?
- What kinds of people appeal most/least to you as work associates?
- How many people have you supervised? What types?
- What are your greatest accomplishments to date?
- What equipment can you work with?
- Why have you changed jobs so frequently?
- Have you ever been fired or asked to resign?
- Describe the biggest crisis in your career.
- What were you doing during the period not covered in your résumé?
- Why were you out of work so long?
- What was the specific nature of your illness during your extended hospitalization?
- Why did you leave your previous jobs?
- Do you have any particular weaknesses on or off the job I should know about?
- Could I see samples of your work?

Objections

- We prefer younger people / college graduates / more experience / people willing to start at lower pay / people with shorter hair / people who own property in this community / people who have lived in the area more than a year, etc. (Anticipate those most likely to come up in your case.)

Regarding pay

- What do you require?
- What is the *minimum* pay you will accept?
- What is your pay record for the last five years?
- Why do you believe you are qualified for so much more?
- We can't pay the salary you should have. Would you be willing to start lower and work up to that figure?
- What do you expect to be earning five years from now?

Other questions

- What public figures do you most admire and why?
- What books have you read in the last three months?
- What periodicals do you subscribe to?
- What are your primary outside activities?
- Do you belong to any organizations?
- What kind of security clearance do you have?
- Have you ever applied for unemployment compensation?
- Will you tell me the circumstances of your divorce?
- Have you ever been arrested?
- Would you have any concern whatever about a full background investigation?
- How many days have you been off the job for illness in the past two years?
- Describe your health for me.
- What is your wife's (husband's) attitude toward your work?
- What do you think of women's lib? Black power?
- Do you own your own home, car?
- What is your net worth?
- What is your insurance / indebtedness situation?
- Will you be able to put in extensive overtime or travel extensively on the job?
- Whom can we check as references?

QUESTIONS FOR THE EMPLOYER

Openers

- (After the usual cordialities:) Have you had a chance to review my qualifications brief?
- Did it raise any questions about my qualifications that I can answer?
- Did (the previous interviewer) give you the full story on my experience?

Regarding job content

- Would you mind describing the duties of the job for me, please?
- Could you show me where it fits in the organization?
- What characteristics do you most like to find in people on this assignment?
- Is this a new position?
- What do you consider ideal experience for this job?
- Was the previous incumbent promoted?
- Could you tell me about the people who would be reporting to me?
- How does their pay compare with that in other sections/companies?
- Are you happy with their performance?
- Have there been any outstanding cases of dissatisfaction among them?
- What is the largest single problem facing your staff now?
- Is there anything unusually demanding about the job I should know about?
- What have been some of the best results produced by people in this job?
- Could you tell me about the primary people I would be dealing with?
- What are their strengths and limitations as you see them?
- What are the primary results you would like to see me produce?
- May I talk with the person who last held this job? Other members of the staff?

Regarding the employer's problems
(And reflecting your ideas)

- Is there any problem on this job with waste/quality/accuracy/ public acceptance/meeting quotas/inventory, etc.?
- Have you considered...(some equipment or technique to improve operations)?
- I have often wondered why...

- Do any factors prevent action along this line . . . ?
- Have any recent steps been taken regarding the problem of . . . ?
- How is the current marketing program going?
- Is there an untapped market for your service in . . . ?
- Would this approach produce good results . . . ?

Regarding your bid for the job, pay, and other closing questions

- Is there anything else I can tell you about my qualifications?
- From what I've told you, don't you think I could do an excellent job for you?
- I can be ready to go to work in – – days. Should I plan on that?
- Based on my qualifications, don't you think $– – – a year would be appropriate for me in this job?
- Would you mind telling me the pay *range* the company has in mind for this job?
- Do you think more could be justified in light of my particular experience?
- Can you tell me the prospects for advancement beyond that level?
- I greatly appreciate your offer. How soon do you need a decision?
- Will it be all right if I let you know by (date)?

Regarding benefits
(Raise only after it looks like you will be offered the job—or separately with the personnel department)

- Could you tell me briefly about your benefits program? (Vacations, insurance, retirement, profit sharing, bonuses, hospitalization, etc.)

If the employer is undecided

- May I check back with you on (day of the week)?

If the employer finally says "no"

- Do you know of others in the organization or elsewhere who would be interested in my experience?
- I very much like what you are doing. Could you keep my qualifications brief on hand for other openings in your office or referral to others?
- If the situation changes, please let me know.

14 Stanford Court
Palo Alto, CA 98716
March 4, 1968

Mr. Tushiro Akari, President
Celestial Graphics, Inc.
4300 Oldlane
Carmel, CA 94341

Dear Mr. Akari:

I want you to know that I am
interested in the position of
Print-Production Director we
discussed today. Based on
the cost experience you
outlined in our talk, I am
sure that my wide knowledge
of printing capabilities in
this area can be used to
bring about significant
reductions in production
expense while still preserv-
ing the beautiful quality
that typifies work done by
Celestial.

In any event, I do want to
thank you for the consideration shown me today. It was
indeed a pleasure to meet you.

Sincerely,

Sophie Bernstein

Sophie Bernstein

After-interview letters are important, regardless of the
outcome of the interview. They set you apart from most

14 Stanford Court
Palo Alto, CA 98716
March 4, 1986

Mr. Tushiro Akari, President
Celestial Graphics, Inc.
4300 Oldlane
Carmel, CA 94341

Dear Mr. Akari:

I greatly enjoyed our discussion
today regarding your current
opening. Although we agreed
that my qualifications are not
in line with your needs at this
time, I wanted you to know that
I am tremendously impressed by
the quality of work being done
by Celestial Graphics. Consequently, I do hope you will
keep me in mind in the event
a more suitable opening should
occur.

And if you should hear of others
in need of talents like mine, I
will greatly appreciate your
action to call my qualbrief to
their attention.

Again, my warm thanks for your
consideration today. I do
hope we will have the opportunity to meet again.

Sincerely yours,

Sophie Bernstein

Sophie Bernstein

applicants and help to expand your friendships in the
job market in addition to helping to lock up job offers.

Employers normally have a pay <u>range</u> in mind
when they talk with you.
Your aim should be to get as close to the top of that range
as you possibly can.
Whether you are aiming for an entry
or executive job
here's how to determine your best pay level
and how to get it.

10
You are entitled
to top pay
for your talents

"What pay do you want?"

It's a question that faces all applicants sooner or later. And it throws most. Few know how to answer it.

Unless you know the rules, this can pose a terrible dilemma. Knowing them starts with the realization (1) that, in most instances, *pay is negotiable*, (2) that employers normally have a pay *range* in mind when they talk with you, and (3) that they are often quite flexible with regard to pay for any particular job.

Knowing the rules can produce results far beyond anything you expected. Sometimes inadvertently.

For example, one candidate we know coolly put her figure at $15,000—$2,000 above the level she expected to get. "Fifteen," she said simply when the employer asked her about pay. However, the employer thought she meant fifteen hundred a month. That, of course, adds up to *eighteen* thousand a year.

His response?

"Eighteen thou (the term he used) is higher than we expected to go but I guess we can swing it."

She floated out of that office on a golden cloud of elation. With a job at $5,000 more than she expected to get and $3,000 higher than she had specified, it was clear that she had done a better job of convincing the employer of her value than she knew.

Was she worth that much?

Of course. The employer was convinced of it and he should know. The fact that he was most pleased with her work after she came aboard proved it.

Her example helps to show how much flexibility often exists in pay matters.

But let's back up a minute to put down some additional rules. The pay negotiation problem divides itself into two broad categories requiring slightly different treatment. One is the situation where you are applying for a job in which pay levels are fairly well established for people who can do what you can do. The other involves dealing with the question when standard pay rates do *not* exist for people with your talents.

Aim for pay at the peak of your qualifications

Let's suppose that you fit the first category.

If you are seeking a job for which many others have been trained, if you aim to apply learned skills to your employer's problems where little or no initiative is required (carpentry and accounting are good examples), then determining the pay range for the work you want to do is relatively easy. Public and private employment agencies will be able to tell you what the local rates are. The pay you get within that general range will depend entirely on the length and quality of your experience plus your ability to persuade the employer that you are good enough to be hired at or near the top of the established pay range. And *planning* your approach to the question of pay is most likely to get you there.

Such planning starts with a good qualifications brief, coming in knowing something about the employer's operations, and handling your interview so that the employer takes an immediate liking to you in the context of the job to be filled. Those are the things that will decide how the employer looks at the length and quality of your experience. If you handle them right, the employer may conclude that you probably could run circles around most of the crew already in the shop long before the question of pay comes up.

Next comes the problem of persuading him/her that you should be paid *more* than most of the on-board crew.

When the question first comes up, give the employer a level look and say, "I was thinking of . . ." and then name a figure five percent *higher* than the top of the established pay range. Of course, the employer is unlikely to go along with this and will say so in one way or another. But keep your cool. When that happens, simply ask, "Then, what is the *best* you can do for me in the way of pay?"

If there is any leeway at all, the employer's impulse will be to put the rate as high as possible—maybe at the top of the range —because you obviously attach strong value to the quality of your work and certainly must have a reason for it. Some also do it just to keep from feeling cheap.

But it may not come out that well, after all. If the employer still specifies pay at or near the bottom of the range, try one more time. Let the employer know that you hate to go that low and ask, "Could you possibly swing...?" naming a figure somewhere in the middle.

Suppose even that doesn't work, are you trapped into turning down the job and leaving in a huff?

Not at all.

If you really want the job, you can indicate that you would like to sleep on it. Then call the next day saying, "I am a little disappointed about the pay but the important thing is that I definitely would like working for you. When should I start?" Or you can say it then and there.

The point is, you really *are* entitled to top pay for your talents. And you should aim to get it. On the other hand, the employer has the responsibility not to pay you one cent more than you are worth. If your negotiations produce higher pay than the employer originally had in mind (and they will more often than not) or even higher than you expected to get, accept that as solid and authoritative proof that you are worth every cent of it and may be worth more than you thought.

Negotiating in the dark

Now let's suppose you fit the second category—the one where pay ranges are *not* well fixed for people who can do what you can do.

If you want work that requires the ability to analyze, to develop new things and techniques, to influence others, then your pay level will depend almost entirely on (1) the extent of your ability to do these things, (2) the need of employers for such ability, and (3) your ability to convince employers that you can fill their need.

It boils down to this: *In creative, influential, and executive types of work, you are not worth thus-and-so and that's it. Your worth to various employers who would like to put all of your talents to full use may vary by many thousands of dollars between them.*

The general idea, of course, is to find those employers who have the greatest need for your particular abilities. They are likely to put the highest value on your services.

If you are eyeing a flexible-pay type of job, the following example will give you a good idea of how to determine the appropriate salary considering your abilities and the employer's need.

Let's suppose it comes out this way in true button-down fashion: "Well, Joe, what do you require?" Clearly Smith is actively interested in employing you and is at the point of final negotiation or the talk wouldn't have turned to money in this way. And your evaluation of your own worth is one of the best indicators for Smith of the level of your abilities. So, if you say that $5,200 a year will get you by quite adequately with your outside income, Smith is not likely to think you would be any bargain even at that low figure.

To tell the truth, it probably would be a good idea not to answer his question immediately because a few well-chosen words at this crucial point may well mean $20,000 or more to you over a period of time.

Instead, your answer might be something like this: "To be perfectly candid about it, the content of the job is far more important to me than the pay. I wonder if we might go into that in a little detail before we get down to specifics." (How's *that* for a tactful dodge?) "For example, where is the job in the organization?"

Then Smith sketches a rough organizational chart, which gives you the opportunity to ask all sorts of questions about the job's content, associates, relationships, importance in the eyes of the primary executives, and so forth. And these questions also give you time to do some fast mental arithmetic.

You note that Smith has pegged you as Assistant Director of a major division four echelons down from the top. You know the company, while small, is prosperous and assume that the President gets at least $50,000 a year. The Executive Vice

President probably gets $35,000 to $45,000. The next man, a Vice President, is probably in the $25,000 to $35,000 range. This puts Smith, your immediate boss, on the chart at about $20,000. Evidently the job Smith has in mind pays between $14,000 and $20,000.

Making your bid

Then you begin to ask Smith about the subordinate staff— their strengths, limitations, how they are organized, etc. You ask for an indication of the top supervisory positions immediately under the job you are being considered for, whether he is pleased with their performance, and who he considers the best of the lot. When Smith indicates Helen Brown, you ask what Brown's pay is and how this compares with others at the same level. When Smith tells you that Helen is getting $12,000 but Henderson, over here, is at fourteen, you've got it pegged. Pay for the job is definitely above $14,000 and probably below $20,000.

Having figured all this in your head, you throw out a feeler. "To get back to your question, Mr. Smith, I believe pay at about the eighteen to twenty thousand level fits both my experience and this job. Don't you agree?" You say this even though you might be quite happy with three thousand less. And then you sit back and watch Smith.

He may not even flicker an eyelid. In that case, chances are excellent that you are in the range the company has set for the job. Or he may look quite pleased. In either of those instances, aim for $20,000 in the discussion that follows. Or he may drop his teeth.

If he blanches at the thought, then this is your cue to follow through with something like this: "However, the position you have described sounds more interesting to me. The important thing, of course, is the great satisfaction that I would gain from a job of this kind and, as you know, many other factors enter the determination of pay needed for any particular work. What pay range did the company have in mind?"

Now, it is up to Smith to make a commitment. He will be motivated to put the figure as high as he can in the hope that you will be interested. And he may fortify his figure with considerable amplification on opportunities and the company's fringe benefits. So when he says, "To tell you the truth, Joe, seventeen is our top for this opening," the job is very likely to be yours for the asking. *But don't seize on it too eagerly.* Instead, tell him you would like to give it serious consideration and ask how much time you can have.

Of course, there is a calculated risk in this approach. Sure, Smith's offer is $2,000 above your minimum. Even so, if you defer your final decision, you will make new job contacts with greatly increased confidence as a result of the firm offer already in your pocket. The end result may be a final offer at significantly better pay—far better than you ever dreamed possible.

Looking at what happened to Joe Jones, as described above, some more basic rules regarding pay negotiations come clear:

- Always state your pay requirement in a *range* while indicating that where you settle, finally, within that range depends on a multitude of factors regarding that job and others you may have under consideration.

- Always put your minimum pay in the range ten percent *higher* than the absolute minimum you will accept. It's easy to back off a figure that's too high (as Joe tentatively did) but impossible to recover from one that's too low.

- Never hesitate to ask employers what pay range *they* have in mind—especially after you have indicated your requirements. If the top of their range is within yours, say that you could consider accepting the top figure specified.

- And remember this: Paradoxically, it is generally easier to get a pay raise *before* you accept a job than after. Now is the time to start out from the strongest possible base.

One more thing:

If you sense that the employer is terrifically interested in bringing you aboard or simply terribly anxious to get that job filled, other benefits are also highly negotiable *before* you finally commit yourself to the job. For example:

- Where the policy is no vacation during the first year and one week in the second, you might negotiate two weeks during the first year and three thereafter. Or better.

- You may win annual cost-of-living raises tied to the Consumer Price Index where the organization has no policy on such raises.

- You may secure the right to a semi-annual or annual review of your performance with specified merit raises to follow such reviews as long as you remain with the organization.

- Stock options are another benefit that may be extended to you as a result of negotiation.

- You may secure the right to fully or partially subsidized training or education in line with the requirements of your job.

- Even full refurbishing of the office you are to occupy (and where it is to be located) along with a key to the executive john may be specified—especially where you are able to persuade the employer that such "image" factors are important to your success on the job.

Whatever they ask, ask for written confirmation of any such benefits that are out of line with the organization's normal policy before finally entering the job.

$20,000 for a few choice words

Because most job seekers fail to recognize the tremendous potential in sound pay-negotiation techniques, we can't stress their importance too heavily. A well-informed and careful approach can readily lead to substantially increased compensation—a differential that may well add up to $20,000.00 or more in a few short years. All as a result of a few choice words during interviews.

Such benefits negotiated now tend to carry themselves forward and multiply as you advance in your career. And any such arrangements negotiated with another company can have a profound impact on your present employer (if you have one). Their impulse, frequently, is to match the terms of the employer who would pirate you away.

Or to top them.

And that's good for you.

Don't let the "greener pastures" mirage fool you.
If your present employer is not
in an active state of decline,
the odds are excellent
that your best opportunities exist where you are now.
Explore these possibilities first
to see whether you can move up
before deciding to move out.
Here's how to do it.

11

Double your pay
with your
present employer

The message in the letter was clear and like many others we
get. It said this: "My present job is OK, I guess, but I don't
think I'm going to light any new candles in this company.
I feel solidly walled in with no place to go. I've got to find
a new employer who will recognize that, while I'm no para-
gon, I'm no pariah either—somebody who will make better
use of my abilities."

Maybe you have this feeling.

If you do, you have a lot of company. But, very frequently,
the feeling isn't really justified by the facts.

It is often hard to tell from inside an organization just how it
stacks up in terms of operating efficiency, good management
practices, and opportunities as compared with others. This is
especially true if your current trend is to concentrate on the
negative aspects of your job and to overlook positive factors
in your career. Hence, if your present employer seems less
than perfect in terms of using your abilities, the one you are
eyeing for new opportunities may be considerably worse.

Well, then, should you just sit there?

By all means, no. When it's time to move, *move.* But this
doesn't necessarily mean you should move *out.* Keep in mind
that tenure and experience with one organization is a highly
valuable asset and not to be discarded lightly. It's a reservoir
of security—like a trust fund from a rich uncle.

For one thing, your current dissatisfaction with the way
things are done may be of tremendous value to your employer
if you put it to work in a constructive way. We have seen
businesses fail simply because employees down the line didn't
know how to see that their ideas were considered where they
could count. And we have seen some saved—to the great credit

and everlasting reward of the individuals who had the initiative and good sense to bring up their suggestions, and to the credit of the management members who listened to them.

Try first to move up, not out

It adds up to this: you have a duty to yourself and to your employer to have ideas about how the work can be better done and an obligation to discuss these ideas. If you aren't talking to your employer openly and frankly about growth where you are now, that's a clear indication that you are not giving your company an opportunity to take advantage of your full potential. And you are throwing away opportunities that are readily within reach.

So, before you decide to move out, ask yourself this: "How can I make myself more useful here? In what ways can I make a more positive (and noticeable) contribution?" Use the self-exploration techniques outlined in Chapter 4 to find the broad answers. Relate what you find to your present job. Then develop your qualifications brief. When this is done, you will be ready to move.

Your first approach should be to your present boss—unless he/she is clearly a hopeless case. Maybe in a casual contact you could say something like this: "Sam, I've been wondering about some things we might do to expand the department's production while cutting unit costs. When you have time to talk about it, I'd like very much to get your advice on whether they might work."

Now, normally, Sam is interested in expanding the department's production. (If it goes up, maybe Sam will, too.) So you are talking the right language. On top of that, Sam normally likes to give advice.

If Sam is receptive to the discussion and you take the "I wondered about the possibility of doing this" approach in your talk, your initiative in making the suggestions is likely to produce some highly positive results. At least Sam will learn that you have more than a routine interest in her success and that you value her advice. (Sorry about that, Sam's full name is Samantha.) It should help to establish a new and more positive relationship with her that can only help to open doors to your advancement.

With this new relationship, the opportunity should soon present itself to take on Sam with yet another approach. Sometime when you catch her in a mellow mood, let her think about this question: "Sam, sometime in the next few days, I would appreciate your guidance on ways in which I can improve my performance on the job." One of two things is likely to come out of such a discussion. First, Sam may not be able to think of anything needed to improve your work. Then this will be a clue to her and to you that a raise may be due. Second, Sam may come up with a number of suggestions—some of which may well be off the beam. But don't argue. Just be sure in the future that there is never any cause for Sam to form such erroneous impressions again. Follow her suggestions to the best of your ability in ways that make it clear to Sam that this is what you are doing—even those suggestions that you really think have no merit.

There's a fairly complicated consideration behind this approach: when you get right down to it, excellent performance on the job is not usually the basic consideration in advancement. Instead, it's the *impression* of excellence that you create with your superiors. You may very well be turning in the best, most thorough, most conscientious, and most productive performance of all, but if this is not the *impression* created by your efforts, others will move ahead of you.

Maybe you have seen it happen.

So look to your personal public relations on the job. Work to establish a friendly, supportive, cooperative relationship with everyone who can play a role in your advancement. And don't quietly leave it to others to discover the good results of your work. See that they are made known where they count.

While all this is well and good, there is also the possibility that Sam's advice when you first approach her with this tack in mind will be of the "where-you-can-go" variety. Then it will be clear that the direction you should be moving (contrary to Sam's advice) is *out.* And that problem will be settled.
But, still, *out* is not necessarily out of the organization.

What about other departments?

If your present department holds no promise for you, look around at the other departments. Which ones seem to be expanding, well run, doing interesting things, staffed with people who enjoy their jobs? How do your abilities fit in?

When you find one that looks good for you, study it in detail so you will have a good idea about the problems and personalities involved. And start to move.

You might initiate action by dropping a note to the department head (or by bringing it up in a casual contact) that says that you have been terrifically interested in watching the growth of his/her operation and think you may have some abilities that will contribute to its expansion. When there is time you would like to talk about some of the things you might be able to do along that line. Obviously, Brown (we'll call him) likes that word "expansion" and can only conclude from your approach that you have energy, self-confidence, interest and, above all, ideas—all qualities that he wants in his staff. On top of that, you know the company's operations— a highly important factor. He is likely to welcome the chance to talk with you.

Then you see him, fully prepared in line with everything said up to now in these pages, to show him how you can serve his interests. When you ask him what characteristics he most likes to find in his staff and then show him the remarkable resemblance between his needs and your abilities, he very well may reach for the telephone to arrange your transfer.

One more point.

Volunteer for "impossible" jobs

We have seen people skyrocket their careers by deliberately volunteering for the most impossible jobs they could find— the ones that others had repeatedly tackled and repeatedly failed to conquer.

Obviously, if you do this, you're a hero in the organization the day you bid for the job. You can hardly do worse than your predecessors since you have their experience to go by. And you'll probably do better—a development that can only make you famous in the front office. Even if you finally fail, it's unlikely to be held against you. (After all, others didn't do as well.) Instead, the courage and initiative you displayed in taking on the job in the first place may very well produce a whole series of gold stars by your name in the company's personnel roster as the one most likely to solve the most serious problems facing the organization—even if such solution finally rests in a decision (based on your recommendation) to by-pass the problem.

The basic point is this: Knowing an organization, its "personality," strengths, and limitations will normally give you a strong edge over anyone applying from outside. Because of this, it may be a great deal easier (and a lot less costly) to land the job you want right there than to look for it outside. Most companies tend to favor their present personnel when it comes to picking people for their better openings—and this often applies even when the "on board" experience is less strong than that offered by new applicants.

If you play your cards right, you may **double** your pay with your present employer in a quick series of promotions over a short time. It happens much more often than you think. And it happens most to the people who *plan* to do it.

But suppose you have concluded that, for any of a number of reasons, there really is no hope of getting ahead where you are now. What then?

This is clearly the time to decide to move out of the organization and it's time to make up your mind not to be half-hearted about it. Sitting there while your hair turns gray and frustration and hopelessness work to bring you down can only spoil your chances for a happy and rewarding career. And every day you put off doing something about it only makes matters worse.

So *move.*

There's plenty of help available—for fees or free.
When going for such help, remember that
some job-market services
are much better than they look.
Others look much better than they are.
This guide will tell you which are which.
The good ones among them can play
a major role in your success.

12

Make wise use of
professional
help

His elation was poorly suppressed as Joe sat down in our office.

"I've found a firm to help me," he said, "that is exactly what I've been looking for. They'll write up my résumé and send it to their affiliates all over the country. The affiliates have a dramatic system—they showed it to me—for projecting résumés onto a screen right in the offices of the employers they serve so that immediate interest is aroused. Best part is that I can get all this for $1,200 and *every cent* will be refunded when the employer who hires me pays their fee. It's right here in the contract. I don't have a thing to lose."

We muttered some misgivings to the effect that it looked a little too good to be true and that $1,200 might be what he had to lose. Plus some irreplaceable time, energy, and hope. "In fact, right while I was explaining my experience to the director of the firm," Joe pressed on, "one of their executive counselors whom I'd never seen before came in and asked if he could interrupt. Said it was urgent. Said he had just received a crash call from a company in Fort Lauderdale . . . I've always wanted to work in Florida . . . and they wanted a man immediately for $22,000, all expenses paid. That's $3,000 above what I hoped to get. But the interesting part is that the qualifications required by the Fort Lauderdale company match mine—*almost on the nose.* Only difference is that my experience is a shade stronger than they need."

We wondered out loud whether there might have been an open intercom carrying Joe's description of his experience between the office of the director and the counselor with the on-the-nose "job order." We didn't wonder whether Joe had signed the $1,200 contract because we felt reasonably certain he had. We asked to see it.

Sure enough, there it was. In plain language. The firm agreed to refund every cent of Joe's $1,200 fee when he was hired through their system by a company that paid their employment fee. It was ironclad language. One catch (among several we found in the deal) is that *most* applicants who use job-search services of this kind don't connect with employers who are willing to pay a fee or any other employment expenses. Some do, of course, but they are a very small percentage of the whole. In fact, the odds against your connecting with a good job through such services are at least 10 to 1.

As it turned out, nothing ever came of this firm's services to Joe—not even an interview. Yet they fulfilled their contract and he had no recourse. He was out $1,200 which he certainly couldn't afford to lose.

We cite this example only to make one critically important point: *Traps for the unwary are deliberately and skillfully laid throughout the job market.* It is the purpose of this chapter to help you avoid these traps while making wise use of the valuable help offered by ethical and well-conceived services and other resources.

As we said before, most people never get adequate experience in dealing with the problems posed by the job market. But there are some who do, some who devote their lives to handling career questions. These specialists can help you avoid many pitfalls and speed your entry into a new position that lines up with your requirements and long-term interests. Because wise use of job-market services can be highly beneficial in your job campaign, here is a quick rundown on the more important services available to you, their value for you, and the ways to go about selecting those that can serve you best.

Résumé writers

Hopefully, the point has been made clear in this book that you do not want to handicap your job search with what is known as a résumé. You want something quite different— a qualifications brief. Sure, they *look* much the same, but the internal structure, content, and impact of a qualifications brief is basically different from that of a résumé. Chapter 5 goes into those differences in detail.

To give them their due, some of the widely advertised résumé writing services turn out presentations that look great. They often sound great, too. Especially to people who don't know much about résumés and the job market. Moreover, such services generally produce their product for less than $50.

But, for all of the reasons given in Chapter 5, avoid them.

But what if you *really* need help with development of your qualifications brief?

Our suggestion, then, is that you seek out a professional career specialist and ask for such help. The best list of services staffed with such specialists is in a book called *What Color Is Your Parachute?* by Richard Nelson Bolles. (More on this book later.) You can probably find it at your library. If not, check the library of any college placement office on a major campus near you. When you find such a specialist, indicate that you want your brief developed under the WHW standards.

However, be prepared for considerable cost. The reason is that development of a good qualifications brief usually involves ten to fifteen hours of exacting professional analysis and writing, and fees for talent of that kind normally run $10 an hour or more.

Private employment agencies

As indicated earlier, very few people, on the whole, find their jobs through private employment agencies. One major reason for this is that few applicants know how to use them. If you do, odds are roughly one in five that you will succeed through a private agency.

Surveys show that large numbers of employers rely on employment agencies to fill vacant jobs. A few do *all* of their hiring through agencies. As a result, employment agencies have many job-finding contacts throughout the business community—in some cases, thousands. Because of these contacts, often established at considerable expense over many years, good agencies can sometimes locate satisfactory positions very quickly—positions that otherwise might take weeks or months to find, if found at all.

Because well-run agencies offer help that considerably expands the scope of your own efforts in the job market, a thorough job-finding campaign should include filing with one or more reputable agencies serving applicants in your category. In addition to the direct placement help they provide, you will find that agencies offer fine training ground for brushing up on your interviewing techniques.

When you apply to a private employment agency, you should clearly understand the fee arrangement. Agency fees are either paid by the applicant or employer. The only consistent rule governing who pays is this: If the employer doesn't agree to pay the fee, you are liable for it. Of course, reputable agencies spell out all obligations of this kind well in advance of any commitment you might make. In general, employers pay agency fees for applicants with qualifications that are in short supply. They may pay such fees (or share in them) to obtain unusually well qualified applicants in other categories, but they seldom pay fees to find people with qualifications in abundant supply.

If you fall in the latter group, you will find that agency fees usually range in the area of five percent of annual salary at $5,000 per year, and ten percent and up at $10,000 and above. Some are lower, some higher.

Beyond any doubt, such fees can seem impressive—especially when it comes time to pay them. However, due consideration should be given the fact that a great deal of skillful—and often extremely difficult—work normally lies behind each successful placement. If such effort produces an opening you want—and accept—the agency has performed an important service for you and is entitled to prompt payment of its fee. On the other hand, you may (and should) decline any opening found by an agency if you have reservations about the job or feel that it is not worth the fee. In that case, you will owe the agency nothing.

Two important factors determine whether you will succeed through a private agency. One is to find a good counselor. The second is to keep in touch. Neither is hard to do.

For example, during your rounds, you are very likely to find yourself talking with an employment officer of a sizeable company that employs people in your category. (If not, call one.) When you are putting away your pen after being told, "Awfully sorry, but we just don't have any suitable openings now," ask the employment officer to recommend the employment-agency counselor he/she considers best for people with your qualifications. Then call or go see that counselor with the word that Sam Smith (or whoever) of ABC Company recommended him/her as the best counselor in town. After that introduction, the counselor is likely to do handsprings, if necessary, to find you the job you want.

But don't let that interest die. Call *once a week* to check the current status of your counselor's efforts and let it be known that you are still available and looking. Don't let repeated assertions that nothing has turned up yet discourage you. Keep in mind that making a successful placement is a highly demanding task and often takes time.

Again, whenever possible, be sure the counselor is highly recommended either by an employment official or a close friend. Otherwise, you may find yourself in the hands of an individual who will attempt to scare you into accepting an unsuitable job simply to collect a fee.

Or, if such prior checking is not possible (when you are responding to agency-advertised openings, for example), try to assess the professional competence of your counselors yourself so that you will know how much reliance to put on their activity in your behalf. One way to do this, after you've first met and before getting down to cases, is to ask—lightly—whether they've read WHW and what they think of it. Or what they think of the qualbrief vs. résumé approach or some other aspect of this book that is new to you.

If your would-be counselor pulls a blank on such questions or comes through with views that just don't make sense to you, then the chances are good that you are in the hands of someone who knows even less about the job market and how to deal with it than you do—someone not likely to be very productive in your job search and with whom you should not waste too much time. On the other hand, a with-it counselor is likely to welcome your familiarity with WHW simply because you are more likely to land the job(s) to which he/she refers you—and at better pay—than would be the case with less-informed applicants.

Meanwhile, continue to pour all the energy you can muster into your own job-finding efforts. Never proceed on the assumption that applying to an agency, or even a whole string of them, has solved your job problems—no matter how reassuring the counselor(s) may be.

Public employment agencies

Public employment agencies are operated by state governments and offer essentially the same kind of help as private agencies. Because such agencies are tax supported, they charge no fees for their services—a factor that certainly has its appeal. To find the public employment office(s) in your area, look under the state government listings in the white pages of the telephone directory. Or dial 411 and ask for the number of the state employment office.

Research shows that three times as many people attribute their employment to help from public employment offices as to private agencies—at least at the lower pay levels. Still, a very small part of the total find their jobs this way. One of the major reasons for this is that public employment offices are charged with a gigantic job but are given very little money to do it with.

Counseling with regard to career choice for people entering the job market for the first time is probably the most valuable service offered by state employment services—one that certainly is not adequately available in private employment agencies. But even that is terribly underfunded. The Job Bank —a computerized system in which employers may list their daily openings without cost—is another unique service found in larger state employment offices. However, in the final analysis, the Job Bank offers you less value than the help-wanted ads in your daily newspaper, and certainly is less convenient to use. Still, the Job Bank does contain listings not found elsewhere and is worth checking out when you are in the office for other reasons.

As indicated at considerable length in prior chapters, if you can find a wise and sympathetic counselor in the state employment office to help guide your own job-search efforts, that is the best use you can make of their services. And one you should play for all it is worth.

Temporary-help agencies

Temporary-help agencies are employment contractors who may hire you in any of a broad number of job categories. These may range from laborer through various categories of office, industrial, and professional help to administrator. The agency puts you on its payroll (usually at fair pay for the work you do) and then farms you out under contract to employers who need people with the kind of qualifications you have. Such agencies are a rich source of part-time and temporary work while looking for a permanent location. If you accept such work, you may luck out and be assigned to an employer who wants to put you on permanently. If that happens, there often is a fee involved that either you or your new employer will have to pay. To find such agencies, look under "Employment Contractors" in the Yellow Pages.

Job shops

Job shops are engineering service organizations that move in under contract to complete projects ranging from small to huge (such as building a subway system, steel plant, or airport in Africa). As each new contract is won, they gear up in terms of personnel to meet the specific needs of the task ahead. Their requirements are usually for engineers, designers, draftsmen, programmers, technical writers, etc., in all areas of specialization. The people employed (who usually call themselves job shoppers) are normally hired on a per diem (PD) basis ranging to $120.00 a day or more. Some such organizations have numerous projects going throughout the U.S. and around the world. Because of the nature of this particular part of the world of work. job shoppers tend to lead (and like) a nomadic existence. To obtain a good idea of the scope and flavor of opportunities available among job shops at any particular time, send $1.50 for the latest issue of *P. D. News.* Address: Box 371W, Grand Prairie, Texas 75051. Also, if you would like to know which organizations are expanding operations to fill new defense contracts (sometimes ranging to hundreds of millions in cost), *P. D. News* includes the current list.

Job-search agencies

Some specialists have flat-fee-in-advance arrangements for handling the details of your job search. They may be variously identified in their advertising as career counselors or professional placement specialists or management consultants or executive search firms. The single characteristic that identifies a job search firm is this: it will, for a fee, send your résumé to a number of employers. Such fees generally range upward from about $350 for processing 100 résumés. The sky's the limit.

211

The proposal most generally made by job-search firms is that they will take over all details of your job-finding campaign—determining your best job field, preparing a résumé, reproducing it, developing a list of likely employer prospects, sending your résumé to them, guiding you on how to handle any employer queries that may result, etc.

Reputable job-search agencies can be helpful if you simply do not have the time to handle the details yourself in line with the guides in this book and are prepared to pay for the service. However, if you are not careful and fall into the wrong hands, you may find that all that has been done for you was the mailing out of less than 200 inadequate résumés to an indifferent list of employers under a form letter from a firm that most employers have long ago learned to ignore. And no job. Or if, by a stroke of good fortune, you should find employment down this path, you may still owe another whopping fee because, unfortunately, the employer didn't pay the search firm's placement fee in your case as they (allegedly) normally do. And you'll have no recourse but to pay it, or go to court—and lose.

To avoid an experience that would only make you sadder, wiser, and poorer, take these steps before signing a contract with a job-search firm:

- Proceed with caution if the firm's contract specifies a fee at both ends—when you retain their services and when they find you a job. This can be all right but, as often as not, it's a matter of working both ends against the middle with you in the middle.

- Don't engage their services in the absence of compelling reasons if you have strong qualifications in a scarce-skills category. Professional placement services will be glad to give you roughly the same kind of help without charging you anything. (See below.)

- Back away if you get the strong feeling in the exploratory interview that all of your job-finding problems will be solved once you are in their capable hands or if their procedures vary substantially from those recommended in this book.

- Check the Better Business Bureau and local licensing agencies. Do not proceed unless you get a good report.

Executive-search specialists

"Don't call us, we'll call you," is the distinguishing cry of most executive-search specialists. The reason is that they are set up to serve employers—not applicants.

In behalf of employers, executive-search specialists usually concentrate their efforts on people who already have jobs and are very happy with them, not on those who are looking for new employment. That's their role in life—to find executives whose talents are coveted by other executives, ones who are otherwise not available, and to entice them to leave their present unsuspecting employers for a headier environment. Consequently, your direct application to an executive-search firm is not likely to get much direct play.

Even so, executive-search specialists are often acutely aware of vacancies at top levels (some of which they are just about to create) in which they have no fee interest. As a result, they can provide helpful advice to applicants at the executive level. And they sometimes do.

However, the best way to get employment interest from one of these firms is to apply for a job on their immediate staff.

To find these people, check "Executive Search Consultants" in the Yellow Pages. Unfortunately, that listing covers a motley crew along with the true executive recruiters. If any you contact want to charge you a fee, either immediately or prospectively, you are in the wrong pew.

Professional placement services

Professional placement services are for critically needed applicants—fully qualified engineers, scientists, technicians, and others who fall into shortage categories. If you are qualified, good professional placement services will provide help with your qualifications brief, reproduce it, and send it out to employers while maintaining the strictest confidence in the whole operation. Although you pay no fees for their services anywhere along the line, obviously this doesn't stem from their great-hearted devotion to the interests of humankind. Employers pay them for everything they do. Your associates in the same professional field or employment officers of large companies that hire professional people can identify the

services they rely on. If you are qualified for the services of
a professional placement service, by all means use them. But
avoid letting any such agency talk you into "exclusive"
handling of your application. This is not in your interest.

Vocational counselors

Vocational counselors attempt to determine your suitability
for employment in various job fields on the basis of your
aptitudes, attitudes, abilities, and personality. Generally, they
know little about the job market's operations and how to go
about pursuing the opening you want. If you retain a vocational
counselor (at fees that generally range from $10 to $50 an
hour), you will be tested, interviewed, and analyzed in an
effort to help you with the choice of a career. Their fees are
likely to be money well spent if you have completed the
Career Analysis Guidelines exercise in Chapter 4 and have
concluded that you still don't know where your primary
abilities lie or where they might be put to best use. Call the
student placement director of the nearest college or university to locate reputable services of this kind.

Career counselors

Career counseling is a growing profession that fills a major
need created by chaotic conditions in the national job market
and rapidly accelerating change. The focus of career counselors
is on the needs of people who must make a major career shift
because of declining demand for their experience or simply
because they got started in the wrong field to begin with (as
often happens). Their aim—as the profession is now evolving
—is to equip their clients with the information, understanding,
and techniques needed to cope successfully with career questions in the interest of maximum personal development
throughout a lifetime. The principles developed by leaders in
this field also have wide applicability in orientation of high
school and college students to the world of work and how to
make the most of it and are being used on an expanding basis
in educational systems throughout the nation.

Career counselors operating at the professional level work
within a "life/work planning" context to uncover basic abilities
sought by employers—abilities frequently overlooked by the

people who possess them because they are not fully aware of them or have an inadequate appreciation of their value. The counselors specialize in techniques for uncovering each client's strongest qualifications and for communicating such qualifications to employers in ways that produce employment at or near the peak of ability, earning power, and potential consistent with the client's personality, interests, and location preferences.

Fees for career counselors start at about $1,000 for fully competent individual counseling. They are sometimes less for group sessions which, in some respects, can be even more effective. Often such fees are considerably higher.

Are they worth it?

If the help received enables an individual at the $20,000 a year level to save two months of frustrating effort and expense before success (not at all unlikely), then substantially more than the fee will be recovered in salary alone. In addition, an immediate or potential increase in earning power is an expected result. Finally, a permanent increase in the client's own appreciation of his/her value in the job market normally stems from such advisory services.

We have seen people enter professional career counseling programs desperately hoping to land a job at one figure and coming out with firm offers at *double* the pay they previously would have accepted most happily. In such cases, the fee paid is a bargain by any standard. But, like the physician who unexpectedly loses a patient or the lawyer who loses a case, no career counselor can assure such success. Factors beyond the counselor's control—including the approach each client brings to such programs—may get in the way. On the other hand, it is a rare individual who is not permanently benefitted by a fully competent career counseling program conducted at a professional and ethical level.

Many highly exploitative enterprises mask themselves as career counselors—some on a national basis. Those organizations that gear themselves to high ethical standards are rare and hard to find. Here are ways to go about it.

- Check with the Better Business Bureau and local business licensing agencies to determine the record of complaints against any firm under consideration.

- If you are in military service, consult a military personnel officer or the office of any military association in the city in which the counselor is located.

- In the exploratory interview with the counselor, look for questions that probe your attitudes as well as experience. You should get the strong impression that you may not be accepted as a client.

- During the interview, look for volunteered statements that much hard work will be required of you and success definitely is *not* guaranteed.

- If the offices of your would-be counselor are unusually baronial in style and furnishings, be doubly cautious in your checking.

If you want a standard against which to weigh what you learn, write to John Crystal, Life Management Services, Inc., Box W-11, 6825 Redmond Drive, McLean, Va. 22101. Basic discoveries and new development by Crystal have had a massive impact on how counseling is perceived and approached—not only in this country but abroad as well—and have greatly expanded the potential for accomplishment to be found in it. (People now in the field—and those who would enter it—should understand that, in Crystal's perception, counseling is not simply a process of analyzing, guiding, and advising. Instead, he says, it is—most of all—*loving*.) Educators, employment specialists, and others concerned with problems of career orientation and development who want to learn more about the potential in such programs should also write to the National Career Development Project of the United Ministries in Higher Education, Box 379-H, Walnut Creek, Calif. 94596. Two books, *What Color Is Your Parachute?* and *Where Do I Go from Here with My Life?* (see *Outside Reading* below) will give strong insight to both individuals and professionals on what counseling has recently become under the influence of their authors. Both are likely to be available in your library.

The National Center for Job-Market Studies

The National Center, sponsor of this book, is concerned with developing and fostering programs, resources, and methods to:

- Correct major job-market malfunctions that impede hiring action.

- Accelerate communications between applicants and employers regarding available candidates and job openings, and increase their impact.
- Reduce the cost of employment operations for both applicants and employers.
- Provide basic professional services to support applicants in the interest of faster and more satisfactory relocation and make such services available nationally regardless of location.
- Develop methods looking to more effective disclosure of openings in the "hidden job market" and dissemination of information concerning such openings.
- Offer low-cost information and reports not readily available elsewhere concerning particular aspects of the job market, e.g., federal employment, career education programs, summer employment, etc.
- Encourage the development of increased professionalism in job-market operations.
- Stimulate study of the job market in the nation's educational system.

One career service offered by the National Center provides a summary, but expert, judgement on whether your qualifications brief is in the "superior" group for applicants at your experience level and, if not, general guides on how to proceed to improve it. This service, designed solely to indicate whether your brief needs more work, may be obtained by sending a copy of your brief, a long, stamped, self-addressed envelope and $2.00 to cover costs to: WHW QualBrief Check, Box 3651, Washington, D.C. 20007. (Please do not expect specific suggestions at this token cost. A much more detailed review is also available, if desired.)

If you want information concerning *all* aspects of the National Center's applicant-support program and the costs involved, send a long, stamped, self-addressed envelope to NCJMS-WHW at the same address.

Business, trade, and technical school placement services

Placement services offered by business, trade, and technical schools are severely handicapped in their operations by the reluctance of employers to publicly reveal more than a small percentage of their job openings. As a result, such offices are able to provide effective placement help only to a very small number of graduates. While such offices list those employers who *do* report suitable openings (and should be consulted for that reason), it is safe to say that many more opportunities exist at any given time than are ever listed. For that reason, finding a good job after graduation will depend almost entirely on your efforts (not the school's) in making direct contacts with employers who employ people in the field for which you have been trained. When you make such contacts, follow the guides in the previous chapters for best results.

College placement offices

Until recently, almost all college placement offices were run like employment agencies—that is, they attempted to squeeze graduates into those few openings reported by employers. However, such practices offered little help to most graduates —those who were not in high-demand categories. In addition, research has proved that a high percentage of the placements achieved were short lived. These factors have recently caused a number of such offices to shift to a "career-center" approach while deemphasizing the job-brokerage aspects of their operations. Where the job-brokerage concept focuses on the needs of employers, the career-center approach concentrates on the needs of students in terms of their career orientation, aspirations, and the problems facing them in coping with the job market. The latter approach, in line with the principles of this book, assumes that graduates who are adequately informed with regard to the job market and the problems it poses will be substantially more effective in achieving satisfactory employment than any job-brokerage system that can be devised. If your placement office is still operating along employment-agency lines, it would be wise to give it short shrift and concentrate on the measures recommended in this book to find the work you want. If it is taking the career-center approach, rely heavily on it. You picked the right school.

Personnel and employment officers

Most sizeable organizations have personnel or employment offices. They can play a major role in your success. It is important to know what they do and how they can help you.

Employment officers offer valuable assistance to management officials in filling job openings. They recruit applicants when needed and screen them to eliminate the least qualified. They then refer the applications of the rest to the "hiring official" (usually the person who will supervise the new employee) for a decision on who should be finally selected. Their recommendations regarding the applicants may carry considerable weight with the hiring official—especially at entry levels. However, employment or personnel officers seldom *hire* people—except those who will work in their own offices. Even so, it is important to create a favorable impression in any contacts with them since they can exercise substantial influence on the final selection.

Employment officers are normally the best single source of information in most organizations regarding the job openings that exist there. However, especially in larger organizations, they cannot know about *all* openings—particularly those that hiring officials are only thinking about, those that will be created only when the right applicant comes along, and those that have not yet been referred to the employment office for action. (In some organizations, the employment office only hears about the openings that are least desirable, least important, or most difficult to fill, but they are in the minority.)

In view of these factors, always check with the employment office to determine whether they have any openings to be filled in your category, but don't let this forestall your direct contact with the hiring official(s) most likely to have people with qualifications like yours working for them. In fact, many employment officers will be glad to tell you, if you ask, which hiring officials in the organization *do* have people with talents like yours on their staffs or crews.

In addition, employment officers are frequently good sources of information on other organizations likely to use people with your abilities, and are normally glad to provide such information when they have no suitable openings. Very often, they can also identify employment agency counselors whom they find most effective for applicants in your category. Give them a chance to help you along these lines by asking for their advice.

Chambers of commerce

If you want information concerning the major employers in any distant locality plus an indication of what they do, write the Chamber of Commerce in that town and ask for the information. (Your letter is likely to be delivered even without the street address if you don't have it.) Such information is often available for the asking. If not, you will probably be given a guide by the Chamber on how to get it.

Professional and trade associations

Professional and trade associations often maintain employment clearing houses for their members. Openings are often available through such facilities that are otherwise not publicized—especially at the higher levels. Check the associations related to your career field to determine the types of services available. (To determine these, ask your librarian for the directory called *National Trade and Professional Associations of the United States* published by Columbia Books, Inc., Washington, D.C.) The placement help available through such association clearing houses, along with openings specified in their periodicals, is often worth a great deal more than the price of membership.

Your librarian

Finally, there are librarians. Lean heavily on them. (The "frail and cloistered" image for librarians couldn't be more misleading. They are giants as educators and towers of strength for job seekers.) Tell your librarian the occupational field you are exploring. Be specific in naming the kind of enterprise you want to enter. Ask to be led to the pertinent references, periodicals, and directories that will give you the best information on the occupation, companies, products, and officials that are targets in your job search. Ask whether similar resources are available elsewhere in town. (Often a call will produce the information you need, if it can be briefly given.)

Outside reading

You will find a number of books on job-finding in your library. Most, however, have been overtaken by recent, strong progress in the field of career management—progress achieved most notably by John C. Crystal (see page 216) and Richard N. Bolles, Director of the National Career Development Project of the United Ministries in Higher Education (see the reference to *Parachute* below), along with others who think as they do. However, if you want a comprehensive rundown on the best books available, *Parachute* contains it. Beyond that, the few highly selected resources listed below are most likely to be influential in your choice of work and how you go about finding it.

- *What Color Is Your Parachute?* An incisive and highly definitive book on the job market and the services and resources to be found in it. Probably the most influential book to date on career management and how problems of the individual vis-a-vis the job market are best handled. Not, primarily, a guide to practical job-finding techniques, however. Instead, an insightful survey of the questions to be answered by people facing a career choice or a major career change; provides an important conceptual perspective on how to go about the job hunt—one strongly antithetical to traditional systems which produce such poor results. Essential reading for career-minded people and those who are professionally engaged in helping applicants. Author: Richard N. Bolles. Publisher: Ten Speed Press, Box 7123W, Berkeley, Calif. 94707. Usually available in public libraries and college placement offices.

- *Where Do I Go from Here with My Life?* Where WHW is a practical guide to finding work that aligns with your strongest abilities, *Where Do I Go from Here* is an intensely detailed guide to the whole highly demanding process of self-discovery that must occur if you are to find and pursue a career (whether at the beginning or in midstream) that aligns with a precise definition of your highest aspirations and potential. Based on John Crystal's discoveries in the field of career counseling (see page 216), this is really three books in one. It offers side-by-side guidance for students (individuals who want to go through the process by themselves), counselors (those advising individuals on a one-to-one basis), and instructors who are leading groups through the process. Individuals who might want to undertake this process alone should first review a copy of WDIGFHWML at the library. For professionals who want to gain a full understanding of the potential in counseling for inspiring maximum self-realization, this is *the* basic book. Authors: John C. Crystal and Richard N. Bolles. Publisher: The Seabury Press, 815 Second Avenue, New York, N.Y. 10017.

- *The Quick Job-Hunting Map.* Based on discoveries by John L. Holland regarding the primary determinants that make for success (and joy) in any particular occupational category (see *Basic Resources* in Appendix B). Provides strong direction in assessing past experience to determine your specific job-related skills and, hence, the best kind of work for you. Outlines the exploratory techniques most likely to uncover such work. Comes in two versions: (1) The *Beginning Version*—best for students and others newly entering the job market; (2) the *Advanced Version* —for those who have had substantial work experience. Author: Richard N. Bolles. Publisher: Ten Speed Press, Box 7123W, Berkeley, Calif. 94707.

- *You, Inc.* Subtitled "A detailed escape route to being your own boss," this book is exactly that. Provides a wealth of practical information on the steps to take to establish an independent enterprise created in your own image. Basic reading for everyone who suspects that he/she is never likely to reach maximum productivity in a formal administrative hierarchy. Author: Peter Weaver. Publisher: Doubleday & Co. (For a short, sharp charge of inspiration along the same lines, also read *Breaking Out* by Donn Biggs, David McKay Co., Inc.)

- *The Occupational Outlook Handbook.* Better described as a "two-handbook" (842 pages). Covers the outlook for employment through the mid-1980s in some 850 occupations. (See the next chapter for a sampling.) Describes the nature of work involved, places of employment, training and other qualifications required, prospects for advancement, earning, working conditions, and the number of openings anticipated each year. (Numbers of openings shown are highly conservative since those created by turnover are often ignored.) Especially valuable for young people mapping their careers. Also good as a broad survey of opportunities in the nation's major industries for those facing a career change. Published by the U.S. Department of Labor. For sale by the Superintendent of Documents, Washington, D.C. 20402. Almost always available in libraries, campus placement offices, public employment offices, and in the offices of student guidance counselors.

- *The College Placement Annual.* A heavily cross-indexed listing of opportunities for college graduates by major field of study. Includes an alphabetical listing describing the functions, products, services, and dominant applicant needs (among white collar types) of most of the nation's major companies. Valuable as a survey of employers, where they are, and what they do. Published by the College Placement Council, Inc., Box 2263, Bethlehem, Pa. 18001. Available in the placement offices of sizeable colleges and universities, major military separation centers, and some libraries.

- *Contact.* A literate, highly readable, slick, quarterly magazine on opportunities for black college graduates and degree candidates. As of this writing, subscriptions are entered without cost for men and women in that category. To enter yours, write to Contact Resources, Inc., Box 10W, 1270 Sixth Ave., New York, N.Y. 10020. Specify degree level (attained or being sought), date, and major field of study when ordering.

- *Help-wanted ads.* Across-the-board coverage of job openings. Best, normally, in Sunday editions of daily newspapers. Enough wheat among the chaff to merit daily review and deep digging on Sundays. (Prospects are about 1 in 20 that you will find your next job in such listings.) Business and Education sections of the Sunday *New York Times* leads in display advertising of this type, primarily for professional and administrative applicants. *The Wall Street Journal* is another good source of advertised management openings. If looking for employment elsewhere, subscribe to the Sunday issues of a daily paper in the town you have in mind. Your librarian can tell you the name of the paper and where to write.

- *WHO'S HIRING WHO, Vol. II—The Job Directory.* An A-to-Z directory covering projected applicant needs as reported by employers nationally. Covers openings ranging from those for messengers and mechanics to top administrators (about 2,000 job categories), education and experience requirements, pay levels, part-time and temporary jobs, summer employment, overseas openings, functions of the employers, benefits offered, and where to apply.

Provides a broad profile of opportunities nationally and the weight of demand for applicants in various categories. Valuable as a guide on where to focus your efforts. As of this writing, out of print. For advice on where and how the new edition can be obtained when published, send a long, stamped, self-addressed envelope to WHW-JD, Box 3651, Washington, D.C. 20007.

One more important point.

Expense will be an important factor in your job search, so spend wisely. Use only those fee services that promise the greatest long-term value and use them only after you have thoroughly checked them out. But be sure to weigh the need for expenditures in terms of your career goals—not immediate convenience. Tighten your belt in other areas, not in your job search. Taking a threadbare approach to job hunting is likely to produce threadbare results.

And a threadbare future.

225

There are many more job openings out there
than most people realize
—in far more categories,
at every level, and in every location.
Here's proof that they exist
even when times are bad.
Unquestionably, the best jobs go to those applicants
who know best how to get them.

As we said at the beginning of this book, the job market knows very little about its stock in trade—job openings. Except for a small fraction, almost nothing is known about where available openings are, what they are, how many exist, and who offers them. Since jobs keep our whole system going, this absence of adequate data on available openings keeps us all much poorer than we need to be.

All kinds of evil stem from it.

Because of this lack of data, people now take much longer than necessary (averaging ten weeks in the ten years prior to this writing) to find employment. Because of it, their prospects for finding really suitable work are substantially lowered. And because of it, millions—literally—are added to the unemployment count each year, productivity is curtailed, inflationary pressures are increased, and the quality of our national life is eroded.

It's not exaggerating to say that a permanent and significant reduction in unemployment rates will certainly follow a successful effort to develop better information on available openings. If that effort is coupled with improved guidance to applicants on how to land such openings, the rates will drop even further. (Collaterally, mental hospitalization, suicide, crime, drug addiction, and death by heart disease will also go down.) There's little question that we can do a great deal more on both scores than we are now doing. For example, developing much better data on turnover rates in various industries, occupations, and geographic areas would be a long leap in that direction even though not a perfect solution. The massive national benefits resulting from it would be worth many times the relatively small cost involved.

Employee turnover — prime opportunity pump

Suppose people never got promoted, never changed jobs, never quit or got fired. Suppose, even, that no new jobs were ever created and that no one ever left work for a while to raise a family. What would happen then?

The answer is that at least 244,000 jobs would have to be filled *each month* simply to replace those people who were disabled along with those who retired and died.

But people do get promoted, change jobs, quit, and get fired. Some just disappear and never show up again. Usually, they must be replaced.

For example.

Sarah Stein, executive secretary to the president of the Cramp Clamp Co., resigns to have a baby and raise a family. Her departure opens up a job to be filled—a highly desirable one. Ruth Cowan, secretary to the Vice President for Operations of Smith & Company (and a good friend of Sarah's) gets it. Now Ruth's job is open. Joe Black, a recently hired copy-writer for Smith & Company's advertising agency (Promos-West, it's called) hears about Ruth's job. Since he has a degree in business administration plus shorthand aptitude, he wants it so he can get front-office experience that will expose him to all of Smith & Company's operating problems. He gets it. Corrine Jackson, a pool typist who works across the hall from Promos-West and writes far-out poetry on the side, gets Joe's job. Another opening—in fact, the fourth one. That goes to Kelly Girl Delmarva Washington, who is asked to stay on permanently. Job number five is open. Mark Pryzbcynsky who has just graduated from high school, and is big enough to stand the gaff, exercises his rights under the Equal Employment Opportunity Act and gets taken on as a Kelly Girl. One resignation. Five jobs to be filled. That's turnover.

Obviously, the Steins conceived more than they realized when they decided to raise a family.

That sort of thing goes on all the time. Turnover is an inexorable process that continuously opens up job opportunities at a fantastic and more or less predictable rate. Year in and year out. In good times and bad. And it is not hard to measure. In fact, the Bureau of Labor Statistics has been doing it for years, although on a very limited basis.

What do such measurements show?

They show, for example, that *new* hires in manufacturing industry over the 10 years prior to this writing averaged 38 percent of the total payroll.[12] Thirty-eight percent per year! Based on the latest data available on people at work in manufacturing, that translates to 7.6 million men and women who found new jobs—in manufacturing industry alone. In one year. And that doesn't count about 2.6 million people who were laid off and rehired. Nor does it count millions more who moved into better jobs without changing payrolls. It certainly isn't due to new jobs being created since the total actually declined over the year we are talking about.

The new hire rate can fluctuate widely over a period of time. In 1973, for example, it stood at 46.8 percent, almost half of the total payroll. Then a decline set in. In the recession year of 1975, new hires dropped sharply. But even then, well over 2,000,000 people found new jobs in manufacturing industry alone. People like Sarah Stein continued to create countless new opportunities.

Do such high turnover rates apply to the economy as a whole? Probably not, but no one really knows. We certainly need to know.

We need to know turnover rates for all major fields of work and for their occupational categories. With that kind of information in hand, we will know at a minimum how many job openings will occur each month, what kind they are; generally, where they will be, and which occupations are growing, which are declining, and what needs to be done to see that adequately trained people are available.

And when we have that rather easily obtained information in hand, we can work to develop even better methods for disclosing the great bulk of openings in the hidden job market.

WHERE THE JOBS ARE

The tables at the end of this chapter show the *minimum* number of new job openings *per month* (barring a 1930s-type depression) in various occupations, fields of work, and in each of the 50 states and key cities. If you are like most people,

---

12. See Appendix A: Footnotes, page 258.

you will probably find these figures hard to believe—especially if you are reading this at a time when jobs are supposed to be scarce. But believe. In fact, if unemployment goes below 6 percent, you can safely *double* the figures in the last column showing openings to be filled and you will still be well below the actual total. If it drops below 4 percent, *triple* them. On top of all that, you can safely add an *equal* number of job openings still unfilled from prior months for the minimum existing when you look for work. Even so, there are some things you should know about these figures:

- Our estimates of the minimum number of new openings are monthly *averages*. Because hiring goes up with the temperature, the figures are relatively low for the summer months. Although new hiring drops during the winter (and practically stops dead in its tracks between December 20 and January 2), the figures given are still well below probable numbers of jobs to be filled in the October-April period.

- Although the figures showing total employment in column 2 of each of the following tables are based on the latest information available as this is being written, they may be a little higher than the actual numbers if unemployment is ranging above 6 percent when you read this.

- Table 1 covers a broad variety of occupations. Yet it shows a very small sampling (only about 3 percent) of the kinds of jobs that are out there. Because the American job market offers riches almost beyond imagining in terms of the variety of things you can do, Table 1 only hints at that variety. Experts estimate that there are about 35,000 different *kinds* of jobs to be done in the U.S. and that they carry some 42,500 titles. So you won't find specific data in Table 1 on cat chasers or crown pouncers or chicken sexers or bung-hole reamers—all recognized job categories —or countless others with equally exotic titles. (However, we do mention "upsetters.")

- You will see that the data in Table 1 is quite specific in some occupational categories (for example, farm equipment mechanics) and quite general in others. (Numerous job categories, for example, are covered by the heading "forge-shop workers" without pinning down the number employed in each category.) Much more research is needed to produce better data than this so applicants can know the numbers and kinds of job openings available to them in such fields.

- And, quite probably, passing time will show distortions in our crystal ball. For example, who knows what effect deepening recession or major recovery (if it occurs) will have on the need of the military services for new people? We suspect such requirements will prove to be lower than those shown but an explosive world or a new economic boom may determine otherwise.

Table 1 has yet another value. It provides a good sampling of the occupations covered in the Department of Labor's *Occupational Outlook Handbook* (OOH). If you want to know more about any of the occupations listed in Table 1 (plus others), the *Handbook* covers them all.

In our view, OOH is an extremely valuable book for job seekers. But we have misgivings about one major aspect of it. Statements on the numbers of openings occurring each year are painfully cautious. Usually, OOH indicates only those openings expected to result from business expansion or when people leave the occupation entirely for one reason or another (like death). It pays little heed to the largest single source of job opportunities—simple turnover of the chain reaction type like that caused when Sarah Stein resigned to have her baby. So, if we have counted a great many more openings than the Bureau of Labor Statistics did when it wrote OOH, Sarah Stein's case explains it. Even so, the figures we have given on numbers of openings each month assume depression levels of hiring. They are *very* conservative, indeed. Even if mind boggling.

Who's Hiring Who

Even with the limitations just mentioned, the following tables show who's hiring who and, in general, where. They will help you to focus your efforts. With this information in hand, you can properly evaluate any remarks you hear from employment-agency counselors or others that "there just are no openings now."

There are *always* openings. And they occur in massive numbers. Barring a depression, there are at least two million jobs available today. *Right now.* As you read this. The best go to those applicants who know best how to get them.

And even where no formally established openings exist, employers always have needs. Find such a need and persuade an employer that you can fill it and you will have a job—more than likely one specifically tailored to your image. Countless people do it every day. They use the methods described in this book to accomplish it. When they do, they *create* job openings.

And that's one more reason why we need new systems to give people much more guidance than they now get when they look for work. Applicants who understand the job market and how to cope with it *expand* the nation's job supply.

We hope you are one of them.

Table 1
Who's Hiring Who — New Monthly Openings by Occupation

Occupation	Total employment	Minimum number of new openings per month
Accountants	700,000	5,833
Actors and actresses	9,000	95
Actuaries	5,500	45
Advertising specialists	150,000	1,375
Aerospace engineers	60,000	500
Agricultural engineers	12,000	100
Agricultural scientists	55,000	458
Air-conditioning, refrigeration, and heating mechanics	135,000	1,125
Air Force (total)	726,000	7,218
■ Cadets	—	135
■ Enlisted personnel	—	6,308
■ Officers	—	775
Aircraft mechanics	123,000	1,025
Air traffic controllers	20,000	166
Airline dispatchers	800	6
Anthropologists	3,700	30
Appliance servicers	130,000	1,083
Architects	37,000	308
Army (total)	811,000	18,268
■ Cadets	—	119
■ Enlisted personnel	—	18,441
■ Officers	—	708
Asbestos and insulation workers	30,000	250
Assemblers	1,000,000	8,333
Astronomers	2,000	16
Automobile body repairers	160,000	1,333
Automobile mechanics	700,000	5,833
Automobile painters	25,000	208
Automobile parts counter workers	72,000	600
Automobile sales people	130,000	1,083
Automobile service advisors	20,000	166

SOURCE: Column 2 data: *Occupational Outlook Handbook*, U.S. Dept. of Labor, 1974–75 Edition. Column 3 data assumes a 10% annual turnover rate in the occupations indicated except when adjusted downward where greater job stability is expected to exist.

Occupation	Total employment	Minimum number of new openings per month
Automobile upholsterers	9,000	75
Bank clerks	475,000	3,958
Bank officers	220,000	1,833
Barbers and cosmetologists	700,000	5,833
Bartenders	200,000	1,666
Bell staff and captains (hotel)	16,000	133
Biochemists	12,500	104
Biological scientists	75,000	625
Biomedical engineers	3,000	25
Blacksmiths	10,000	42
Boat motor mechanics	10,000	83
Boilermaking occupations	31,000	258
Bookbinders	33,000	275
Bowling pin machine mechanics	6,000	50
Brakemen, railroad	73,000	608
Bridge and building workers, railroad	10,500	87
Broadcast technicians (TV, radio)	22,000	183
Bricklayers	180,000	1,500
Building custodians	1,900,000	15,833
Bulldozer operators	125,000	1,041
Busdrivers, intercity	25,000	205
Busdrivers, local	68,000	566
Bus mechanics	20,000	166
Business machine servicers	70,000	583
Cable splicers, telephone	31,000	258
Carpenters	1,045,000	8,708
Cashiers	1,000,000	8,333
Cement masons	75,000	625
Central office equipment installers	30,000	250
Ceramic engineers	12,000	100
Chemical engineers	50,000	416
Chemists	134,000	1,116
Chiropracters	16,000	53
City managers	2,500	20
Civil engineers	180,000	1,500
Claims adjusters, insurance	128,000	1,066

Occupation	Total employment	Minimum number of new openings per month
Claims examiners, insurance	29,000	241
Cleaning workers	2,000,000	16,666
Clerical workers	14,000,000	116,666
Clerks, railroad	83,000	691
College career planning specialists	3,800	31
College professors and instructors	620,000	5,166
Commercial artists	60,000	500
Composing room occupations	170,000	1,416
Computer operators	480,000	4,000
Computer service technicians	45,000	375
Conductors, railroad	38,000	316
Construction inspectors, government	23,000	191
Construction laborers	875,000	7,291
Construction machinery operators	310,000	2,583
Cooks and chefs	870,000	7,250
Cooperative extensive service workers	15,600	130
Caseworkers	23,000	191
Credit specialists	110,000	916
Dancers	4,000	33
Dental assistants	115,000	958
Dental hygienists	17,000	141
Dental laboratory technicians	32,000	266
Dentists	105,000	350
Diesel mechanics	90,000	750
Dietitians	33,000	275
Display specialists, retail	33,000	275
Drafting technicians	327,000	2,725
Economists	36,000	300
Electric sign servicers	8,000	66
Electricians (construction)	240,000	2,000
Electrocardiographic technicians	10,000	83
Electroencephalographic technicians	3,500	29
Electroplaters	17,000	141
Electrotypers and stereotypers	4,000	33
Elevator constructors	17,000	141
Employment counselors, agency	20,000	173
Entertainment specialists	100,000	833

Occupation	Total employment	Minimum number of new openings per month
Executives (managers, officials, proprietors)	8,200,000	68,330
Exterminators	25,000	208
Farm equipment mechanics	47,000	391
FBI agents	8,600	35
File clerks	270,000	2,250
Firefighters	200,000	1,666
Flight attendants	39,000	325
Flight engineers	7,000	58
Floor covering installers	60,000	500
Floral designers	30,000	250
Food processing technicians	4,500	37
Food scientists	7,500	62
Food service personnel	3,000,000	25,000
Foremen and forewomen	1,400,000	11,666
Foresters	22,000	183
Forestry aides and technicians	14,500	120
Forge-shop workers	63,000	525
Funeral specialists	45,000	375
Furniture upholsterers	35,000	291
Gasoline service attendants	435,000	3,625
Geographers	7,500	62
Geologists	23,000	266
Geophysicists	8,000	66
Glaziers	12,000	100
Ground radio operators and teletypists, airline	5,700	47
Guards and watchmen	250,000	2,083
Health and regulatory inspectors	25,000	208
Health service specialists	1,500,000	12,500
Historians	24,000	200
Home economists	92,300	769
Hospital administrators	17,000	141
Hotel front-office clerks	49,000	408
Hotel housekeepers and assistants	16,000	133
Hotel managers and assistants	110,000	916
Industrial designers	10,000	83
Industrial engineers	125,000	1,041
Industrial machinery mechanics	430,000	3,583
Industrial traffic managers	20,000	166
Inspectors, manufacturing	725,000	6,041

Table 1 continued
Who's Hiring Who — New Monthly Openings by Occupation

Occupation	Total employment	Minimum number of new openings per month
Instrument makers	5,000	41
Instrument repairers	100,000	833
Insurance agents and brokers	385,000	3,208
Insurance underwriters	60,000	500
Interior designers	18,000	150
Interpreters	150	1
Iron workers	95,000	791
Jewelers	18,000	150
Landscape architects	12,000	100
Lathers	30,000	250
Lawyers	300,000	2,500
Librarians	125,000	1,041
Library technicians	25,000	208
Lithographic workers	80,000	666
Lineworkers, telephone	15,000	125
Locksmiths	8,000	66
Locomotive engineers	35,000	291
Machine set-up workers	45,000	375
Machine-tool operators	573,000	4,775
Machinists	320,000	2,666
Mail carriers	263,000	2,191
Maintenance electricians	260,000	2,166
Manufacturers' sales specialists	42,000	350
Marine Corps enlisted personnel	198,000	5,066
Marine Corps officers	60,500	158
Market researchers	25,000	208
Mathematicians	76,000	633
Meat cutters	200,000	1,666
Mechanical engineers	210,000	1,750
Medical assistants	200,000	1,666
Medical laboratory workers	165,000	1,375
Medical record administrators	11,600	96
Medical record clerks	39,000	325
Medical record technicians	8,000	66
Medical scientists	55,000	458
Merchant marine officers	8,500	70
Merchant seafarers	23,500	195
Metallurgical engineers	10,000	83
Meteorologists	5,000	41
Millwrights	85,000	708
Mining engineers	5,000	41

Occupation	Total employment	Minimum number of new openings per month
Models	7,000	58
Molders	56,000	466
Motion picture projectionists	16,000	133
Motorcycle mechanics	9,500	79
Musicians	85,000	708
Navy (total)	588,000	10,100
■ Enlisted personnel	—	9,391
■ Midshipmen	—	126
■ Officers	—	583
Newspaper reporters	39,000	325
Nursing aides, orderlies, and attendants	900,000	7,500
Oceanographers	4,500	37
Occupational therapists	7,500	62
Occupational therapy assistants	6,000	50
Office machine operators	200,000	1,666
Operating room technicians	25,000	208
Optical technicians	16,000	133
Opticians	12,000	100
Optometric assistants	11,000	91
Optometrists	18,700	155
Osteopathic physicians	13,800	46
Painters and paperhangers	410,000	3,416
Parking attendants	33,000	275
Patternmakers	19,000	158
Personnel specialists	235,000	1,958
Pharmacists	131,000	1,091
Photoengravers	16,000	133
Photographers	77,000	641
Photographic laboratory workers	38,000	316
Physical therapists	18,000	150
Physical therapy assistants	10,500	87
Physicians	316,500	1,053
Physicists	49,000	408
Piano and organ technicians	7,000	58
Pilots and copilots, aircraft	54,000	450
Plasterers	30,000	250
Plumbers and pipe fitters	400,000	3,333
Podiatrists	7,300	24
Police officers, municipal	370,000	3,083
Police officers, state	44,000	366
Political scientists	10,000	83

Occupation	Total Employment	Minimum Number of new openings per month
Postal clerks	286,000	2,383
Power truck operators	300,000	2,500
Practical nurses, licensed	430,000	3,583
Private household workers	1,700,000	14,166
Production painters	180,000	1,500
Printing press operators	140,000	1,166
Programmers	186,000	1,550
Protective service specialists	1,000,000	8,333
Psychologists	57,000	475
Public relations specialists	85,000	708
Purchasing agents	180,000	1,500
Radio and television announcers	17,000	141
Railroad telegraphers, telephoners, and tower controllers	11,000	91
Range managers	4,000	33
Real estate brokers and sales specialists	350,000	2,916
Receptionists	435,000	3,625
Recreation workers	55,000	458
Registered nurses	750,000	2,916
Rehabilitation counselors	16,000	133
Reservation agents, airline	60,000	500
Respiratory therapists	17,000	141
Retail salesworkers	2,800,000	23,333
Roofers	80,000	666
Salesworkers	5,400,000	45,000
Sanitarians	17,000	141
School counselors	43,000	358
Securities sales specialists	220,000	1,833
Sewage-plant operators	20,000	166
Shipping and receiving clerks	450,000	3,750
Shoe repairers	25,000	208
Signal workers and maintainers	11,000	91
Singers	36,000	300
Social service aides	100,000	833
Social workers	185,000	1,541
Sociologists	15,000	125
Soil conservationists	12,000	100
Soil scientists	5,000	41
Speech pathologists and audiologists	27,000	225
Station agents, railroad	8,700	72

Table 1 continued
Who's Hiring Who — New Monthly Openings by Occupation

Occupation	Total Employment	Minimum number of new openings per month
Stationary engineers	175,000	1,458
Stationary fire maintainers	93,000	775
Statistical clerks	300,000	2,500
Statisticians	23,000	191
Stenographers	3,000,000	25,000
Stock clerks	500,000	4,166
Student personnel workers	35,000	291
Surveyors	58,000	483
Systems analysts	100,000	833
Taxi drivers	92,000	766
Teachers, elementary	1,300,000	10,833
Teachers, secondary	1,000,000	8,333
Technical writers	20,000	166
Technicians	700,000	5,833
Telephone operators	400,000	3,333
Telephone technicians	105,000	875
Telephone service technicians	110,000	916
Television and radio service technicians	140,000	1,166
Tellers	250,000	2,083
Tile setters	35,000	291
Tool and die workers	170,000	1,416
Track workers, railroad	53,000	441
Truck drivers, long distance	570,000	4,750
Truck mechanics	115,000	958
Typists	1,000,000	8,333
Urban planners	12,000	100
Vending machine mechanics	29,000	241
Veterinarians	26,000	108
Waiters and waitresses	1,120,000	9,333
Watch repairers	16,000	133
Welders and flame cutters	555,000	4,625
Wholesale sales specialists	690,000	5,750
X-ray technologists	55,000	458

Index to Other Occupations Included in the Above Categories

Able seafarers	See merchant seafarers
Account executives	See advertising specialists
Accounting clerks	See bookkeeping workers
Acquisition librarians	See librarians

Index to Other Occupations Included in the Above Categories

Index to Other Occupations Included in the Above Categories

Index to Other Occupations Included in the Above Categories

Index to Other Occupations Included in the Above Categories

Research directors	See advertising specialists
Reservation clerks	See hotel managers and assistants
Resistance welding operators	See welders
Room clerks	See hotel managers and assistants
Scheduling clerks	See statistical clerks
School media specialists	See librarians
Secretaries	See stenographers
Security guards	See protective service specialists
Shorthand reporters	See stenographers
Shotblasters	See forge shop workers
Ski instructors	See entertainment specialists
Slide mounters	See photographic laboratory workers
Social secretaries	See stenographers
Sorters	See bank clerks
Statistical assistants	See statistical clerks
Stewards and stewardesses	See flight attendants
Stewards, chief	See merchant seafarers
Structural ironworkers	See ironworkers
Student counselors	See student personnel workers
Student financial aid personnel	See student personnel workers
Student housing officers	See student personnel workers
Switching equipment technicians	See telephone technicians
Synoptic meteorologists	See meteorologists
Tabulating machine operators	See office machine operators
Tape-to-card converter operators	See computer operators
Technical secretaries	See stenographers
Technical stenographers	See stenographers
Teletypists	See ground radio operators
Terrazzo workers	See tile setters
Testboard technicians	See telephone technicians
Traffic agents, airline	See reservation clerks
Transit clerks	See bank clerks
Trimmers	See forge-shop occupations
Trust officers	See bank officers
Tune-up specialists	See automobile mechanics
Typesetters	See composing room occupations
Typesetting machine operators	See composing room occupations
Upholstery trimmers, automobile	See automobile upholsterers
Upsetters	See forge-shop workers
Ushers, theater	See entertainment specialists
Wipers	See merchant seafarers
Zoologists	See biological scientists

Table 2
Who's Hiring Who — New Monthly Openings by Field of Work

Occupational or Industrial Field	Total employment	Minimum number of new openings per month
Advertising	118,000	983
Air transportation	332,300	2,889
Apparel and accessory stores	725,900	6,049
Armed forces	2,393,000	41,808
Banking	1,180,200	9,835
Bakery operators	265,600	2,213
Beverage production	235,900	1,965
Coal mining	172,000	1,433
Colleges and universities	695,000	5,791
Department stores	1,690,000	14,083
Eating and drinking places	2,942,500	24,516
Electric companies and systems	330,400	2,753
Elementary and secondary schools	433,500	3,625
Engineering and architectural services	381,900	3,182
Farming	3,400,000	8,333
Food store operations	1,954,200	16,285
Furniture and home furnishings stores	488,500	4,076
Gas companies and systems	166,000	1,383
Gasoline service stations	579,900	4,832
General building contractors	1,055,100	8,792
Government, local	7,643,800	63,698
Government, state	3,105,200	25,876
Government, U.S. executive branch	2,706,000	22,550
Government, U.S. judiciary	8,700	72
Government, U.S. legislative branch	34,500	287
Heavy construction contractors	789,600	6,580
Hospitality operations (hotels, motels, etc.)	885,900	7,382
Insurance operations	1,144,700	9,539
Laundries and dry-cleaning plants	399,200	3,326
Legal services	292,300	2,435
Local and interurban passenger transit	277,000	2,308
Manufacturing		
■ Apparel	1,300,000	10,833
■ Aircraft and parts	572,400	4,270

SOURCE: Column 2 data: *Employment and Earnings*, U.S. Dept. of Labor, Vol. 21, No. 2, August, 1974. Column 3 data assumes a 10% rate of annual turnover in the industrial fields indicated.

Occupational or Industrial Field	Total employment	Minimum number of new openings per month
■ Blast furnace and basic steel products	608,600	5,063
■ Broadcast and other communications equipment	437,700	3,647
■ Canned, cured, and frozen foods	257,400	2,145
■ Chemicals and allied products	1,048,300	8,735
■ Construction and related machinery	330,700	2,755
■ Dairy products	209,800	1,748
■ Electric lighting and wiring equipment	218,400	1,820
■ Electric test and distributing equipment	223,400	1,861
■ Electronic components and accessories	414,100	3,451
■ Engines and turbines	113,900	949
■ Fabricated metal products	1,450,400	12,086
■ Furniture and fixtures	518,000	4,316
■ General industrial machinery	301,100	2,508
■ Grain mill products	137,900	1,149
■ Hardware	163,700	1,364
■ Household appliances	209,400	1,745
■ Instruments and related products	522,100	4,350
■ Leather and leather products	294,100	2,450
■ Lumber and wood products	644,000	5,366
■ Machinery (nonelectrical)	2,141,200	17,843
■ Meat products	335,700	2,797
■ Metal stampings	233,500	1,945
■ Metal working machinery	322,100	2,684
■ Miscellaneous (jewelry, toys, etc.)	440,000	3,666
■ Motor vehicles and equipment	860,500	7,170
■ Motors and generators	128,900	1,074
■ Office and computing machines	289,100	2,408
■ Ordnance	187,600	1,563
■ Paper and allied products	722,800	6,020
■ Petroleum and coal products	192,700	1,605
■ Primary metal production	1,333,400	11,111
■ Radio and TV	139,200	1,160
■ Railroad equipment	43,700	364
■ Stone, clay, and glass products	700,600	5,838
■ Structural metal products	462,600	3,855

Occupational or industrial field	Total employment	Minimum number of new openings per month
Manufacturing (cont.)		
■ Rubber and plastics (NEC)	184,275	1,535
■ Textile mill products	1,011,200	8,426
■ Tobacco	67,400	561
Medical and other health services	3,704,100	30,866
Merchant marine	60,000	500
Metal mining (iron, copper)	96,600	805
Motion picture theaters and services	187,400	1,561
Motor vehicle dealers	767,600	6,396
Oil and gas extraction	275,000	2,291
Printing and publishing	1,103,800	9,198
Radio and television broadcasting	136,700	1,139
Railroad transportation	586,200	4,885
Real estate operations	732,200	6,101
Retail merchandising, general	2,570,200	21,418
Shipbuilding and repair	190,600	1,588
Special building trade contractors (plumbing, painting, electrical, etc.)	1,813,600	15,113
Telephone operations	995,800	8,298
Stone, sand, gravel mining	120,500	1,004
Trucking and trucking terminals	1,095,000	9,125
Warehousing, public	86,500	720
Water, steam, and sanitary systems	61,200	510
Wholesale trade	4,177,000	34,808

Table 3
Who's Hiring Who—New Monthly Openings
by Location

Location	Total employment	Minimum number of new openings per month
ALABAMA	1,144,900	9,540
Birmingham	304,100	2,534
Mobile	117,100	976
ALASKA	113,200	943
ARIZONA	726,800	6,056
Phoenix	437,400	3,645
Tucson	135,300	1,127
ARKANSAS	633,900	5,282
Little Rock—North Little Rock	152,400	1,270
CALIFORNIA	7,840,500	65,337
Anaheim—Santa Ana—Garden Grove	549,400	4,561
Los Angeles—Long Beach	3,063,200	25,526
Riverside—San Bernardino—Ontario	334,400	2,786
Sacramento	296,000	2,466
San Diego	462,800	3,856
San Francisco—Oakland	1,310,800	10,972
San Jose	443,500	3,815
COLORADO	914,600	7,621
Denver	590,800	4,952
CONNECTICUT	1,277,900	10,649
Hartford	344,700	2,872
New Haven	164,300	1,369
DELAWARE	233,700	1,947
Wilmington	204,600	1,705
FLORIDA	2,778,200	23,151
Fort Lauderdale—Hollywood	237,900	1,982
Jacksonville	241,600	2,013
Miami	608,500	5,070
Orlando	228,500	1,904
Tampa—St. Petersburg	428,000	3,566
GEORGIA	1,807,400	15,061
Atlanta	763,400	6,136
Augusta	96,800	806
HAWAII	329,700	2,747
Honolulu	278,800	2,323

SOURCE: Column 2 data: *Employment and Earnings*, U.S. Dept. of Labor, Vol. 21, No. 2, August 1974. Column 3 data assumes a 10% annual rate of turnover in employment in the geographic areas indicated.

Table 3 continued
Who's Hiring Who—New Monthly Openings
by Location

Location	Total employment	Minimum number of new openings per month
IDAHO	252,800	2,106
Boise	55,200	460
ILLINOIS	4,444,000	37,033
Chicago Metropolitan Area	3,000,200	25,008
Davenport—Rock Island—Moline	142,800	1,190
Peoria	137,800	1,148
INDIANA	2,030,200	16,918
Fort Wayne	162,400	1,353
Indianapolis	453,600	3,780
IOWA	998,800	8,323
Des Moines	145,500	1,212
KANSAS	772,700	6,439
Wichita	162,000	1,350
KENTUCKY	1,065,600	8,880
Lexington—Fayette	120,200	1,001
Louisville	369,600	3,080
LOUISIANA	1,173,400	9,778
Baton Rouge	143,600	1,196
New Orleans	413,800	3,448
MAINE	351,600	2,930
Portland	70,600	588
MARYLAND	1,456,500	12,237
Baltimore	870,400	7,253
MASSACHUSETTS	2,374,100	19,784
Boston	1,301,000	10,841
Springfield—Chicopee—Holyoke	193,100	1,609
Worcester	134,700	1,122
MICHIGAN	3,203,400	26,695
Detroit	1,588,000	13,233
Flint	157,900	1,315
Grand Rapids	209,600	1,746
Lansing—East Lansing	144,000	1,200
MINNESOTA	1,492,100	12,434
Minneapolis—St. Paul	904,800	7,540
MISSISSIPPI	691,700	5,764
Jackson	113,200	943
MISSOURI	1,776,500	14,804
Kansas City	550,200	4,585
St. Louis	856,300	7,135

Table 3 continued
Who's Hiring Who — New Monthly Openings by Location

Location	Total employment	Minimum number of new openings per month
MONTANA	244,400	2,036
Billings	37,400	311
NEBRASKA	554,800	4,623
Omaha	237,000	1,975
NEVADA	258,700	2,155
Reno	72,500	604
NEW HAMPSHIRE	300,000	2,500
Manchester	52,900	440
NEW JERSEY	2,797,100	23,309
Long Beach—Asbury Park	138,400	1,153
Trenton	147,300	1,227
(See New York for N.E. New Jersey)		
NEW MEXICO	359,100	2,992
Albuquerque	145,800	1,215
NEW YORK	7,160,800	59,673
Albany—Schenectady—Troy	314,600	2,621
Buffalo	500,600	4,171
Nassau—Suffolk	818,000	6,816
New York—Northeastern N.J.	6,641,300	55,344
Rochester	391,200	3,260
Syracuse	244,600	2,038
NORTH CAROLINA	2,023,800	16,865
Charlotte—Gastonia	274,600	2,263
Greensboro—Winston Salem—High Point	337,400	2,811
Raleigh—Durham	205,000	1,708
NORTH DAKOTA	188,900	1,574
Fargo—Moorhead	49,800	415
OHIO	4,198,200	34,985
Cincinnati	541,400	4,511
Cleveland	880,300	7,335
Columbus	430,200	3,585
Dayton	336,200	2,811
OKLAHOMA	875,900	7,299
Oklahoma City	312,000	2,600
Tulsa	215,100	1,791
OREGON	833,600	6,946
Portland	437,200	3,644

Table 3 continued
Who's Hiring Who — New Monthly Openings
by Location

Location	Total employment	Minimum number of new openings per month
PENNSYLVANIA	4,511,300	37,594
Harrisburg	207,600	1,730
Philadelphia Metropolitan Area	1,841,600	15,346
Pittsburgh	886,100	7,384
RHODE ISLAND	359,300	2,994
Providence Metropolitan Area	373,600	3,113
SOUTH CAROLINA	1,044,000	8,700
Columbia	145,400	1,211
Greenville—Spartanburg	232,900	1,940
SOUTH DAKOTA	211,500	1,762
Sioux Falls	42,100	350
TENNESSEE	1,563,300	13,027
Memphis	324,100	2,700
Nashville—Davidson	306,200	2,551
TEXAS	4,325,800	36,048
Dallas	762,600	6,355
Fort Worth	298,300	2,485
Houston	929,900	7,749
San Antonio	306,100	2,550
UTAH	435,500	3,629
Salt Lake City—Ogden	316,500	2,637
VERMONT	164,100	1,367
Burlington	40,900	339
VIRGINIA	1,424,800	11,873
(See Washington, D.C. for Northern Virginia)		
Norfolk-Virginia Beach—Portsmouth	247,100	2,175
Richmond	273,300	2,277
WASHINGTON	1,197,500	10,099
Seattle—Everett	549,000	4,575
Tacoma	112,800	940
Washington, D.C. Metropolitan Area	1,328,000	11,066
WEST VIRGINIA	562,400	4,806
Charleston	97,100	929
Huntington—Ashland	90,400	873
WISCONSIN	1,694,100	14,175
Madison	136,900	1,140
Milwaukee	611,800	5,098
WYOMING	130,100	1,084
Cheyenne	23,600	196

Afterword:
Resolve!

The dictionary defines an expert as "a person with a high degree of skill in or knowledge of a certain subject." You may find this hard to believe but, if you have studied this book, you are a true expert in the dynamics of the job market—especially if you have tested WHW's premises and guides in practice.

In truth, you know much more about the job market—its gross failings, its heavy bias, its incentive systems, its opportunities, and the measures needed to succeed in it—than *most* of the "experts" who earn their living ostensibly helping applicants. You know far more, for example, than almost all job counselors in school placement offices and public and private employment agencies. And, tragically, even more—in most instances—than the experts who determine the direction of national employment programs.

The reason is simple enough. Such experts focus on the manpower market (as it is called), not the job market. Their concern is with job filling, not job finding. While these two approaches *sound* much the same, there is a vast difference between them in terms of potential for solving your employment problems (and the nation's). The reason for *that* is that the job fillers focus their attention on the very small number of openings revealed to them by employers. (One in five, remember.) Because of their limited view of the opportunities available, they are forced to try—with might and main—to squeeze you into one of the few openings they do hear about, no matter how unsuitable it may be.

The job finders, on the other hand, zero in on the *total* job supply—many millions upon millions more openings than ever come to the attention of the job fillers.

In view of all this, we hope you will resolve—here and now—to apply your expert knowledge in the future to achieve two important results:

1. We hope you will resolve to use the principles and guides in this book during the rest of your life to move ahead in your career as fast as your personal development allows and to maintain employment as close as possible to the peak of your abilities from here on out. If you do, all of us will be better for it—at least to some small degree. Both your productivity and the satisfaction you get from your work will be increased. And you will do more than simply serve yourself. You will be helping in your own way to pump new strength and vitality into our economic system and to reduce the quality-of-life crisis in the United States that now weighs so heavily on us all. So *resolve*.

2. Because you know a great deal more than most about the uncertainties, critical questions, and genuine agonies that face almost all job seekers—*and* how to deal with them—we hope you will also resolve, here and now, to lend your strong support to everyone you know or meet in the future who needs employment or a better job. Let them lean on you. Give them the benefit of your unique experience and expert knowledge. Support them with evidence of your interest and concern. Actively assist them in uncovering leads to employment that will solve this crisis in their lives. When you do, you will do more than serve them alone. You will serve all of us. You will help strengthen our society. And—figuratively or literally—you may even save a life. So *resolve*.

And we hope you will resolve one more thing.

When you enter the job market, you inevitably enter a period of intense research—a testing time that determines which measures, which principles, which steps in your approach are most successful for you. Consequently, when your job search is successfully concluded, we hope you will resolve to let us know which approaches worked best for you—whether or not they are covered in this book—and which measures you tried that proved ineffective for you even though common sense (or this book) said they would work. And where you encountered problems *not* covered by WHW on which you think applicants should have guidance.

Give us the benefit of *your* experience as an expert, and we will be better able to help countless others. Working together, we just may bring the job market—that "mindless monster in our midst"—under control.

Please help. Send your critical views and suggestions to: WHW—II, Box 3651, Washington, D.C. 20007. If incorporated in the next edition of WHW, the views you express may be a crucial factor in determining, finally, whether or not the job market in the United States can be shifted in its emphasis to serve, *first,* the needs of job seekers—and consequently those of employers who will benefit directly from the lower hiring costs and higher productivity such a system will achieve.

We will be grateful for the help you give. And so, we think, will countless others.

Appendix A:
Footnotes

This book puts considerable stress on the fact that serious but correctable malfunctions in the national job market stemming primarily from poor guidance to applicants add significant and unnecessary increments to national unemployment rates in both good times and bad. The primary research and expert opinion supporting such a conclusion is cited below:

1. **Unemployment is reduced approximately 50 percent when applicants are counseled.** Source: *Counseling and Placement Services for Older Workers,* page 66, Bureau of Employment Security Study No. E-152, U.S. Department of Labor, 1956. Subsequent unpublished studies by State employment offices also show approximately doubled employment rates for counseled applicants even when not restricted to older workers.

2. **The duration of unemployment averages 70 days; 20 million annually suffer such unemployment.** Source: *Employment and Earnings,* Bureau of Labor Statistics, U.S. Department of Labor, Issue No. 7 of Vols. 11-21, 1965-1975, during which period average duration of unemployment ranged from 8.0 to 12.1 weeks. Total annual unemployment is obtained by dividing 365 by the average duration of unemployment in days and multiplying the quotient by the average monthly unemployment for the year as reported by BLS.

3. **Reduction of the average duration of unemployment by 4 days will reduce the annual unemployment count by more than 1 million; reduction by 7 days (from 70 to 63 days) will cut annual unemployment 2 million—i.e. 10 percent.** Under the system used by the Bureau of Labor Statistics for measuring unemployment, any method that reduces the average duration of unemployment will reduce total unemployment proportionately. Thus, a 4-day reduction in average duration from 70 to 66 days (5.7 percent) will subtract more than 1 million from the annual count of 20 million unemployed during "normal" years.

4. **Professional job-market analysts observe that most applicants make serious job-hunting mistakes that inevitably delay employment.** This conclusion stems from the author's own observation in dealing with thousands of job seekers and is fortified by similar observations of numerous other job-market analysts—most notably Richard N. Bolles, Director of the National Career Development Project of the United Ministries in Higher Education, Walnut Creek, Calif.; John C. Crystal, Life Management Services, Inc., McLean, Va.; and Barton M. Lloyd, Director, Mid-Atlantic Career Center, Washington, D.C.

5. **A short job supply is typically only half of the nation's unemployment problem.** According to the Chief, Division of Employment and Unemployment Statistics, Bureau of Labor Statistics, BLS has traditionally used unemployment of less than 5 weeks as a "rule-of-thumb" indicator of that part of unemployment that results from malfunctioning job-market operations ("friction") rather than an inadequate job supply. During 1973 and 1974 (more or less "normal") years) such unemployment stood at 51.6 percent and 50.5 percent, respectively, of the total. See *Employment and Earnings,* Vol. 21, No. 7, January 1975.

6. **Malfunctioning job-market operations are the nation's number 1 public-health problem.** Source: *Work in America,* W. E. Upjohn Institute for Employment Research, published by Massachusetts Institute of Technology, 1973. This report of a special task force to the Secretary of Health, Education, and Welfare cites numerous studies indicating that inadequate applicant guidance and resultant poor employment are primary contributors to heart disease, mental hospitalization, and suicide. See, particularly, pages 77-87, 153, and 186.

7. **Barring a depression at least 1 million new job openings occur each month with 2 million in "normal" times and 3 million in boom times.** This estimate is supported by: (1) Bureau of Labor Statistics estimates of unemployment due to "friction"—i.e. poor communications—in the job market, and (2) analysis of rates of turnover in manufacturing industry reported monthly in *Employment and Earnings* published by the Bureau of Labor Statistics plus other available personnel turnover data. (See footnote 12 below.)

8. **Only 1 in 5 job openings are likely to be advertised, listed with employment agencies, or otherwise broadly publicized.** The best confirmation for this conclusion is found in the data cited in footnote 9 below showing that only 15 percent of job seekers find employment through formal job-publicizing systems. Eli Djeddah (*Moving Up,* pages 57, 58, Lippincott, 1971) and Richard K. Irish (*Go Hire Yourself an Employer,* page 41, Anchor Press/Doubleday, 1973) have arrived at an identical conclusion.

9. **Employers typically use an "insider" system—not formal job-help systems—to fill most of their job openings.** Source: *Career Thresholds,* Vol. 1, Manpower Research Monograph No. 16, Manpower Administration, U.S. Department of Labor, 1970. This data regarding hiring methods is derived from Tables 4.13 through 4.15, *Method Used to Find Current Job.*

10. **Applicants typically are most successful in finding work if they rely on friends and direct contacts with employers.** Ibid.

11. **Major employers consider an average of 245 résumés for every interview granted.** Source: Study by Deutsch, Shea, and Evans, Inc., a New York recruitment advertising firm, cited by Richard N. Bolles in *What Color Is Your Parachute?,* page 14, 1976 Edition, Ten Speed Press, Berkeley, Calif.

12. **New hires in manufacturing industry average 38 percent of payroll annually.** Source: *Employment and Earnings,* Vol. 21, No. 7, January 1975.

Appendix B:
Key elements in courses on the job market and how to cope with it

Job-market operations have a heavy impact on the vitality of our entire economic system. Yet, to the best of our knowledge as of this writing, no formal study is being undertaken at any academic level anywhere in the United States regarding the job market in terms of its effect as an institutional and operating system on the people it theoretically should be designed to serve—job seekers and employers.

Perhaps with good reason.

Some people who have looked into this question wonder whether a genuine job market—an applicant-serving entity—actually exists at all in this country. (So what is there to study?) While they don't question the reality of a "manpower" or "labor" or "human resources" market (an employer-serving entity, by whatever name), John Crystal and Richard N. Bolles, for example, both express doubt that any real national system to serve the urgent needs of job seekers can be found in the United States. Bolles asserts that there are as many job markets as there are employers. Which is to say, of course, that there is no national job market. Crystal almost always refers to the "so-called" job market whenever he mentions whatever is out there.*

The implication is strong in both of those views that we have no national systems to serve the needs of applicants—only systems to exploit those needs.

---

*Crystal's "so-called job market" is the operation that this book so heavily criticizes. It is the one we refer to, mixed-metaphorically, elsewhere as a "mindless monster" and a "jungle." It exists to fill only those few openings employers choose to publicize. It only incidentally and ostensibly helps job seekers. The "genuine job market," on the other hand, focuses entirely on the needs of applicants (and the millions upon millions of openings never brought to the attention of the "so-called" job market). Its full development, the evidence indicates, will not only serve critical needs of job seekers that are not now met but should also much better serve employers as well.

We agree, in the main, with such views but with an important reservation. A genuine job market *does* exist, we think, but only in an embryonic state.

We think that more than the germ of a job market exists in a number of career guidance centers across the country that focus entirely on the needs of their clients as they confront the imponderables of employment. We think it exists in the life/work planning now studied in many colleges and universities in the U.S. (and brought into being by Crystal and Bolles). We think it exists in this book and as a strong reality in the experience of many who have used WHW to guide their job search.

What that embryo needs now, we think, is greatly increased understanding and nurturing. And that will begin to occur as the job market is brought under direct study in order to determine its needs and potential while we move deliberately to foster its growth. Such study, we think, should start at the high-school level, if not before.

Our suggestions:

BASIC RESOURCES

In addition to all of the publications cited in Chapter 12 under *Outside Reading,* the following, *at least,* should be well thumbed and annotated in the library of anyone who would guide others with regard to the job market and how to cope with it (see Appendix A of *What Color Is Your Parachute?* for many more to be considered):

- *Work in America,* W. E. Upjohn Institute for Employment Research, MIT Press, Cambridge, Mass.
- *Making Vocational Choices: A theory of careers,* John L. Holland, Prentice-Hall, Englewood Cliffs, N.J. 07632.
- *The Three Boxes of Life and How to Get Out of Them,* Richard Nelson Bolles, Ten Speed Press, Box 7123W, Berkeley, Calif. 94707.
- *Career World,* The Continuing Guide to Career Education, Curriculum Innovations, Inc., Highwood, Ill. 60040. (Exposes students to intrinsically interesting information on opportunities in various career fields. Substantially updates and improves upon the *Occupational Outlook Handbook* with regard to the occupational categories covered.)

- *Newsletter about life/work planning,* The National Career Development Project of the United Ministries in Higher Education, Box 379W, Walnut Creek, Calif. 94596.

- *Employment and Earnings,** Bureau of Labor Statistics, January issue (latest year)—particularly for annual data regarding duration of unemployment, job-search methods used, turnover rates, and current extent of frictional unemployment (estimated by BLS to be roughly equivalent to unemployment less than five weeks).

- *Career Thresholds,* Vols. 1-5,* Manpower Research Monograph No. 16, United States Department of Labor covering the year-by-year experience of 5,225 young males in the job market.

- *Merchandising Your Job Talents,** Employment and Training Administration, U.S. Department of Labor, for review as an important example of applicant misguidance. (Note: editions revised after 1976 may not serve that function.)

- *WHW, Vol. II—The Job Directory,* National Center for Job-Market Studies. (Note: Send a long stamped, self-addressed envelope to WHW–JD, Box 3651, Washington, D.C. 20007, for advice when this publication again becomes available.)

KEY COURSE ELEMENTS
AT THE HIGH SCHOOL LEVEL

- **TEXTS:** *WHW, The Quick Job-Hunting Map—Beginning Version, Career World.*

- **SUPPLEMENTARY READING:** *The Occupational Outlook Handbook, WHW—Vol. II* (when available).

- **ELEMENTS:** Broad survey of the job market as an operating system; guidance on determination of strongest abilities, interests, and most likely occupational fields; completion of the *Abilities Checklist* (WHW chap. 3) and *The Quick Job-Hunting Map;* guidance on qualbrief development followed by preparation, exchange of briefs among students for review using the *Qualbrief Checklist* (WHW chap. 5)

---

*Available from the Superintendent of Documents, Washington, D.C. 20402.

followed by discussion and redrafting;* discussion of the various and most effective methods of contacting employers including review and analysis of current help-wanted ads; development of a letter or note to cover mailed or hand-delivered qualbriefs with cross-evaluation by fellow students; determining types of employers most likely to hire; exploration of techniques for determining most likely pay level and negotiating pay; interview role-playing with suggestions by class members; dry-run interviews in the field to seek a summer job or after-graduation employment divided among class members to assure coverage of public and private employment agencies, plus employment officers and operating officials of local employers followed by classroom discussion of impressions and results; and review of methods for keeping agency and employer interest alive while continuing to work to win a strong job offer.

KEY COURSE ELEMENTS AT THE COLLEGE LEVEL

- **TEXTS:** *WHW, Parachute, The Quick Job-Hunting Map—Advanced Version, Merchandising Your Job Skills,* and *WHW Vol. II—The Job Directory* (when available).

- **SUPPLEMENTARY READING:** *The Occupational Outlook Handbook, Work in America, Employment and Earnings, Career Thresholds, You, Inc.* (or *Breaking Out*), *Making Vocational Choices,* and *Where Do I Go from Here with My Life?*

- **ELEMENTS:** All of those listed above for high-school students plus the following as feasible: Completion of the *Career Analysis Guidelines* (WHW chap. 4) and/or *The Quick Job-Hunting Map;* assessment of the incentive systems (motivation and sources of support) controlling actions of the job market's major groups (applicants, employers, employment agencies, job-search and executive-search specialists, counselors, etc.); analysis of the structural and motivational causes of failure of major job-market components; assessment of the state of communications in the job market and

---

*Instructors who want to provide their students with a more definitive assessment may order the *Qualbrief Review* form from NCJMS. To obtain a sample and learn about costs, send a long stamped, self-addressed envelope to Qualbrief Review–Students, Box 3651, Washington, D.C. 20007.

remedies needed; analysis of factors that cause employers to be secretive about their openings and possible remedies therefor; review of the effect of national neglect of the job market as an operating system on public health, increased social program costs, lost productivity, and accelerated inflation; determination of why the job-bank concept was doomed before its inception and assessment of the prospects for success of computerized job-applicant matching services; analysis of the factors that cause job seekers to focus their energies largely on the least productive sources of employment and corrective measures needed; exploration of alternatives available to students who are unlikely to be productive in a formal administrative hierarchy; general evaluation of the quality of services rendered by public and private employment agencies as observed during dry-run interviews; study of *Merchandising Your Job Talents* to discover all of the instances in which it leads applicants to action likely to lessen their prospects for employment and general assessment of factors that produced such poor guidance; general survey of areas in which major research and development are needed if a job market that is adequately responsive to the needs of applicants and employers is to be achieved.

So the field is wide open. You and your students will be opening up virgin territory as you explore the job market to see what exists there, why it does, and what needs to be done about it. The potential in your efforts—and theirs—for immensely important new discovery is great. Meanwhile, simply by focusing attention on the job market's major malfunctions, you will stimulate needed changes in approach by its institutional components that have never before been brought under such broad analytical review.

If, in the process, you develop a teacher's manual along the above (or other) lines that outlines formal courses on the job market and how to cope with it to be offered at the high school and/or college level, please send us a copy. While we will not be able to critique it, we would like to consider it for publication as a guide to others under your name and with appropriate compensation for your efforts. If interested, please submit your manuscript with a long stamped, self-addressed envelope and your qualbrief to: WHW Teacher's Manual, Box 3651, Washington, D.C. 20007.

Appendix C:
Job-search research — we need your help!

WHO'S HIRING WHO covers highly persuasive evidence showing that authoritative job-search guidance (like that in WHW)
can dramatically increase your prospects for finding rewarding
employment in much less time than it otherwise would take.
More, it shows that such help—if broadly applied—promises to
produce a significant reduction in national jobless rates. Consequently, WHW urges that such guidance be made available
to *all* applicants as a matter of right and in the national interest.

However, we need additional evidence to make such a case
before national employment planners. Although we have received thousands of letters roundly applauding WHW for the
strong job-finding support given its readers, few have included
precise facts of the kind needed to determine the true value
of such guidance. *That's where you may be of major help.*

For example, one reader kept specific records of the results
of his employer contacts before and after reading WHW. Then
he wrote us citing facts showing that his interviews per contact
increased 1000 percent (literally) after applying WHW's pre-
cepts while his job offers per contact increased six times.

Because WHW focuses on ways to overcome factors that
actively *prevent* success in gaining interviews and strong job
offers, we were—of course— highly gratified to learn that it
apparently produced such dramatic results in that applicant's
case. However, in truth, we have no way of knowing whether
his experience was highly unusual, or typical, or the result of
other factors having little or nothing to do with WHW itself.
We hope you can help us to find out.

If you have kept careful records of the number and results of
your employer contacts before and after receiving WHW—
numbers of such contacts, interviews granted, and job offers
received—we will greatly appreciate your action to complete
and return the report on the next page. (Please do it even if
your post-WHW experience has been negative.) The information you give us may prove to be of very substantial importance in determining the future direction of national programs
to assist job seekers.

THE NATIONAL CENTER FOR JOB-MARKET STUDIES

Report your job-search experience

Note: If you have kept accurate records of the results of employer contacts prior to and after exposure to WHW, your completion and return of this form will be greatly appreciated. All responses will be held in confidence and will be used only to determine the direction of new programs to assist job seekers.

1. Please indicate your experience *prior* to exposure to WHW in the spaces indicated:

    a. Dates of prior job-search activity:

    From _____ to _____

    Number of weeks spanned by such activity: _____

    b. Total number of employing organizations contacted in that period (excluding those contacted by or through employment agencies): _____

    c. Total number of interviews granted as a result of such contacts: _____

    d. Total number of positions offered as a result of such contacts: _____

    e. Average pay (to extent known) offered with such positions: $_____
       ☐ per year   ☐ per month   ☐ per day

2. Now, please indicate your experience *after* exposure to WHW:

    a. Dates of post-WHW job-search activity:

    From _____ to _____

    Number of weeks spanned by such activity: _____

    b. Total number of employing organizations contacted in the post-WHW period (excluding agency contacts): _____

    c. Total number of interviews granted as a result of such contacts: _____

    d. Total number of positions offered as a result of such contacts: _____

    e. Average pay (to extent known) offered with such positions: $_____
       ☐ per year   ☐ per month   ☐ per day

    f. Have you finally accepted employment? ☐ Yes   ☐ No

    If so, at what pay level? $_____
       ☐ per year   ☐ per month   ☐ per day

3. Please check off those *five* elements or premises of WHW listed below which you believe most heavily influenced your approach to your job search:

☐ Exposure to factual information showing the channels by which people most often find jobs and employers most often fill them.

☐ Getting the value of various job-help services (employment agencies, etc.) in proper perspective and knowing how to use them for best results.

☐ Completion of the ☐ *Career Analysis Guidelines* (WHW chap. 4) or ☐ *The Quick Job-Hunting Map* (WHW chap. 12).

☐ Recognizing the importance of abilities (vs. experience) as a major factor in determining job-search success.

☐ Development and use of a qualifications brief in lieu of a résumé.

☐ Guides on how to write effective letters of application.

☐ Knowing when *not* to use a qualifications brief.

☐ Directly asking for interviews rather than leaving it to employers to initiate interview action.

☐ Recognizing that employers seldom have suitable openings on the day of first contact but, more than likely, soon will.

☐ Using each contact to develop more when possible.

☐ Entering interviews ready to talk knowledgeably about the employers' activities and problems.

☐ Focusing on employer needs and interests (rather than your own) in all written and oral contacts.

☐ Knowing how to control interviews when necessary.

☐ Learning the governing principles determining pay levels.

☐ Knowing how to negotiate pay.

☐ Knowing how to use the CORE approach (WHW chap. 8) to uncover or create job opportunities.

☐ Offering help to (and getting it from) other applicants (WHW chap. 8).

☐ Knowing that suitable openings exist for applicants who know how to pursue them.

☐ Having a strong plan of action that enabled you to proceed efficiently knowing that you are on the right track.

☐ Other (please specify): _____

_____

4. Your name (printed): _____

Address: _____

City, state, zip _____

Telephone _____

If you have additional comments on your experience that you believe may be of value to other job seekers, please enclose them with this report and mail to: WHW Job-Search Research, Box 3651, Washington, D.C. 20007.

WHAT COLOR IS YOUR PARACHUTE?
A practical manual for job-hunters and career-changers by Richard N. Bolles
New 1978 Edition, 6 x 9" 233 pages
paper $4.95, cloth $8.95

"One of the finest contributions to the literature on life/work planning, this book is written in a light tone, which serves to hold the reader's interest, while showing that job hunting, self-assessment, and career planning need not be dull, arduous, awesome tasks... Bolles presents a practical combination of exercises for self-discovery and resources for consultation, and his appendixes of books and organizations for further investigation are very detailed..."
—Harvard Business Review

THE THREE BOXES OF LIFE
And How to Get Out of Them by Richard Bolles
6 x 9" 300 pages, paper $6.95, cloth $9.95
The three stages of our lives: education, then work and then retirement, have tended to become three boxes for learning, achievement and leisure, argues Richard Bolles. Illustrating and giving substance to the instinctive feeling we all have about this, he proceeds to describe some very effective tools which everyone can use to blend learning, achieving, and playing during all the stages of our lives. A long awaited breakthrough in the area of deciding what you want to do with your life.

THE QUICK JOB-HUNTING MAP
by Richard N. Bolles, 8½ x 11" 24 pages, $1.25
A practical booklet of exercises designed to give the job-hunter or career-changer most useful and detailed help in shortening the time it takes to find a job or change careers. This "map" will help the reader to identify his or her skills in detail, and the places he or she wants to use those skills, as well as a method for getting hired in those chosen places.
Also: **BEGINNING VERSION of**
THE QUICK JOB-HUNTING MAP—an even-quicker presentation for less experienced job-seekers. 8½ x 11", 24 pages, $1.25

MOVING UP by Eli Djeddah
5½ x 8" 190 pages $3.95 paper   NEW EDITION
A master in the employment counseling field publishes for the first time in paperback his program for job relocation and advancement which has been available until now only to fee-paying clients. For the man or woman who is between jobs, over 45, or just starting out, Djeddah offers an invaluable guide to finding a job providing maximum compensation and personal effectiveness.

 TEN SPEED PRESS 900 MODOC • BERKELEY, CALIF. 94707

When ordering, please include 50¢ additional for each book, for shipping & handling.